AS WE SAW THEM

AS WE SAW THEM

The First Japanese Embassy to the United States

Masao Miyoshi

KODANSHA INTERNATIONAL
New York • Tokyo • London

Kodansha America, Inc.
114 Fifth Avenue, New York, New York 10011, U.S.A.

Kodansha International Ltd.
17-14 Otowa 1-chome, Bunkyo-ku, Tokyo 112, Japan

Published in 1994 by Kodansha America, Inc.
This is a Kodansha Globe book.

Copyright © 1979 by Masao Miyoshi.
All rights reserved.

Printed in the United States of America

95 96 97 98 6 5 4 3 2

Library of Congress Cataloging-in-Publication Data
Miyoshi, Masao.
As we saw them : the first Japanese Embassy to the United States /
Masao Miyoshi.
p.   cm.—(Kodansha Globe)
Includes bibliographical references and index.
ISBN 1-56836-028-2
1. Man'en Gannen Kenbei Shisetsu (Japan)   2. United States—
Relations—Japan.   3. Japan—Relations—United States.
4. Japan—Foreign relations—To 1868.   I. Title.
E183.8.J3M57   1994
303.48'252073—dc20   94-21572
CIP

In Memoriam Mark Schorer

Contents

Illustrations

Acknowledgments

Many friends and colleagues have read the manuscript of this book in various forms at various stages. I am grateful to John Anson, Marti Archibald, Robert Bellah, James Cahill, Albert M. Craig, Melina Cybele, Howard Hibbett, S.-Y. Kuroda, Elizabeth Lester, Owen Malcolm, Leonard Michaels, Kathy Michele, Earl Miner, C. C. Miyoshi, John Nathan, John Raleigh, Wayne Shumaker, and Thomas C. Smith. I must single out for special thanks Irwin Scheiner, who has been a patient tutor and a walking bibliography for several years to an often unwilling and rebellious pupil. I would like to thank the participants in the seminars at Michigan, Princeton, Berkeley, Chicago, Washington, and Harvard, where a part of this book was presented; I am especially in debt to Harry Harootunian, Tetsuo Najita, and Akira Iriye of Chicago and Dan Henderson of Washington for their fine discernments that made me reconsider some of my earlier ideas. Several Japanese scholars similarly helped me in numerous ways. I owe a great deal to Maruyama Masao, who was unstinting with comments and suggestions on so many occasions at Berkeley and in Tokyo. I must also mention Ishii Takashi, Nakajima Fumio, Ōno Susumu, Kanai Madoka, Tamamushi Bun'ichi, Muramatsu Sadataka, Sakata Seiichi, and Kawakita Nobuo for their kind assistance. I am in debt to the staff of the East Asiatic Library of the University of California, Berkeley, particularly Eiji Yutani and Kiyoko Yamada, who graciously let me feel as if I had been reading *kokiroku* at the Tokyo University Shiryō Hensanjo or writing on Dickens at the Victoria and Albert Museum; similarly, to Henry Hayase, Lynne Miyake, and Rob Wilson for their quick and meticulous scholarship as research assistants, and to Grace O'Connell for not having written me off after typing two previous books. Finally, I would like to express my gratitude to the John Simon Guggenheim Memorial Foundation and the University of California, both of which came to my aid once again by providing me with free time, that precious source of inspiration.

Prologue

The talks dragged on at the Institute for the Study of Barbarian Books located on the outer rim of Edo Castle.* In the conventional straw-matted room, several tables and chairs made especially for the occasion had been brought, and Townsend Harris, America's first Consul General in Japan, and Henry Heusken, his Dutch interpreter, sat down on one side facing Inoue Shinano-no-Kami Kiyonao and Iwase Higo-no-Kami Tadanari, Commissioners for Foreign Affairs for the Shogun government, and their Dutch interpreter Moriyama Taki-chirō (Einosuke), on the other.† As usual, several secretaries and

*The Bansho Shirabesho evolved from the Tenmonjo (Observatory), Yōgakusho (Institute for Western Learning), etc. Established in 1856 for the purpose of studying and translating Western documents and books for the government, it later merged with the Confucian Shōheikō College and the Seiyō Igakkō (Western School of Medicine) to form the Imperial University of Tokyo. The Tokugawa government assigned the building for Harris's lodgings during his stay in Edo. Often spelled "Yedo," Edo is the pre-Meiji name for Tokyo.

†The names of Japanese officials are hopelessly complicated. They have various titles and official names in addition to several personal names (childhood names [yōshō], literary names [gō], common names [tsūshō], nicknames [azana], etc.); they change their names frequently; and they are known variously either by their surnames, official names and titles, or any of their first names; finally, they are pronounced in several ways. I will restrict myself to those names essential for identification, indicating the official's main title as though it were a middle name. I have little doubt that the convention of a man having a plethora of names, changeable in accordance with his particular social roles, has a significant relationship with the makeup of the Japanese self and identity. Compare it, for instance, with the modern Western convention where one's name does not essentially alter with one's changing roles in society. In this book, Japanese names are always referred to with the family name first. Thus, Moriyama is a surname, and Takichirō a given name. (Actually, it was not a name "given" by his parents, since they named him originally Einosuke, later replaced by Tak-ichirō presumably by himself upon his promotion to a higher rank in the office of interpreters.)

1

"spies" were busy, by order of the Council of State, taking down every word spoken in the room. Direct negotiations had begun barely twenty days before, and Harris had already been given the opportunity to represent the President of the United States to the Shogun, or His Majesty the Tycoon as he used to be called by the Westerners. It was a feat no other Western diplomat had ever been able to boast of. And yet for Harris it had been a wait of almost a year and a half since his landing in Shimoda in August 1856, his determined efforts to open trade with Japan having been frustrated at every step by the country's procrastinating authorities. He was worn out and felt sick every day. Now once again they reviewed Harris's treaty draft, article by article, word by word.

Today, however, Saturday, February 6, 1858 (or, according to the Japanese calendar, the twenty-third day of the twelfth month, the fourth year of Ansei), progress was smooth for once. And after both sides agreed on several articles and proceeded to discuss conditions for the exchange of ratifications, the Commissioners took the Consul General by surprise. Harris reports, "They proposed, if I was willing, to send an ambassador in their steamer to Washington *via* California for that purpose."[1]

The idea of sending students or an ambassador to the West was not new to the Japanese. Though Harris didn't know this at the time, the Council of State had already considered the possibility, and there had been a number of proposals submitted on the subject.[2] In fact, Inoue had once intimated to Harris that someday the Japanese would go abroad, and Harris himself had suggested it at least twice. On the first occasion in November 1856 the Japanese officials replied, "The time will soon come when we will build ships like yours, and then we can visit the United States in a proper manner."[3] At the early stage of the Edo talks, Harris once again hinted at such a possibility when he delivered a long, impassioned lecture on world conditions and the "laws of nations" to Hotta Bitchū-no-Kami Masayoshi, the Minister of Foreign Affairs and Chief of the Council of State. Heusken records Harris's plea to Counselor Hotta: " 'Why,' he added, 'should not the Japanese who are courageous and not lacking in personal energy send their ships to take their flags to the distant American coasts?' "[4] But this was mere diplomatic rhetoric: Harris was only being "playful." For the resolute and irascible New York diplomat, the Japanese were too slow, too moribund; they would never venture forth. Even the open-minded Heusken thought at first that the Commissioner's proposal was "idle chatter."[5] But the Japanese were serious, the record on their side being, as usual, quite matter of fact. Meanwhile, discussion of other matters resumed and continued until seven that evening. When they dispersed, the Commissioners left Harris with a gift, a handsome lacquered box with 260 eggs packed in closely among innumerable small black beans.

The Commercial Treaty was signed on July 29, 1858, on the U.S. frigate *Powhatan* in Edo Bay. Another long postponement and the treaty ratifications were at last exchanged in Washington, D.C., on May 22, 1860, where the large entourage of Japan's first Ambassadors brought the Shogun's message and gifts along with the treaty documents to the President of the United States, James Buchanan. This visit by the Envoys was not only the first such tour by any Japanese to America, but also the first trip anywhere abroad after a two-centuries-long seclusion.* American civil War 1861 —1865

Union(N) versus Confederacy (S)

Many members of the 1860 mission—usually called Man'en Gannen Ken-Bei Shisetsu (The Embassy to the United States in the first year of the era of Man'en)—left copious records of the event. Other contemporary accounts, direct or indirect, of the Embassy are also available on both sides of the Pacific. As these diaries and memoirs written by the members of the Embassy are examined both in themselves and in the broader context of outside materials, a fascinating picture begins to emerge. What lay behind the dispatch of the legation, what the retinue experienced in encountering the mysterious West, and finally how they wrote about their experience—such are the concerns of this book.

The first chapter, "Travelers," is largely a factual and background discussion: mid-nineteenth-century Japan's knowledge of the West (especially its languages), the domestic political situation, the formation of the Embassy, the itinerary, practical problems faced in America, and so on. The second chapter, "Views," presents opinions the travelers expressed about Americans. I have culled from the diaries and travelogues (about forty altogether) remarks particularly related to race, women, and democracy so that we may gauge the general feelings of the samurai toward the new and the unaccustomed. In the third chapter, "Minds," the most speculative of the four, I try to surmise the minds of these travelers as they struggled to grasp the meaning of their experience. My method here is a close examination of the form and language of their records. The chapter makes a number of stylistic and grammatical observations (such as the general

---

*There was some traveling in Asia during the seclusion, but it was quite limited and insignificant.

absence of first-person singular pronouns, or the almost obsessively uninterrupted temporal sequentiality), and ponders their significance. The chapter ends with a comparison of the Vice-Ambassador's record of his reception at the White House with Townsend Harris's of his audience with the Shogun in Edo Castle. The two documents describe strikingly similar diplomatic situations, and yet are utterly different in crucial perceptual and philosophical aspects. In the final chapter, "Lives," I return again to the factual, setting out the lives of some of the more prominent members of the Embassy after their return home. One became a military leader in the government of the last Shogun only to be decapitated by the new imperial (Meiji) government; several were forced to commit harakiri; two survived the Restoration to become leaders of modern Japan (one of them being Fukuzawa Yukichi, the founder of Keio University and one of the most important writers of nineteenth-century Japan). I then try to relate these archetypal travelers to the tourists from today's Japan. There are obviously some blurrings of chapter outlines, but the divisions are kept, more or less.

Throughout, I make comparisons between these 1860 accounts and some dozens left by Western visitors to Japan around the same time (including Goncharov and Laurence Oliphant). When relevant, reference is made to the traditions of both the Western travelogue and the Japanese (*tabi nikki* or *kikō bun*, evolving since the tenth century). My aim is to recall the Japanese mind at that moment when it first began to face the Western world after centuries of introspection. It is also hoped that the book will offer the reader a sort of journey in itself, from outside to inside, and then back to the outside again.

America, the lands inhabited by the Negro, the Spice Islands, the Cape, etc., were at the time of their discovery considered by these civilized intruders as lands without owners, for they counted the inhabitants as nothing. In East India (Hindustan), under the pretense of establishing economic undertakings, they brought in foreign soldiers and used them to oppress the natives, excited widespread wars among the various states, spread famine, rebellion, perfidy, and the whole litany of evils which afflict mankind. China and Japan (Nippon), who have had experience with such guests, have wisely refused them entry, the former permitting their approach to their shores but not their entry, while the latter permit this approach to only one European people, the Dutch, but treat them like prisoners, not allowing them any communication with the inhabitants.

— Immanuel Kant, *Perpetual Peace* (1795)

You have to deal with barbarians as barbarians.

— Senator William Mangum of North Carolina, on the Perry Mission

I am therefore convinced that our policy should be to stake everything on the present opportunity, to conclude friendly alliances, to send ships to foreign countries everywhere and conduct trade, to copy the foreigners where they are at their best and so repair our own shortcomings, to foster our national strength and complete our armaments, and so gradually subject the foreigners to our influence until in the end all the countries of the world know the blessings of perfect tranquility and our hegemony is acknowledged throughout the globe.

— Hotta Masayoshi's memorandum on foreign policy
(circa December 1857)

Chapter One

Travelers

Far off, methinks, I hear the beaten drum.
King Lear

Eastern morality, Western technology.
Sakuma Shōzan

Even during seclusion, Japan kept a tiny crack open to the rest of the world. There were always a few Chinese traders. And under the most humiliating conditions, several members of the Dutch East India Company persisted in living on the small man-made island of Deshima in Nagasaki. At every ship's arrival, the Dutch director of the trading post was required to write the Tokugawa authorities a newsletter (*fūsetsugaki*) setting out recent events in the world outside. He was also ordered to pay homage each spring to the Shogun in Edo. As the Dutch director's entourage stayed in the capital, scholars and intellectuals flocked to their lodgings asking questions and comparing notes. If the traders were not all well educated, there were a few learned men like Engelbert Kämpfer, who published the long standard *History of Japan* after his stay between 1690 and 1692, or Carl Peter Thumberg, who later became the President of the University of Uppsala, or Philipp Franz von Siebold, the author of several outstanding works on Japan. Despite the rigidly conservative Tokugawa orthodoxy, the Shogun's capital did have some opportunity to hear about the steadily evolving Western events. At times with governmental encouragement but often under the severest strictures (aimed against Christianity and domestic subversion), knowledge of the West gradually spread.

By the end of the eighteenth century, the impact of "Dutch

7

learning" (*rangaku*) was real enough in fields ranging from medicine, geography, and chemistry to military science, economics, and painting. And excited avant-garde students were traveling all over Japan in search of accomplished masters, exchanging scanty information among themselves. And by the mid-nineteenth century there was a considerable amount of literature available on the West, largely deriving from Dutch and Chinese sources.[1] When the officers of Commodore Perry's *Susquehanna* made their first contact with the Japanese in 1853, they were surprised by the Tokugawa officials' grasp of the "general principles of science and of the facts of the geography of the world": they knew something, for instance, about American and European cities and the mechanism of the steam engine.* The importance of Western technology was by then unchallengeable even to those ultra-xenophobes who were increasing in number and intensity as traffic with the Westerners grew.

As to traveling abroad, Tokugawa Iemitsu's ban (the Third Prohibition Decree) in 1635 on navigation beyond the coastal waters was effectively enforced: so much so that the large fleet of ships—ranging from 300 to 800 tons, which had been freely sailing in the Southeast Asian seas for generations—was completely demolished. And for centuries hardly anyone left the island country. Shipwrecked sailors and fishermen lucky enough to be saved by foreign ships were forbidden to return.[2] As the Russian and other Western ships began to put in their unwelcomed appearances in the second half of the eighteenth century, the prohibition had to be relaxed, and a few sailors were not only permitted to come back but were also asked to brief officials on the conditions of the strange countries they had witnessed. Daikokuya Kōdayū, an energetic cargo boat captain who had been

---

*Francis L. Hawks, *Narrative of the Expedition*, 1:248. Perry commissioned Hawks to write this official account after strictly forbidding everyone, during the voyage, to leave any private records. (Of course, Perry's high-handed command was disobeyed by several, such as Samuel Wells Williams and George Henry Preble.) Although valuable in many ways, Hawks's account is nonetheless a regrettably undistinguished piece of writing. According to Nathaniel Hawthorne, "[Perry] called to see me this morning . . . He soon introduced his particular business with me — it being to inquire whether I would recommend some suitable person to prepare his notes and materials for the publication of an account of his voyage. He was good enough to say that he had fixed upon me, in his own mind, for this office; but that my public duties would of course prevent me from engaging in it. I spoke of Herman Melville, and one or two others; but he seems to have some acquaintance with the literature of the day, and did not grasp very cordially at any name that I could think of." *Notes of Travel*, 1:172, December 1854. Had America's first contact with Japan been described by Hawthorne, or, better still, by Melville!

rescued by the Russians and sent to St. Petersburg to become something of a celebrity in Empress Catherine's court, was granted an audience by the Shogun himself upon his return in 1792, and his story of Russia was avidly listened to. He was even provided a residence in the Shogun's herbary. Regarded as a potentially dangerous figure in the eyes of ever watchful officials, however, he was never allowed to return to his native village. After thirty years of virtual house arrest, he died in 1828.[3]

In the next fifty years things improved a bit. And as more and more Western ships arrived in the northeastern Pacific, dozens of shipwrecked waifs were handed back to Japan.[4] The most famous of these was Nakahama Manjirō (John Mung), who was saved in 1841 by an American whaleboat from New Bedford. The captain of the ship took a great interest in the intelligent boy and put him to school in Fairhaven, Massachusetts, making Manjirō the first identifiable Japanese to live in the United States. He returned eventually to Japan in 1851. Hamada Hikozō (Joseph Heco), shipwrecked in 1851, was also brought to the United States. After various experiences, including his conversion to the Catholic Church and interviews with Presidents Pierce and Buchanan, he went back to Japan in 1859 as an American citizen attached to the U.S. Consulate in Kanagawa. Manjirō and Heco left accounts of their adventures, and were to become two of the rarely available Japanese-English interpreters. Heco worked on the Western side (he had met both Harris and British Minister Alcock before his return), Manjirō on the Japanese, and both had a role to play in the history of the 1860 Embassy, as we shall see later on.[5]

And yet, in spite of such rising curiosity about the West and gradual relaxation of seclusion, a little more than a century ago and on the eve of Japan's reopening of her ports, there was in the entire empire not one man—not to say woman—who fluently spoke or wrote a European language. Of course, the returned sailors were exceptions, but they were too lowly to contribute significantly to the affairs of state. Besides, even their information about the West was not comprehensive, nor was it often reliable. After the Westerners' arrival, officials—commissioners for foreign affairs (*gaikoku bugyō*), magistrates (*bugyō*) of important port towns, inspectors, and interpreters—came to have fairly clear ideas about several specific aspects of the West through repeated negotiations and informal get-togethers. But as to any authentic understanding of the West—either by actually living in the heathen territory or by vicariously experiencing it through reading and studying in its language—such intimate familiarity was denied to the entire Japanese population. Even the most advanced "Dutch scholars" of those times were forbidden anything but the most rudimentary acquaintance with the West.

Take, for instance, the matter of verbal communication at the time of Perry's and Harris's arrivals in the 1850s. What were the Japanese interpreters like? How were they trained during the centuries of seclusion? The Japanese interpreters in Nagasaki were originally trained in Portuguese, the language that had been familiar for a century since the coming of traders in 1543 and of the Catholic missionaries like Francis Xavier soon after. The Shogunate, increasingly concerned with religious, and even territorial, aggression by the Catholic countries, banished the Portuguese and Spanish traders and priests from Japan, permitting only the Protestant Dutch traders to stay. The official interpreters after a while sensed the need to switch to Dutch, and in time a corps of linguists grew to a size of 100 to 150. Like most other feudal offices, the position of interpreter was hereditary, and its ranks were finely graded between the "major interpreter" (*dai tsūji*) and the "apprentice" (*keiko tsūji*), via "minor interpreter" (*shō tsūji*) and many others.[6] A higher rank did not necessarily indicate greater proficiency in the language, just as the title of "interpreter" did not always guarantee the command of even a modicum of Dutch. For a long time, most did not read the language, and only in the earlier decades of the eighteenth century were the interpreters generally learned enough to deserve their titles. Even then progress was slow. The attempts to compile a Dutch-Japanese dictionary began for the first time in the late eighteenth century. And not until 1834—almost two hundred years after the exclusive Dutch trade began—did the first Dutch-Japanese dictionary, a translation of François Halma's *Nieuw Nederduitsch en Fransch Woordenboek,* appear under the guidance of Hendrik Doeff.[7]

How good was the interpreter's Dutch at mid-century? Moriyama Takichirō, who mediated between Harris and the Tokugawa negotiators and attended almost every important diplomatic bargaining, provides the best yardstick. Be it Ranald MacDonald, Samuel Wells Williams, Laurence Oliphant, Rutherford Alcock, Ernest Satow, Ivan Goncharov, or Léon Roches, all the Westerners who wrote about the interminable sessions around that time praised Moriyama, referring to his exceptional proficiency and superior intelligence. Some, like Williams, even pointed out that Moriyama often served as virtually the sole negotiator for the Tokugawa government.[8] That he was the best Dutch interpreter Japan could offer at the time is beyond doubt. And yet one does note that none of these Moriyama admirers knew Dutch well, and the only native speaker who mentioned him, Henry Heusken, held considerable reservations. Heusken registered in his journal a long complaint about Moriyama's poor grasp of Dutch grammar, and, reflecting his aide's view no doubt, Harris wrote the following day: "To add to my difficulties, their Dutch interpreter is very imperfectly acquainted with the *idioms* of that language, [while] his self-sufficiency is in the exact ratio of his ignorance."[9] Furthermore, some extant Tokugawa documents translated by Moriyama confirm Heusken's criticism.[10] It is more than probable that Moriyama, while excellent in normal conversation, had not fully mastered those subtle and complicated legal terms which he had come to learn only very recently. And if Moriyama's Dutch was not impeccable, what must an ordinary session with a less accomplished interpreter have been like? A Japanese official speaking in Japanese to his Dutch interpreter, who would speak an approximation of Dutch to, say, Admiral Putiatin's Dutch interpreter, who would in turn communicate in Russian to the Admiral, and then all the way back to the Japanese official!

The introduction of English into Japan was much later. Although there were some signs of interest in English in the later eighteenth century, it was not until the English frigate H.M.S. *Phaeton* invaded Nagasaki in search of the Dutch in 1808—during the Napoleonic War—that the Tokugawa government ordered a dozen Dutch interpreters to study English from a Dutch trader. Several vocabulary books and conversation guides—such as *Anguria kokugo wage* (The Japanese interpretation of the English language, 1811) and *Anguria gorin taisei* (A collection of English words, 1814)—were written in the following years.[11] But there was as yet no marked progress before Ranald MacDonald's arrival in Nagasaki in 1848. The son of a Chinook Indian chief's daughter (Princess Sunday) and a Scottish official of the Hudson's Bay Company, MacDonald had come to believe, after some confusion about his racial identity, that American Indians had originated in Japan, and in order to be with his people he sailed to the island country. Landing in Hakodate, he was swiftly arrested and sent to Nagasaki for repatriation. During his half-year's stay there, he taught a number of interpreters, including Moriyama Einosuke, who had been studying English alongside Dutch. Some of the Japanese Dutch interpreters, in short, did know a smattering of English, as Western visitors at the time often testified.[12]

Nevertheless, surviving documents in English show their command of the language as less than adequate. Here is an official letter to the captain of the *Saracen,* which sailed into Uraga in 1822:

You have us explained, that you have been long at sea and you was in want of water fruit and refreshment, and you have any sick on board, there fore stepped you necessary on shore of our country, to obtain the upper said thing, there fore give we you the thing after your asking, there fore you must depart as speeding as you can, and you must come no more near by Jappan, chiefly by this place, you must warn to all and other peoples, they must not come to Jappan.[13]

Perfectly intelligible, and certainly quite charming—but grammatic and idiomatic? In fact, even Nakahama Manjirō, who was in English what Moriyama was in Dutch, cannot be called a fluent writer. The following is a paragraph from his letter—written in Hawaii while a member of the 1860 Embassy—to the Fairhaven benefactor describing his reunion with his mother:

In the month of July get on board junk and went into Harbour of Nagasaki Island, off Kieu-Seeu, waiting to get permition for 30 month before we get to our residense. After all the things is properly regulated we were send to our residence. I was great joy for mother and all the relation. I have stayed with my mother only 3 day and nights the Emperor called me to Jedo. Now I became one emperor's officer. At this time I am only attached this vessel.[14]

Or take another example, this one from Joseph Heco, the first Japanese-American whom Harris and Alcock fought over for their consulates:

Dear Sir
Since Uniting waiting to-day for "Ida D Royers" I have nothing in my of receipt to acknowledge. By the "Kioka" I sent you my Price Current of this market . . .[15]

One final specimen, Shogun Iesada's official letter sent to President Pierce in May 1858:

To his Majesty Franklin Pierce,
President of the United States of America
&ca &ca &ca
I Minamoto Ië Sada, Taikoon of the Japanese Empire respond with satisfaction to what you have lately at times written in relation to peace and friendship between both Empires, and make known to you my honest-gratification at the Mission of his Excellency Townsend Harris Consul General of the United States of America with your friendly letter, which has been placed before in relation to the opening of Commerce and the hence forth enduring Peace between both nations, but the impossibility of

the speedy exchange of ratifications of this seasonable Treaty arises from the circumstance that it is requisite that the gathering and consultation of my whole Empire take it into favorable consideration.

I wish your Majesty good fortune in the prosperity of your Empire.

The sixth day of the fifth Month of the fifth year of Ansei Tsutsenoye Uma[16]

Until the 1870s, all negotiations were still conducted in Dutch, the language the Japanese felt more comfortable with. English was simply too new, too difficult.

If all this sounds overly negative toward the Japanese mastery of Western languages at the time, such is not at all the intention. No Western power had produced anyone who came close to having a satisfactory grasp of Japanese. Although a Walter Henry Medhurst published in Batavia *An English and Japanese, and Japanese and English Vocabulary* in 1830, he had no knowledge whatsoever of Japanese, surely not the best lexicographic procedure.[17] Perry had read some forty books on Japan available in New York and London, yet the best he could do was bring along "Sam Patch," a rescued Japanese fisherman (who, however, refused to talk to the Japanese officials in absolute fear of the Tokugawa samurai),[18] and Samuel Wells Williams, a noted linguist indeed, but of Chinese. (He had studied Japanese from a shipwrecked sailor years back, but seems to have barely risen to the conversational level.)[19] Rutherford Alcock, Britain's first Minister to Japan, bravely took on the language after settling in Edo in 1859. But in the light of his ambitious but less than competent *Japanese Grammar* (1861), his command cannot have been too advanced. He, too, had brought a Japanese sailor, saved along with Joseph Heco; defensively arrogant and swaggeringly Westernized in manner, Dankichi quickly antagonized the sword-happy samurai of Edo and was found slain at the gate of the British Consulate.[20] The Westerners had to wait a decade or more until Ernest Satow and his like began to learn the language firsthand. In the meantime, we might do well to recall a Japanese official's boast recorded by Laurence Oliphant in 1858: " 'Oh,' said one of the Commissioners, 'you had better make English the official language; there is no telling how long it will be before you will be able to write a despatch in Japanese; but give us five years, and we shall be quite competent to correspond with you in English.' "[21]

I am not at all sure if this bragging was backed up by actual achievement. At any rate, the East-West understanding commenced

Lord Elgin's retinue and the Tokugawa officials in 1858. The samurai prostrate between the two sides is an interpreter, probably Moriyama.

Commodore Perry meeting the "Imperial Commissioners" at Yokohama, March 8, 1854.

in this fashion with difficulties on both sides being nearly insurmountable, at least at this early stage.*

Japan was in the midst of a great turmoil at the arrival of Perry's flotilla in 1853. Very much a result of the increasing recognition of Japan's vulnerability to Western naval threats, the crisis was also indigenous in its making. After two and a half centuries, the Tokugawa political structure had by then clearly outlived its initial purpose and function. The cost of maintaining the huge unproductive military ruling class (five or six percent of the population) and insuring continued Tokugawa dominion over potential rivals strained the country's financial resources to the danger point. Peasants were suffering chronically from the harshest taxation; samurai's stipends were often drastically reduced; and masterless samurai (*rōnin*) were on the increase. Famines and peasant riots were frequent, and the rising cost of defense against external threats rapidly worsened the financial crunch. The Tokugawa government (*Bakufu*) itself was tottering on the edge of bankruptcy. While the general loyalty to the Shogunate remained unshaken for another decade or so, criticism of the officials in charge was growing clamorous as never before. The Tokugawa bureaucracy had to face internal problems as serious as the menacing demands from the West.

At first the Shogun government was no more willing to open Japan than were the rest of the Japanese. Intercourse with the West was banned by ancestral laws (*sohō*); the officials hated the hairy barbarians as much as anybody else. They hoped the foreigners might somehow go away if only they procrastinated long enough. However, witnessing the overwhelming force and determination of the American warships, the Tokugawa officials were by 1854 forced to acknowledge the impossibility of further resistance. Abe Ise-no-Kami Masahiro, the Chief of the Council of State, took the unusual measure of consulting all the officials, lords (both *fudai* and *tozama*),† and others as to a possible course of action.[22] Inexperienced in offering as well as being asked for advice, they came up with neither satisfactory pro-

---

*Of course, a man's writing proficiency in a foreign language is not always commensurate with his reading proficiency in it. In the case of the Tokugawa Dutch scholars, there is in fact good evidence that their reading in Western *technology* was considerable. At the same time, their understanding of Western culture — institutions and values — was quite something else, as we will see in later chapters.

† *Tozama* (outside) *daimyō* (lords) were lords whose ancestors were hostile to the Tokugawa rule until Tokugawa Ieyasu vanquished the Toyotomis at

posals nor a workable consensus. Abe went ahead and signed the
Perry Convention without fully comprehending what it entailed.
The country reacted in rage. For those who knew little about the
absolute military superiority of the Western nations to the weak and
impoverished Tokugawa Japan, the signing of the Convention was
nothing short of an act of infamy. Those increasingly disgruntled
with the Shogunate, especially among the Mito domain and the
southwestern fiefs, found as their rallying point the stubbornly anti-
foreign imperial court in Kyoto. After all, they reminded themselves,
the title "Shogun" was an abbreviation of the Sei-I-Tai-Shōgun, meaning the "barbarian-subduing generalissimo": the Shogun who abandoned the will to subdue the barbarians was no Shogun. The cries of
"Revere the Emperor" (*sonnō*) and "Expel the barbarians" (*jōi*) re-
sounded throughout the land with more and more vehemence. The
waning of the Tokugawa hegemony was by then unquestionable.

The Western powers that negotiated with the Tokugawa government assumed at first that the Shogun in Edo was the legitimate
political authority in Japan and the Mikado in Kyoto merely the
spiritual head, like the papacy. But as the treaty negotiations lagged
on, they realized that the Tycoon, as they called the Shogun, no
longer possessed delegated sovereignty, since he was compelled to
seek imperial sanction on any crucial issue. The problem was eventually resolved, more or less, by the resignation of the fifteenth
Shogun, Tokugawa Yoshinobu (or Keiki), and political power was
restored to the imperial throne in 1867. But at every step of the treaty
bargainings, the confusion was acutely felt not only by the Westerners but by the Tokugawa officials themselves.

Townsend Harris was at first oblivious—as was every other
Western diplomat—to such complex problems. As far as he was concerned, Japan was ruled by the Shogun and was undemocratic, un-
christian, and uncivilized. To bring the heathen country under the
"laws of nations" was his personal mission, reflecting the Manifest
Destiny of the United States. A diligent student of Perry's gunboat
diplomacy, Harris took every advantage of the Tokugawa men's
knowledge of Japan's military vulnerability. Though Harris, a mere
consul general, was not empowered to act as ambassador plenipotenti-

---

Sekigahara in 1600. They were regarded as possible challengers to the Shogunate
and were kept outside of the administrative offices. *Fudai* (hereditary) *daimyō*
were lords whose ancestors supported the Tokugawas even before the
Sekigawara battle. Senior officers were chosen from the *fudai daimyō,* and lesser
ones from the direct vassals *(hatamoto).*

Townsend Harris in 1855.

Harris has a free hand

ary,[23] he was free to brandish any rhetorical weapon to the Japanese: Washington had no way of knowing what Harris was saying in Edo except through his own communiqués slowly and infrequently transmitted via chance boats and warships. According to Harris, the United States was the only friendly and benevolent Western power—Britain, France, and Russia being more than eager to resort to force to gain their ends. The English navy especially, though temporarily delayed by involvement in the Arrow War (1856–1858) in China, would arrive any day at Edo Bay to make far harsher demands and, in

Hanks diplomacy

U.S - as a lesser evil

case of Japan's refusal, to coerce with devastating military action. Harris often made reference to the Opium War (1840–1842) and other instances of European use of force in Asia, not forgetting to suggest the possible angry response of the magnanimous President of the United States should Japan prove unappreciative. The requests of the peace-loving United States must be accepted without delay before the avaricious European countries humiliated Japan. And he was by and large sincerely convinced of the "justice" and "humanity" of his own undertaking.

If Harris's rhetoric sounds a bit too familiar to us in this last quarter of the twentieth century, it was persuasive enough to the Japanese at the time. Although the Tokugawa officials then headed by Hotta Masayoshi were not as naive as Harris thought them to be, they nonetheless could see no other choice.[24] In our hindsight, it is extremely doubtful that Europe was either interested in or capable of military occupation of Japan. Probably it was more concerned with

Townsend Harris and Henry Heusken in conference with the two Magistrates of Shimoda, about June 17, 1857. A pen and ink sketch by Heusken.

economic domination than political or military.[25] But the Japanese did not know that. Thus, Japan would yield now and learn from the West whatever she could, so that someday soon she might become like the West, behave like the West. Townsend Harris could not have found a better pupil: as he suffered from the isolation and misery of living in Shimoda and complained loudly about the deception and cynicism, inefficiency and unintelligence of the officials, these apparently unresponsive men were quickly absorbing from him the techniques of modern diplomacy. How good a student Japan was is clearly manifest in the history of Japan's Asian policy since: it was less than twenty years before the Japanese began to practice the lesson in Formosa, then Korea, China, and an ever-expanding circle of countries, until World War II demolished the overreaching empire in 1945.

The history of the 1860 Embassy was inextricably enmeshed with the volatile day-to-day developments in domestic politics. Convinced that the only way to silence the anti-foreign, anti-Tokugawa voices was by obtaining imperial endorsement of the treaty (which he was confident he could do without difficulty), Hotta Masayoshi set out for Kyoto in the spring of 1858 with Kawaji Toshiakira and Iwase Tadanari, his aides and chief negotiators with the foreigners. Hotta was completely wrong in his calculation: the court remained adamant in rejecting the Harris treaty, despite a considerable amount of money Hotta took along to Kyoto to bribe the court. Unable to resist the urgent pressure from Harris (who told him that the Anglo-French armada, having settled the Arrow War, was now about to move into Edo Bay), Hotta finally decided to ignore the imperial objection. By then, his control of the cabinet had been badly shaken, and a few days after the signing of the treaty, he was banished from his office by Ii Kamon-no-Kami Naosuke, the powerful Regent (*tairō*) of the Tokugawa government. A fierce loyalist, Ii resolved to strengthen the power of the Tokugawas by ruthlessly jailing and executing the imperial court adherents. In connection with another closely related issue—the nomination of a successor to the childless and diseased Shogun Iesada—he was also determined to purge the Tokugawa government of all his enemies. As a part of this palace intrigue, Ii expelled for one reason or another almost all the able diplomats of the time: Iwase Tadanari, Inoue Kiyonao, Kawaji Toshiakira, Nagai Naomune, and Mizuno Tadanori.[26] It was Iwase who proposed to Harris an envoy to Washington for the purpose of exchanging ratifications of the treaty. An imaginative diplomat with a rare understanding of international affairs, he had been anxious to learn about the

West by personally observing it, hoping to be appointed to the ambassadorship himself by his patron Hotta Masayoshi. All this was now in vain.

Although no internationalist by any means, Regent Ii was nonetheless committed to the opening of ports. And the plan of sending a mission to the United States survived the changeover. The ambassadorial nominations were altered a few times, however, and the final selection was certainly not made from among the best talent in Japan. The situation was less than propitious for other reasons as well. Before the Embassy reached San Francisco, Regent Ii Naosuke was assassinated by activists from the rival Mito domain; and as his severed head was being sewn back onto his body, his Tokugawa-loyalist, anti-imperial, pro-trade policy was replaced by one more placating to the imperial forces. The new administration agreed to slow down the calendar stipulated by the treaties with the Americans and Europeans. It so happened that such trade was having immediate and destructive consequences in the nation's economy. Because of Japan's peculiar gold-silver exchange rate, foreigners bought up gold in huge quantities and sold it elsewhere for staggering profits. Foreign demand for Japanese goods far exceeded the supply, and the result was a rapid and steep rise in prices of domestic commodities. The rude and greedy Western traders angered the Japanese in other ways, too, and their growing resentment soon took the form of a succession of murderous assaults on foreigners and their Japanese associates. In turn, the Westerners were just as enraged by the government's inability to protect their safety and were exasperated by its evasive and delaying tactics. The Tokugawa government was fast losing confidence. The Japan the Ambassadors found on their return was considerably changed from the Japan they had left only seven and a half months earlier.

The Mission was headed by Shimmi Buzen-no-Kami Masaoki as the Chief Ambassador and Muragaki Awaji-no-Kami Norimasa as the Vice-Ambassador. Shimmi, thirty-nine years old, had been in diplomatic service for only a few months, although Muragaki, at forty-seven, had had considerably longer experience as Commissioner for Foreign Affairs and as Magistrate of Hakodate and Kanazawa. Like most bureaucrats, they were committed to the status quo. If in any way curious about America, they were at the same time—unlike Iwase or Nagai—both uninformed and unimaginative. Harris was understandably disturbed by the change, protesting that every official who had previously dealt with him was now dropped from the list of nominees to the ambassadorships, and that this was equivalent to the Shogunate's disapproval of himself as well. According to the Japanese stenographer, he then added that "the dispatch of the Envoys was not for the purpose of exchanging ratifications alone, but of observing the prosperity of cities, the wealth of citizens, the conditions of the army and navy, and the strength and greatness of the United States. If people ignorant about the international situation are sent, they will neither hear nor see what might prove beneficial to the welfare of Japan. There are outstanding officials in Japan, and for the sake of Japan's future these brilliant men should be sent."[27] Though patronizing, it was perfectly reasonable advice, but Wakizaka Chūmu-Tayū Yasutaka, the Counselor in charge, did not bother to respond.

The third man on the Mission was Oguri Bungo-no-Kami Tadamasa, undoubtedly the ablest, as well as the youngest at thirty-two, of the three. He was appointed to be the group's *metsuke,* a position that requires some explanation. Literally a "steady looker" (or, as Algernon Mitford put it, the "eye in attendance"[28]), the office meant at the same time inspector, censor, spy, advisor, attorney general, as the word was variously translated by puzzled American reporters after the Embassy's arrival. The office of *metsuke,* created at the beginning of the Muromachi period, resembled at times that of the police inspector or even the secret police. Reflecting the nature of the office, the Japanese of the period did not leave detailed accounts, but foreign visitors were unanimous in expressing their annoyance with the ubiquity of these policemen. According to Rutherford Alcock, Great Britain's first Consul General to Japan:

Every office is doubled; every man is alternately a watcher and watched. Not only the whole administrative machinery is in duplicate, but the most elaborate system of check and countercheck, on the most approved Machiavellian principle, is here developed with a minuteness and perfection, as regards details, difficult at first to realize. As upon all this is grafted a system of more than Oriental mendacity, one feels launched into a world of shadows and make-believes hard to grapple with in the practical business of life.

You ask for your interpreter, and finding him long in coming, you demand the reason, and receive for conclusive answer that "he could not come without his shadow!" If the objection strikes you as singular or novel, it is explained that his shadow is an "*ometsky,*" literally, the "eye that sees through"; in plain English, a spy, without whom it is not safe for him to enter on the performance of his functions, for the "ometsky" is supposed to be a witness to the loyalty of his action.[29]

And Heusken describes the situation: "I have no doubt either that there are among the Japanese officers secret spies who report all that goes on. In a word, every Japanese spies on another, and it is only by that system of mutual spying that the government can maintain itself in power."[30] Such vigil was indeed universal. And yet, to think of the *metsuke* mainly as a secret police system (as does E. H. Norman in his monumental work *Origins of the Modern Japanese State*[31]) may be mistaken. The Japanese titles and appointments were always loosely defined: a *metsuke* could be as much a diplomat as the foreign service man he was attached to. Iwase Tadanari, one of the most openminded men before Ii's purge, for instance, was officially a *metsuke*. In fact, during the Hotta administration, advisors and commissioners were largely recruited from the offices of *metsuke* and treasurer (*kanjōgata*), and it was almost always the former, not the latter, that expressed progressive and foresighted opinions.[32] Oguri Tadamasa, then, was advisor to the Ambassadors, although obviously he also served as inspector and supervisor of the group, which required—by reason of size alone—fairly rigorous regulation and discipline.

Shimmi, Muragaki, and Oguri were the triumvirate of the Embassy, always acting together, signing every document together, and sharing the final responsibility together. The Embassy had seventy-seven members in all, including treasury officers, foreign affairs officers, inspectors, secretaries, interpreters, physicians, and attendants and servants. As to their selection, eighteen of the nineteen officers were direct Tokugawa vassals (*hatamoto*), the one exception being a Confucian physician chosen from the fief of Hizen after a serious discussion by the Council of State itself.[33] (The fact that they were "Confucian" physicians—and not "Dutch-trained," by then the more dominant of the two—seems to indicate the administration's conservatism.) Retainers of various lords (*daimyō*)—including the "outside lords" (*tozama daimyō*)—joined the Embassy in the capacity of personal attendants and menial servants, and as many as thirty members in the lower ranks came from fiefs such as Hizen, Higo, Chōshū, Tosa, Kaga, Sendai, Jōshū, and Bushū. Preference seems to have been given to those who had some knowledge of the West, but in reality a willingness to travel abroad—a venture frightening enough to many—may have been sufficient in some cases.[34] The members were by and large young, with the majority in their thirties

The principal Ambassadors of 1860: Muragaki Awaji-no-Kami, Shimmi Buzen-no-Kami, and Oguri Bungo-no-Kami.

and twenties. There were even half a dozen teenagers in the group.[35] Some from this group (including the escort crew) later matured into outstanding figures contributing a great deal to the molding of modern Japan, but others dropped quietly into obscurity. The formation of the Embassy as a whole was timidly conceived and haphazardly organized at the end of a long process of change and postponement.

Townsend Harris was thoughtful about the reception of the envoys in the United States. In one of his dispatches to the State Department, dated September 6, 1858, he laid out in detail how the legation should be met at the Isthmus of Panama by a "person having a knowledge of the Dutch and English languages." He also referred to the problem of who was to pay the costs of the visit. Although he emphasized that he had made clear to the Japanese that "envoys in the West always traveled at the expense of their own government," he nonetheless reminded the Secretary of State, Lewis Cass, that while he stayed in Edo for nearly six months, his "servants, guards, Bearers, grooms, & so on, together some fifty persons, were all fed by the Japanese." He further suggested that the Japanese knew that "when the Burmese Ambassadors visited Paris, and when the Siamese Envoy visited England and France, that all the expenses of these three Embassies were born[e] by the [English and French] Governments."[36] If the Japanese had such information, its source is unmistakable. Harris also described the Ambassadors and their retinue somewhat ambiguously as "Princes" and "Governors" and officers of "the first rank" without further details.[37] Whether his description was a result of an honest and unintentional misrepresentation or a deliberate deception is not easy to determine. It is certain, however, that the lordly terms applied by the Consul General gave an impression to the Americans back home that the envoys were great nobles of the empire, which of course was far from the truth. The Tokugawa government was playing its usual game of sending rather humble officials to represent the Shogun, and Harris perhaps was aware of this trick. Possibly he let it go through with exaggerated rank, fully aware that it would enhance the importance and prestige of the occasion and, ultimately, of his own achievement as sponsor. Back in Washington at any rate, Secretary Cass was more than obliging: he appointed to the "Protocol Committee" Captain Samuel Francis DuPont (a grandson of Pierre Samuel DuPont de Nemours, the founder of the industrial dynasty), Commander Sidney S. Lee, and Lieutenant David D. Porter, men who all had served on the Perry Mission. And

Harris indeed swayed Washington into receiving the Embassy in the most sumptuous manner.

The Ambassadors' group was to travel on board the U.S. frigate *Powhatan,* which had served Perry as his flagship in 1854, and on which the Harris Treaty had been concluded. The Japanese had originally wished to send the Embassy aboard a ship of their own. Recognizing the impracticality, those organizing the mission then proposed to send at least one separate ship to carry an escort group and the equipage appropriate to the dignity of a Japanese Embassy.[38] The emerging navy men also had to test and display the nautical skill which they had been learning from Dutch officers for the last five years in the Nagasaki Naval Academy. The *Kanrin Maru,* a 300-ton corvette, built in Holland a few years earlier, was selected for the Japanese crew. They were commanded by Kimura Settsu-no-Kami Yoshitake, the Director of the Academy and Minister of the Navy (*gunkan bugyō*). Primarily an administrator, however, Kimura knew next to nothing about actual navigation. The captain of the *Kanrin Maru* was Katsu Awa-no-Kami Rintarō (or Kaishū), currently the Dean of the same naval school. Katsu was to become the most important naval administrator in the final stage of the Tokugawa government in the late 1860s, but during this voyage at least he, too, was no more competent than Commodore Kimura: throughout the voyage from Uraga to San Francisco he was confined to his quarters continually seasick.[39]

With the principal officers less than ideal, the ninety-six-man crew needed guidance and assistance, which were offered by Lieutenant John M. Brooke of the U.S. Navy (who had helped Joseph Heco return to Japan, and was in Yokohama at the time with the sailor as his interpreter). Brooke's voyage log reveals that the actual work of sailing on the stormy thirty-seven-day voyage to California was mostly carried out by the eleven American sailors aboard plus a few of the more able Japanese.[40]

Still, the selection of the escort group was more professional than that of the Embassy. Kimura and Katsu were naval men, and so were all the officers on board. Students and instructors at the Naval Academy, some were actually skilled navigators, and even the sixty-five common sailors and stokers were carefully selected. The majority came from the Shiaku Islands in the Seto Inland Sea, an area long noted for its reckless and far-faring pirates, and the rest from the Nagasaki area, sufficiently exposed to the comings and goings of

Western ships. Several menservants like Fukuzawa Yukichi were serious students in "Dutch learning." Finally, the interpreter of the group was none other than Nakahama Manjirō, who was, with the sole exception of Joseph Heco, the very best English-Japanese interpreter at that time.

A retinue of over 170 altogether might seem somewhat lavish even for an epoch-making mission. But when Harris traveled the 130 miles from Shimoda to Edo, the Tokugawa government provided him with an escort of some 350 men.[41] If a consul general from a country of barbarians deserved that much splendor for a paltry distance, why not 170 for the Envoys Extraordinary and Ministers Plenipotentiary from the nation of the rising sun all the way across the Pacific? After all, the dispatch of the Embassy itself was the prize pawn in this tit-for-tat game. And, finally, wasn't nineteenth-century diplomacy on both sides of the hemisphere inseparable from such ceremonial fanfare?

Aside from the copies of the 1858 Commerce Treaty ratified by the Council of State, the Embassy carried greetings from the Shogun to President Buchanan. A vague expression of friendship, this document was written in quaint Japanese. It was to be recited by the principal Ambassador, translated by the Japanese interpreter Namura Gohachirō into Dutch, and in turn to be translated into English by the American Dutch interpreter A. C. Portman. In the process, this message, a jumble of clichés saying even less than the usual diplomatic inanities, improved. An English version carefully prepared by the Shogunate translators in Edo and brought by the Ambassadors reads as follows:

To His Majesty the President of the United States of America I express with respect. Lately, the Governor of Simoda, Ino oo ye Sinano no Cami, and the Metske Iawasay Higo no Cami had negotiated and decided, with Townsend Harris, the Minister Plenipotentiary of your country, an affair of Amity and Commerce, and concluded previously the Treaty in the City of Yedo. And, now the Ratification of the Treaty is sent with the Commissioners of Foreign Affairs, Sinmi Buzen no Cami and Muragaki Awage no Cami and the Metske Oguli Bungo no Cami, to exchange the Mutual Treaty; It proceeds from a particular importance of affairs, and a perfectly amicable feeling. Henceforth the intercourse of friendship shall be held between both countries, and benevolent feelings shall be cultivated more and more, and never altered. Because the now deputed three subjects are those, whom I have chosen and confided in for the present post, I desire you to grant them your consideration, charity and respect. Herewith I desire you to spread my sincere wish for friendly relations, and also I have the honor to congratulate you on the security and welfare of your country.

> The 16th day of first month
> of the seventh year of Ansei, Sar[u].
> Minamoto Iyemotsi

The "Letter of Instructions" to the envoys was likewise translated by the Edo experts:

You are ordered to proceed to Washington to exchange the ratification of the Treaty and to be careful about all business matters of importance so that the peace and friendship between both countries be permanent.

If the officers and attendants accompanying you should behave improperly either on board or on shore, they will be punished. You will therefore take care that such do not take place.

Should there be any shipwrecked Japanese desirous to return to their Country, you will see them back after communicating with the Secretary of State of the United States.

> The 16th day of the first month
> of the seventh year of Ansei
> Majesty's Seal
> To Simmi Buzen no Kami
>   Muragaki Adwadgi no Kami
>   Ogure Bungo no Kami[42]

These instructions do not refer to any diplomatic or trade negotiations, and the Tokugawa officials were too inexperienced in foreign affairs and international laws at this stage to detect any injustice and inequality in the 1858 Treaty, which compromised Japan's territorial sovereignty and sole authority in determining tariff rates. Long accustomed to "tributary" relations with China, Holland, and Korea, the Japanese were unacquainted with the concept of a treaty. Of all the records left by the Embassy none makes even a single reference to the content of the 1858 Treaty, and very few mention even the treaty itself. (It took a full decade before the Japanese began to notice the inequities, and yet another forty years elapsed before these were finally rectified. In the meantime, the Japanese had to enter a few skirmishes with Formosa and Korea and launch bloody wars with China and Russia in order to persuade the West that Japan was a civilized enough nation.)[43]

The purpose of the Mission, at any rate, was not for negotiation. Even one of the two original reasons for it, gathering information about the West, was almost forgotten in the minds of the final nominees. The occasion was by now mainly ceremonial, tailored to humor

Harris's relentless demands for larger trade. If at all political, the display of the Shogunate's power (in sending a legation to match the United States's dispatch of Harris) may well have been as much for the domestic audience as for the American.

The Ambassadors on board the *Powhatan* left Yokohama on February 13, 1860. The weather was stormy throughout, and the *Powhatan* had to stop over at the Sandwich Islands (Hawaii) for supplies, delaying its arrival in San Francisco till March 29. Sailing directly to the California coast, the *Kanrin Maru* had arrived there two weeks earlier, and the two groups were united for a while, until the *Powhatan* resumed her travel southward to Panama. With all the storm damages repaired at the naval shipyard in San Francisco Bay, the *Kanrin Maru* left the United States—with five American sailors aboard as advisors—on May 8, and returned home via Hawaii on June 23. Apparently, the task of escort was accomplished by this trip to the West Coast.[44] The Ambassadors, on the other hand, crossed the Isthmus of Panama by train and went aboard the U.S. frigate *Roanoke*, finally reaching Washington on May 14.

Except for the weather, the voyage on the *Powhatan* was eventless, the American crew being civil and friendly toward the passengers aboard.[45] According to James D. Johnston, the executive officer of the ship, they were sufficiently impressed by the importance of the Embassy.[46] There may have been an altogether different set of circumstances making the American sailors appreciative, if not really friendly, toward the Japanese. As reported by Rutherford Alcock, Harris's rival diplomat from Great Britain, the *Powhatan* officers struck it rich while the ship was at anchor in Japan: "An American frigate coming into port was seized with the same epidemic. One officer resigned his commission, and instantly freighted a ship and started a firm; and nearly every other officer in the ship, finding by the favor to the custom-house an unlimited supply of itziboos [silver coins] as they were about to take the embassy over to America, entered largely into profitable operations for converting silver into gold!"[47]

The sanctimonious Lieutenant Johnston says nothing about this. Of course, Alcock may be a little slanderous here, having ample reason for jealousy about the New World hosting the first Japanese legation—regarded as a prize diplomatic coup. But, whether it was an "epidemic" or not, several *Powhatan* officers were undeniably eager to make the best of what their own Consul called in his official dispatch the "peculiar position the ship occupied in the Japanese mind from her having been appointed to convey the Japanese Embassy to Panama."[48] The stern diplomat was very unhappy about the situation. And it may not be too cynical to believe that such profits in the gold trade may have largely inspired the crew's good-natured feelings toward their unfamiliar guests. They might have been easily annoyed by seventy-seven samurai who crowded on board the ship in addition to its normal crew of three hundred.

The envoys and the escort group took along an enormous amount of supplies. One bill from a ship chandler to the Ministry of Foreign Affairs (*gaikoku bugyōsho*) endlessly lists items obtained for the *Powhatan* group: many sets of copper pots, large and small pans, brass kettles, cooking knives, frying pans, personalized tables, rice bowls, tea cups, bamboo baskets, charcoal burners, and so on.[49] They brought food supplies that would last for months. Also, they carried with them a huge supply of Mexican silver coins, not knowing the system of international credit. Fukuzawa Yukichi remembers that during a raging storm 80,000 Mexican silver dollars burst open their containers and practically covered Commodore Kimura's cabin, where they had been stored.[50]

The envoys were welcomed with a spectacular show of enthusiasm in the capital, where they stayed till June 8 attending various state functions, including a formal presentation to President Buchanan and a presidential banquet, as well as the exchange of the

A view of Philadelphia from across the Delaware River. A drawing by Kimura Tetsuta.

treaty ratifications with Secretary of State Lewis Cass. In Baltimore and Philadelphia, people's curiosity was unabated. In the former, fifteen to twenty thousand strangers journeyed to the city to see the mysterious Orientals and, according to the Baltimore *American,* three-fourths of the population were out in the streets. It was in New York City, however, that America's great display of hospitality and curiosity reached its climax. Hundreds of thousands filled the streets of Manhattan, craning their necks to catch a glimpse of the ambassadorial procession escorted by seven thousand welcoming troops, and the Metropolitan Ball held in their honor on June 25 was attended by more than ten thousand guests. If town sophisticates like George Templeton Strong were cool toward the "first-chop Japanese [who] sat in their carriage like bronze statues, aristocratically calm and indifferent" and "the subordinates [who] grinned, and wagged their ugly heads, and waved their fans to the ladies in the windows,"[51] Walt Whitman, standing on a Broadway corner, celebrated the event in one of his usual longwinded catalogue poems, "The Errand-Bearers":

> Over sea, hither from Niphon,
> Courteous, the Princes of Asia, swart-cheek'd princes,
> First-comers, guests, two-sworded princes,
> Lesson-giving princes, leaning back in their open barouches,
>   bare-headed, impassive,
> This day they ride through Manhattan.
> . . . .
> When million-footed Manhattan, unpent, descends to its pavements,
> When the thunder-cracking guns arouse me with the proud roar I
>   love,
> . . . .
> When every ship is richly drest, and carrying her flag at the peak,
> When pennants trail, and festoons hang from the windows,
> When Broadway is entirely given up to foot-passers and foot-
>   standers—
>   When the mass is densest,
> When the facades of the houses are alive with people . . .
>   . . . When the answer
>   that waited thousands of years, answers,
> I too, arising, answering, descend to the pavements, merge with
>   the crowd, and gaze with them.[52]

After two hectic weeks, they left the city on June 30, as the *Great Eastern,* the world's largest ship, having just arrived from England, was about to replace them in the fickle New Yorkers' curiosity and popularity. Their voyage home was aboard the biggest U.S. warship, *Niagara,* taking the Atlantic course this time. The ceremony and

The Broadway pageant in honor of the Embassy.

The Metropolitan Ball in honor of the Embassy on June 25, 1860.

pomp that greeted them everywhere in the United States were conspicuously missing as the Embassy left the *Niagara* at the port of Shinagawa just outside of Edo.

Throughout their trip, the Ambassadors seem to have been quite passive about their plans. The itinerary was set, the transportation arranged, and the entire expense paid by the United States (that is, federal and city governments and volunteer organizations).[53] The only signs of initiative lay in their persistent attempts to refuse invitations to visit officials and cities. The triumvirate composed as many as four letters to the Secretary of State (out of the total of ten they wrote while in America) in which they stubbornly insisted on the need to hurry back as soon as possible. In fact, they were quite reluctant to visit Baltimore, Philadelphia, and New York.[54] But even this resistance was not really a voluntary decision: they had been ordered by the Council of State to avoid everything but the barest essentials and to return home quickly.[55] While in Hawaii, for instance, the Ambassadors were approached by the Foreign Minister of that island kingdom to discuss the possibility of concluding a treaty similar to the one with the United States. The Ambassadors' response was both brief and decisive: greetings (*aisatsu*) would be sent as soon as they returned home.[56] They did initiate a few local visits on their own, but these short trips—for instance, to the Philadelphia Mint for assaying the Japanese coins or to Grace Church in New York City to observe a private wedding—were not frequent; they usually went to places suggested by the protocol officers. Active travel requires at least some understanding of the land and people one visits, and the 1860 Embassy lacked even minimal knowledge of the United States.

It is not easy now to appreciate these men's difficulties in America. Not to speak English was bad enough; not to know what to expect next was worse. Take their daily diet, for instance. The Japanese are even today extremely attached to their native diet of rice, soy sauce, bean paste, fish, and poultry, and cannot tolerate Western cuisine for any prolonged time. Further, in these pre-Meiji days, the Buddhist taboo on the meat of four-legged beasts was observed by most. If the Commissioners for Foreign Affairs sometimes enjoyed breaking the taboo on their visits to Perry's or Lord Elgin's ships, that was a special treat on a special occasion. As a steady diet, they did not touch milk, nor did they consume cheese, butter, meat, or bread. Thus, the men in the Embassy were unable to eat most of what was served in the hotels, though they grew fond of a few Western delicacies, such as ice cream and champagne, and managed to stomach bread (which they thickly coated with sugar).[57] They did bring along a huge quantity of native food, which they could prepare now and then in a specially assigned kitchen, but their national fare was usually inaccessible.[58] On board the *Roanoke,* the American sailors threw away a great deal of the Japanese provisions for reasons of space and "stench."[59] The envoys were at times famished in the midst of feasts more luxurious than they had ever dreamed of.

Then there were the sleeping arrangements. They admired the luxury and cleanliness of the beds. But these samurai were used to sleeping with a wooden pillow that looked like a brick with a thin cushion on top. They needed it to keep their warrior heads cool and the pistol-shaped hairknots a few inches above the mattress. They could not sleep on down pillows. Some samurai apparently found chamber pots on the shelf, and not knowing the nature of their proper use, placed them under their heads.[60]

Such practical hardships being too numerous and tedious to list, let it suffice here to quote from a memoir of Fukuzawa Yukichi as he recalled the experience some forty years later:

Then we were taken to a hotel. All the floors were covered by carpets— the kind of fabric the richest Japanese splurged on, spending a fortune for square inches so a wallet or pouch could be made. The fabric was spread all over the floor in these huge rooms. And people stepped on them in their street shoes. They didn't change their shoes, so we didn't take off our *zori* either. At once we were served drinks. When a bottle was opened, it exploded with a frightening noise. The strange drink was champagne. There was something floating in our glasses. Of course we didn't know they could have ice in such warm spring weather. Those glasses standing in a row before us, and we trying to drink it up! Some were frightened by the floating objects and spat them out; some were loudly crunching on the cubes. It took us some time before we all realized it was ice. We wanted to smoke. There were no tobacco trays [*tabako bon*], nor ash trays [*hai fuki*]. I lit my pipe from the fire in the stove. I suppose there were matches on the table, but we didn't know what they were. Well, I lit my pipe, but finding no tray to put the ashes in, I pulled out tissue paper from my breast pocket, emptied the ashes into it, and crushing the fire out carefully and twisting the paper into a ball, I put it back into my pocket. I was trying to have another puff, when smoke began to rise from my kimono sleeve. My God! the fire wasn't out, and it was spreading to the pocket![61]

Inexperience, or ignorance, is of course a great incentive for discovery and wonderment. Anything unfamiliar fascinated the men in the Embassy, and practically everything was unfamiliar. Captain Katsu randomly lists his observations in his memoir: the Battery, the city officials, women's clothes, women, ferry boats, gas lights, hospi-

tals, brick buildings, the Mint, printing machines, fire engines, horse
carriages, dance parties, theaters, fencing, the naval shipyard, newspapers, and so on.[62] Most records left by the men in the Embassy
describe at length the appearance, structure, and operation of such
things that happened to catch their eyes.

But even in the gathering of simple data there were serious imped-
iments. The most obvious of these was the unfamiliarity with English. It should be recalled here that the interpreters spoke mainly
Dutch, not English. Although some of them had borrowed a Dutch-
English dictionary from the Institute for the Study of Barbarian
Books, a mere dictionary could not have worked a miracle.[63] As to the
rest, they spoke hardly any English at all. Having made no centralized
plan (as did the 1862 Embassy to Europe or the Iwakura Mission ten
years later),[64] the Mission could conduct no systematic research across
the language barrier. Any American willing to speak to the barely
intelligible guests was a welcome teacher on any subject. But the
chance teacher is by definition apt to be unreliable. Thus, a good deal
of misinformation is scattered among the painstakingly gathered facts
and data, ranging from those of American customs and manners
(according to Fukushima Yoshikoto, "heavy drinking and intoxica-
tion are forbidden in America, but on the days after Sundays such
indulgence is tolerated"[65]) to those of the English language ("the
distinction of married and unmarried women shows," according to Nonomura Tadazane, "not in their clothes, but in their names: unmarried
women are called 'Joan,' 'Bahi'[?], etc., while the married ladies are distinguished by the suffix '-sons' as in 'Joansons' or 'Bahisons' "[66]).

The strict control of the Embassy members' physical movement
was another hindrance to meaningful observation. Before they left
Japan, the Ambassadors and Oguri discussed with the office of *metsuke* the method of regimenting their behavior. The envoys' proposal, which was accepted, was to issue to all lower-ranking men a
special permit for every outing from their lodgings, and to give oral
approval to every higher official's visit out. In accordance with this,
the whole entourage was often ordered to stay inside the premises of
the hotel. Even when allowed to go out, a curfew of 6:00 P.M. was
established, which the Ambassadors themselves were reluctant to
break.[67] Furthermore, members were forbidden to wander out alone.
This rule was merely an extension of their home habit rather than a
specially instituted regulation for foreign travel. No official business was
ever transacted by a single individual at home; it naturally followed that
the same discipline applied abroad.

Still, some of the younger and lower men were impatient, and several voiced their dissatisfaction. Fukushima, an eighteen-year-old attendant of Inspector Oguri, describes how he was prohibited from responding to a great many Americans who wanted to greet and invite him.[68] And Tamamushi Sadayū Yasushige, the Chief Ambassador's manservant (from the northern *tozama* domain of Sendai), is quite vocal about his feelings: "Today I took my first walk out. By a strict order, we had to follow the guide. We were not allowed to leave him for the shortest time. Apparently, the guide was forbidden to take us to a crowded area, for we saw only lonely places. We all complained, but nothing could be done about it." Elsewhere he writes, "The soil of this area seems fertile, so there must be a great variety of plants. But because of the official ban, I cannot go far enough for observation."[69] If these grumblings sound tame, one should remember they were written in the face of possible censorship and punishment.

In fact, Tamamushi, the most articulate of all the diarists in the Embassy, confided his rage to the eighth part of a copy of his *Kō-Bei nichiroku* (The chronicle of the voyage to America). This last section, unlike the preceding seven sections, was clearly marked as "Not to be seen by anybody else."

The Stay in Washington

While in this city, we are prohibited, by the strictest order of our own authorities, from taking even a step outside the hotel. Even when we are allowed to go out for some compelling reason, we are accompanied by our officials. Most officers are wasting their days in the city trying to buy watches and woolen material and velvet, and none are interested in discovering the institutions and conditions of America. People are purchasing things by twos and threes, even by fours and fives, so that they may sell them upon return home. They dash around looking for the cheapest store. How disgraceful it is! Wishing to observe schools and colleges, I asked for permission several times, but I couldn't go since no officer was willing to accompany me there. Needless to say, I couldn't go to charity houses or orphanages, which should be the first on the itinerary if gathering information were the purpose. Among the members of this Mission no one — from the Ambassadors down — is interested in the conditions and customs of the Americans. They [the Americans], on the other hand, are trying to show us everything without any intent of concealment. But no one on our side cares. Some say that the Ambassadors have confined themselves in their rooms never stepping out once and being very cautious. But some people are laughing at them, because they believe that the reason for the Ambassadors' staying home is the fear of the strange American manners, and also the fear that their ignorance and incompetence might lead them into serious trouble. The lower officers, too, decline the Americans' invitations. And only after repeated urgings they consent to

go. Apparently they believe that they are so important that they should
remain aloof. But actually, their behavior shows that they are merely
complying with the Americans' wishes. So how can they be haughty even
if they want to be! In buying watches and woolen fabric, some con-
noisseurs are spending as much as one hundred or even two hundred
silver dollars on one item. These are nothing but toys. If the superiors are
preoccupied with such things, no one should blame their inferiors for
greedily trying to make a profit. Alas, so many things are being done in
this voyage that disgrace our country.[70]

We will note as we go along that those who were serious about seeing
America for what it was were usually among the lower-ranking and
often younger men, like Tamamushi, from the "outside" fiefs. And
their criticism of the Embassy leadership seems to have evolved as
they became increasingly alert to the differences that lay between the
Japanese and the Americans.[71]

The kinds of facts collected by the Embassy members were mechanical and—from our perspective—uninteresting in themselves.
Cooped up in their hotel rooms with only routine work to do, many
wrote about things they could find indoors. The bathroom (especially
running water and flush toilets), gas lights, and call bells received
pages of explanation in many papers. On board ship they com-
pulsively recorded their daily location in longitude and latitude. As-
suming that there was likely to be no second chance, and no doubt
anticipating a future use, they took copious notes often illustrated
with charming sketches drawn with brush and ink which they carried in tiny cases wherever they went. The names and titles of ships'
crew members, the names of the states of America, prices of commodities, tables of wages and salaries of the ship's crew and government officials—many items that are either useless for any general
purpose or easily available in almanacs are tirelessly recorded in a
great number of the diary-travelogues. Later, in Chapter III, I shall
look into the shape of the minds of these men, which inevitably
structured the kinds of observations and descriptions in these documents. Here I would simply like to note those external factors—
linguistic limitations and restriction of physical movement—that
very much influenced the substance of information contained in
them.

As for the dictionaries and almanacs as sources of information,
most of the men would not have been able to read such books. In fact,
the idea of looking for an almanac or encyclopedia may never have

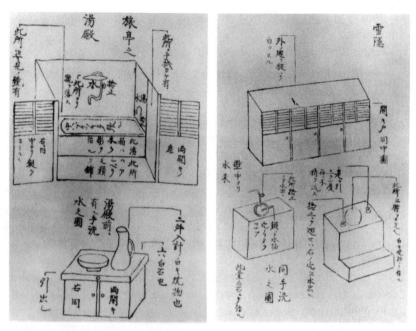

Water closet: bathtub, sink, shelves and toilet. A sketch by Yanagawa Masakiyo.

occurred to many. And although the Ambassadors did purchase dictionaries and other reference books in addition to those given them, they were shelved away upon their return in the libraries of the Institute for the Study of Barbarian Books and other offices, none of them readily accessible places. Two men from the escort group bought copies of the abridged edition of *Webster's Dictionary,* and the purchase has been long hailed as an accomplishment of the time.[72]

The group control of the Embassy seems at the same time to have been eminently successful in preventing any sort of scandal or criminal act. A few sailors died from illnesses that developed during the voyages; swords were stolen; a samurai drew his razor-sharp sword when a gun was fired by a drunk American in his hotel. Such incidents are indeed recorded, but there were no untoward performances on the part of the members of the Embassy—with the sole exception of a drunken menial who had a brawl with an English sailor in San Francisco, and was tried and punished promptly on board.[73] In view of the size of the entourage, the length of their stay, and the unfamiliarity of the travel, their success in maintaining order was quite remarkable.

There were possible occasions for mishaps. In a large city crowd, for instance, shouts of racial insults were unmistakably heard by the samurai, whose splintery pride and acclaimed swordsmanship were soon to become all too clearly manifested: once back in Japan, there were to be numerous bloody assaults on Westerners as well as their Japanese associates. But the visitors seem to have kept their tempers in check and swords well in control. The reserved samurai also took in stride the over-familiar pranks of the easygoing, and at times crude, Americans.[74]

Several men refer to the brothels they visited. The whorehouse is as likely a place to invite trouble as any other. In their home country, such visits were an accepted part of life, and it would have been perfectly natural for the men of the Embassy to expect to include them on their itinerary. But just as Laurence Oliphant seems to have reverted to the native customs while in Japan, forgetting his Victorian prudery—Laurence was a cousin of Mrs. Oliphant, the high priestess of Victorian respectability—these samurai too reverted to the American habits, and turned puritans. Invariably they explain the reasons for their visits as different from the simplest one usually assumed for such an undertaking. Satō Hidenaga, a low-ranking supply officer and cook, for example, went to a brothel—to have a good sleep:

Lord Elgin's retinue being entertained at a tea-house outside Edo.

On the night of the fourteenth, some of us in the lower ranks were not provided with beds. Four or five of us discussed the matter and concluded that now that we finally found ourselves in a good hotel after the voyage of thousands of miles, to sleep without beds or blankets and become sick would be a total folly. We ought to go to a whorehouse and find some beds. We had no erotic interest at all; we only wanted to have a good sleep. We finally found a place after secretly trudging along several blocks and asking questions by signs and gestures. When we asked for rooms, a group of women dashed out who looked like monsters, and holding our hands tried to get us into their rooms. Looking around we saw men and women copulating on the mud floor. At this point, we all became discouraged and ran away. Finding a native going in another direction, we asked him to take us to another whorehouse. But the same thing happened again. So, greatly disappointed we came back and laughed together: even if we became sick from the lack of sleep, it would be better than catch a disease from the devil-like women.[75]

Fukushima, the eighteen-year-old, simply found himself there:

April 10. Fine weather. The three principal Ambassadors went to see the Secretary of State, and in the afternoon, we took a walk. Going south from our hotel for several miles, we came to a six-storeyed house. It sold liquor, and there was a big portrait of a woman in front. The keeper of the house waved his hand and invited us in. He was very happy to see us come in and entertained us with tea and cake. The store looked different from ordinary ones, however; for we noticed on the upper floors women of somewhere around sixteen to twenty-three years. There were no men around, and the women were singing. They looked somehow more uncouth in manners than ordinary women. Thus we began to wonder about the place and asked the man who invited us in. He said it was a whorehouse. We were greatly surprised and thinking of the Ambassadors' strict prohibition, hastily took our leave in fear of severe penalty. After a little more wandering in the streets, we returned to our hotel.[76]

Hirose Kakuzō (Hōan) Kaneaki went to a brothel in Honolulu, but left as soon as he found out that most of the women were infected with a venereal disease.[77] Even Tamamushi, the most candid man on so many matters, seems less than frank when he describes his finding a house of pleasure in Hawaii and repeatedly lists the prices of prostitutes in various cities like San Francisco and New York without once confessing a personal verification of such research. The head of the stokers' gang, Kahachi, one of the two laborers in the Embassy who kept records, alone admits some visits: "I was told that among the young men some [but not he himself!] had been to buy Chinese whores, and that they were no different in character and temperament from the Japanese whores."[78]

Do these accounts mean that the *metsuke* control succeeded in restraining the men? Or failed? Were they told not to go, but went? Did they alter the stories for fear of censorship? At any rate, no one was found in trouble, and the credit—if such disciplining of adult behavior is worthy of praise—was no doubt due to the *metsuke* system.

On a more respectable level, there must have been some personal intercourse between the Japanese travelers and the Americans. And the *Kanrin Maru* crew who had to wait for fifty days for the repair of their ship and the arrival of the Ambassadors in Washington did enjoy informal visits with the families of the Mare Island Naval Shipyard personnel. Commodore Kimura, for instance, invited fifty American officers and their wives to his ship for a feast that lasted three hours.[79] Friendships must have developed between the American crew and the Japanese during the long voyages, and the farewells at the end of a voyage or a prolonged stay in a hotel are often described as emotional.[80] And yet, with the exception of Commodore Kimura and Captain David Stockton McDougal and others of the Mare Island Shipyard, very little is written about any personal relations.*

The silence is explicable in several ways. There may in actuality have been no real friendly exchange. The serious language problem is an obvious reason. But perhaps even more fundamentally, the official Confucian teaching always emphasized the hierarchic relationships (father-son, master-servant, lord-vassal, husband-wife, older brother-younger brother, and so on), ignoring the horizontal friendships.

---

*Informal friendships that grew on Mare Island are best described in Ono Tomogorō's *Kanrin Maru kō-Bei nisshi* (The chronicle of the voyage of the *Kanrin Maru*), reprinted in Fumikura Heijirō's *Bakumatsu gunkan Kanrin Maru*, pp. 530–678. Captain David Stockton McDougal did not forget the friendship, nor did the Japanese. When he voyaged to Japan in 1862, a reception was arranged for him by the Tokugawa protocol officers, and Kimura and Katsu were both invited for a reunion. The Japanese feast, however, consisted of "boiled eggs, boiled potatoes, and angel-food cake," to the consternation of Kimura and Katsu, who felt heavily indebted to the captain for his generosity during their stay in San Francisco Bay. Under the pretext of the anti-foreigner atmosphere in the capital, McDougal was not even allowed a decent chance to take a sightseeing tour of Edo. This may serve as an example of the lack of expertise in diplomatic entertainment among the Japanese of the time (which I will be talking about later on). But Captain McDougal had ample opportunity to pay back the ungrateful hosts. He commanded the U.S. sloop *Wyoming*, which made the successful initial attack on the Chōshū batteries in July 1863, before the allied Western fleet totally demolished them a year later. See Fumikura Heijirō, *Bakumatsu gunkan Kanrin Maru*, chap. 20, pp. 341–346, and Ishikawa Mikiaki, *Fukuzawa Yukichi den*, 1:293; Joseph Heco, who accompanied Captain McDougal at the request of Minister Pruyn, also describes the Shimonoseki Straits attack in his *Narrative of a Japanese*, 1:333–347.

The Mare Island Naval Shipyard in 1860.

Friendship was, if it took the political form of "association" (*totō*), a capital crime tantamount to treason even within a given domain.[81] On board the *Kanrin Maru* and the *Powhatan,* the men were understandably cautious with each other and certainly with the Americans.[82] The still persistent official policy of aloofness, if not isolation, from the foreigners, was undoubtedly an extra deterrent. When it became known that the ever restless Tamamushi had a vigorous "conversation" with a Chinese emigré in Hawaii by writing characters (a procedure somewhat similar to an Englishman and an Italian communicating through writing in Latin), a chilly reprimand was sent down to him from the Chief Ambassador himself.[83] Those daring men who had had some intercourse with Americans may have simply chosen to be mum about it.

Nakahama Manjirō, for example. Having served on an American whaler before his return to Japan, he was one of the few capable seamen on board the *Kanrin Maru.* Lieutenant Brooke found him so fascinating that he wrote Manjirō's life story in his notebook. But Manjirō's position was precarious. A fisherman by birth, he had been promoted to the rank of a Tokugawa vassal (*hatamoto*) on the strength of his Western knowledge. His long stay in the United States, at the same time, made him suspect to the Tokugawa officials. No other than Lord Tokugawa Nariaki himself, the most powerful man in Japan after the Shogun, had written a memo objecting to his recruitment in 1854 on the ground of his dubious loyalty.[84] Thus, Brooke's heartfelt admiration for the sailor interpreter had to be carefully disguised before the eyes of other samurai, as Brooke noted in

Captain David Stockton McDougal, Executive Officer of the Mare Island
Naval Shipyard in 1860.

his journal: "Manjirō talks very freely but at the same time shows a certain uneasiness. He occupies a very dangerous position and has to be very careful to avoid difficulties."[85] Manjirō left no record concerning this travel, and it was a wise decision. Soon after his return to Japan, he was relieved of his instructorship at a navy school on the suspicion of having befriended foreigners too much.[86] The punishment could have been far worse.

There is the peculiar case of "Tommy" in this connection. Tateishi Onojirō Noriyuki, one of the teenagers in the Embassy, was an interpreter trainee who traveled with his interpreter uncle, attached to the envoys. Possibly because of his status as an unpaid apprentice,[87] he seems to have enjoyed much greater freedom than was allowed other members. As early as San Francisco, "Tommy" (so nicknamed by the American sailors aboard the *Powhatan* after his childhood name Tamehachi), attracted the reporters' attention, and he soon emerged as the star among the generally stolid and colorless personalities. Tommy spoke some English—after all, he was an interpreter—and was certainly no repressed Confucian. As the reporters looked for a newsworthy personality, Tommy best fitted the role. He was a "darling fellow," a "Japanese prince."[88] By the time the Embassy arrived in Washington, maidens and ladies of the capital were hysterical about Tommy, who in turn hugely enjoyed the flattery. Wherever the Embassy went, it was not the Ambassadors but Tommy who was surrounded by crowds of women begging for his autograph and mementoes. His movements were described in detail by daily papers and he was reported to have fallen in love with several young damsels in the capital. Even Strong was persuaded that he would be more popular than the Prince of Wales, who was about to visit the United States.[89] A *New York Times* reporter portrayed Tommy's behavior during the voyage home as follows:

Since being on board he has read many articles in the different papers, speaking of the Embassy and himself, that really quite altered the shape of his eyes with astonishment; circumstances that he says never occurred — eccentricities attributed to himself and others, of which he has no recollection whatever. He is anxious to return to Uncle Sam's dominions; speaks of "letting his hair grow — going to the naval school, or to the West Point — and finally of getting Yankee wife"; he has several daguerreotypes, photographs, etc., of feminine individuals, said to be likenesses of American ladies, none of them especially remarkable for good looks, or for modest or intellectual character of visage; but Tommy is highly pleased with his collection, and shows them with great satisfaction.[90]

"Tommy" Tateishi Onojirō.

"Tommy" among the ladies of Washington.

Whenever he found the time, he would compose sentimental love letters on pink stationery to these unremarkable girls of America. What is interesting about all this is not the harebrained young man's foolish conduct itself—although it provides the archetype of the "Americanized" man who is to put in his appearance in the Japanese novel a few decades later—but the attitude of the rest of the group: not a single person, including his uncle, breathes a word about what must have been considered Tommy's reprehensible exhibitionism.[91]

As the lower-ranking officers were continually aware of the eyes of their superiors and colleagues fixed on them, so were the principal Ambassadors conscious of the possible disapproval of their conduct by their superiors back in Edo. They must hurry home because Mr. Harris told the Council of State that the whole voyage would take no more than one hundred fifty days. "We are truly in much haste to return to Japan," their non-sequitur English letter to Secretary of State Cass pleads, "for the views of our Government as to future voyages of Japanese to foreign countries must be taken into consideration."[92] But as long as they were forced to stay in America, they had to play it safe. Tamamushi is accurate: they seem to have practically frozen them-

A dinner given for Tokugawa officials on the deck of the U.S.S.F. *Powhatan* in 1854.

Reception of the Japanese Ambassadors on the deck of the U.S.S. *Roanoke* at Aspinwall.

A meeting of Lord Elgin's retinue and the Tokugawa officials.

selves as they faced Americans. At official occasions, they invariably made the shortest possible speeches. They were always courteous, but their expressions were immovable. "Venerable fossils," a reporter from the *Philadelphia Inquirer* called the Ambassadors.[93] They might not have been able to behave otherwise. Harris's well-intentioned promotion of the Embassy backfired: although seemingly representing the Tokugawa government (which in turn supposedly represented the entire country of Japan), the samurai on the Mission were no more than a group of bureaucrats too humble even to guess where Tokugawa policy might turn next. Their initial instructions from the Shogunate being so vague, they could only perform ceremonially without ever touching on any substantial issues of diplomacy.[94]

For any return of obligations in hospitality, the Ambassadors were largely dependent on the gifts that had been prepared in Edo by the Council of State. These gifts would enable them to avoid the necessity of inviting the hosts back to their temporary lodgings, which would have exposed them to all sorts of difficulties like protocol, food and drinks, conversation, and entertainment. In social (that is, non-ritual) graces, diplomatic expertise was not noticeably developed then even in their own country. The ever wary Council in Edo perhaps wanted the envoys to limit their social intercourse to the absolute minimal performance of gift-giving so as to avoid possible mishaps. They took great care in the choice and preparation of articles. The presents to the President comprised scrolls, folding screens (byōbu), lacquered braziers, an inlaid bookcase, rolls of silk, swords, saddles, and so on, which presumably represented the two ways of samurai: the arts (bun) and the martial skills (bu). In addition, they had a whole store of smaller gifts, ranging from swords to porcelain cups, that were meant for lesser officials (including, as it happened, even the manager of their hotel in New York).[95] The individual men, too, were personally prepared with fans and woodcut prints and sundry items in return for expected acts of hospitality.*

Exchange of gifts is of course a part of the normal diplomatic procedure anywhere, East or West, always coordinated with political objectives. Commodore Perry brought to Japan, among many other things, a set of telegraph equipment, a quarter-sized train locomotive with carriages and tracks, rifles, muskets, pistols, and agricultural instruments to show off Yankee know-how and American might; Lord Elgin presented the Shogun with a 300-ton pleasure yacht as befitted the splendor of the British monarch and her supremacy over the seven seas.[96] There are, however, some features of the Japanese gifts which, especially as gift-giving has since become a sort of institution among Japanese visitors abroad, may require a few comments.

First, the long tradition of tributary diplomacy with Korea, China, and Holland, as well as the feudal structure of Tokugawa Japan, had thoroughly trained the Japanese in the politics of gift-giving—an art in which the relative hierarchic positions were clearly defined and affirmed. That meant the giver and the recipient shared an understanding of a gift in political terms. Second, gift-giving took on a larger significance in human intercourse, diplomatic or personal, for the Japanese than it did for Westerners. Social entertainment was not necessarily absent in Tokugawa Japan, of course. But the system of

---

*According to Katsu Awa-no-Kami Kaishū's reminiscence, some sailors of the *Kanrin Maru* took along pornographic prints as possible presents for their American hosts. Katsu recalls that he was requested one day to appear at the "Consulate" (court?) in San Francisco, where he was told about one of his sailors forcing obscene pictures on a lady. Katsu promised the judge better supervision of his men. Satisfied, the judge then invited Katsu to a dinner with two or three other judges. At the dinner the now relaxed judges wondered if they, too, could all have a few specimens of the oriental fine art. Captain Katsu readily complied with their request. *Kaishū zadan,* p. 131. The story told forty years after the voyage may be no more than his fabrication, but a San Francisco paper does report that the sailors were exhibiting books "full of villainous obscene pictures, very poorly engraved at that." *Daily Evening Bulletin,* March 29, 1860.

Delivery of the American presents brought by Commodore Perry at Yokohama, May 13, 1854.

offering and acceptance had grown to be at least as elaborate as the institution of feast and festivity. [97]

Third, concomitant to these two developments was the enigmatic nature of a Japanese gift for outsiders. The typical Japanese gift even today is, unlike Perry's or Elgin's, often impractical or even useless and its commercial value either absent or inconspicuous.* Its recipient is sometimes at a loss as to its significance. No one knows what Townsend Harris and Heusken did with those 260 eggs; but a certain Lieutenant Wise of the *Niagara* was probably speechless, if not indig-

*Many foreigners commented on this. One interpretation is Samuel Wells Williams': "In the exchange of presents the Japanese have not shown themselves at all generous, whether it is owing to their entire ignorance of the actual cost of the things given them, and therefore inability to judge what would be of corresponding value, or to their petty characters." *Journal*, p. 215. Likewise, Lt. George Henry Preble records: "I found the presents displayed and the Commissioners explaining them. They were chiefly pieces of crepe and silk, and specimens of lacquered ware forming a pretty display, but I should judge of not much value. Not worth over a thousand dollars some thought. I am sure one of our presents, Audubon's Great work on Am Birds, was worth more than all we saw there, and that our miniature railroad engine and car cost several times their value. Everyone, the Commodore included, remarked on the meager display." *The Opening of Japan*, p. 146. For the lists of the Japanese and American gifts, see Arthur Walworth's *Black Ships Off Japan*, pp. 262–265.

nant, when he was handed a large box containing a gift as a token of appreciation for the services rendered to the Embassy when his ship arrived at Yokohama. "This box, when opened, was found to contain shavings, and in the heart of the box, a foot in length, [he found] two pieces of Ribbon!! valued at two dollars." The Lieutenant obviously had not been enlightened about the ceremonial significance of the offering of cloth (*nuno*) as an expression of respect and worship (this still survives in the Shinto rite). The irate reporter who sent this story for the *Daily Alta California* continues: "We have, through great exertions, ascertained the actual amount of presents made to the *Niagara* since her arrival, as a recompense for the kindness shown them. On the second day after their arrival, 23 fish, with a plantain and a clump of boiled rice. Third day—27 radishes, 3 chickens, and 1 rooster. Seventh day—361 catties white beans, and 5 piculs rice. And this is the sum total!"[98]

Many of these gifts are symbolic, their value resting not in their use or consumption but in their salutations. Even today many Americans receive small knicknacks from Japanese visitors, such as paper and bamboo folding fans, without being told what they are for. The fan is not meant as an ecologically superior air conditioner, but is a symbolic message deriving from its shape and name: *suehiro* (literally, greater width, or wealth, toward the end), describing the fan shape, predicts the greater and continuing prosperity of the recipient. Likewise a five-yen coin, which is considered a symbol of friendship by virtue of a pun, *goen*, meaning "relationship." What is interesting about this is that the gift givers seem to take for granted that the foreign recipients will readily understand their intricate symbolic structure. The Tokugawa officials perhaps thought the Americans would know that eggs, fish, and rice stood for fertility and abundance, a roll of silk for respect, and so forth. And for them a high material value would constitute a bribe, a grave insult to an honorable recipient. Another way of explaining this is that there exists a fundamental difference in attitudes toward gifts, a part of that difference which lies between a bourgeois industrial society and a preindustrial feudal community. And yet the tradition seems to linger on in some measure even today when Japan is a full-fledged industrial country.

It is possible, at the same time, that the Japanese never thought that the foreigners would understand their symbolism. A kind of obscurantism, their gift system may be a device aimed at compensating for any psychological disadvantage of being placed in a strange power situation. That is, the giver knows what the recipient doesn't.

The visitor to America brings a bit of Japan, and transplants his host in it. Just as he (the visitor) is in alien territory, so too is the host placed in a strange environ through the receipt of an incomprehensible present. Impenetrable, mysterious East! This is at least a part of the psychological dynamics of gift-giving as Japanese visitors practice it now, and the 1860 Embassy can be seen as having initiated the tradition.

Despite all the physical and psychological difficulties, the members of the Embassy did visit various offices and places. During their stay in Washington, D.C., the Ambassadors, though not overly eager, managed to cover the Patent Office, the Smithsonian Institution, the Washington Navy Shipyard, the Capitol Building. Many men went to photo studios to commemorate their historical voyage, commencing yet another institution of Japanese travelers abroad. Also on the itinerary were the observatory, hospitals, a circus, churches, a printing office, a reservoir, a kindergarten, and a farm. Those high-ranking

The Ambassadors at the Washington Navy Yard. The third from the left is Muragaki, then Shimmi and Oguri. The top-hatted man behind Muragaki is Captain DuPont; Captain Franklin Buchanan is behind Shimmi.

officers who were fortunate enough to have cash to spend roamed around the city shopping, as Tamamushi's angry criticism indicates.

In Philadelphia, some envoys sought out photo studios again. But they could also be found at the Mint, the Custom House, the office of the *Philadelphia Inquirer,* a pharmaceutical factory, watch stores, book stores, an optical instrument store, a theater, the Academy of Music, and Girard College (the well-known boarding school for orphans). The Confucian doctors of the Embassy witnessed a surgical procedure at the Jefferson Medical School. They visited Independence Hall, a spinning mill, and an iron foundry. At Point Breeze Gas Works they saw two balloons carrying two men, along with flags of the United States, England, and Japan, take off to New York to celebrate the opening of Japan.

In New York they stayed at the Metropolitan Hotel on Broadway, which had small theaters on the premises. While in the city they took in Greenwood Cemetery, the naval shipyard again, the deaf and mute school in Yorkville, a museum, the public library, a rubber factory, and entertainment halls. They also went shopping, at Lord and Taylor and at Tiffany, for instance. And the Ambassadors even accepted invitations to two wealthy New Yorkers' residences: one a villa in Washington Heights, which was still a remote suburb of New York City, and the other a townhouse belonging to August Belmont, Commodore Perry's son-in-law. There was a Pekingese at the Belmonts' that was brought back by the Commodore from Japan. The dog, so goes the story, recognized its countrymen at once. Catching sight of this dog's show of affection, Perry's widow was moved to tears. While in New York, the Ambassadors were invited to see Boston and Niagara Falls but declined, as has been mentioned earlier.

Time could have been better spent, no doubt. Still, it was a well-packed schedule for many, especially in view of the Ambassadors' general policy against visiting. Besides, one somehow feels that the specific details of their itinerary might not have made that much difference; except for a few like Tamamushi and Fukuzawa, most men were inexperienced and uninterested in meeting the new. In order to appreciate their predicament, we need to examine their impressions of the people encountered in this unknown land.

Of the habits and manners of the Japanese in regard to the sexes, I see little, for I cannot conquer a feeling that Japs are monkeys, and the women very badly made monkeys; but from others I hear much on the subject, and what I hear is very far from appetizing.

—Henry Adams, letter dated 22 August 1886

We cannot wait for our neighbor countries to become so civilized that all may combine together to make Asia progress. We must rather break out of formation and behave in the same way as the civilized countries of the West are doing . . . We would do better to treat China and Korea in the same way as do the Western nations.

—Fukuzawa Yukichi, "Datsu-A-ron"

Sometimes they meet a lady, or a lady meets with them, which you will—the Japanese waves his hand, the lady benevolently smiles, and demands, "How do you like New York?" A nod or an unintelligible exclamation follows, and both parties appear to perfectly understand each other. "Yerry gooat," exclaims a Japanese on passing the flag of his country. "Yes," returns the nearest stranger; and both are pleased.

—*New York Herald,* June 17, 1860

Chapter Two

Views

Travellers ne'er did lie,
Though fools at home condemn 'em.
The Tempest

"Look ye! master Traveler:
unless ye note something worth the seeing,
and come home wiser than ye went,
I wouldn't give a stag's horn for all your travels."
From an old play quoted
by Rutherford Alcock for the motto
for his *The Capital of the Tycoon*

While the travelers were busy gathering facts and recording events in
their diaries, they seem to have taken very little time out for critical
reflection on their experiences and observations. No matter what the
subject, their analytical comments are usually brief, often cursory—
travelogues vacant of any serious opinion whatever. The absence of
thoughtful commentary in their records is itself an interesting subject, and one which I would like to discuss in the next chapter. At
present, however, I would like to examine those remarks the travelers did choose to make about America around several broad topics
such as race, women, and democracy.

Admittedly, a traveler's general impression is seldom interesting
in itself, prejudice and overgeneralization being the common rule. For
an occasional Lawrence in Mexico or Tocqueville in America, there
are dozens whose cliché comments merely show that they are not
really seeing what they have come all the way to see. Vice-Ambas-

sador Muragaki, for instance, is convinced that all foreigners are barbarians, and this assurance colors nearly every specific observation he makes. After a jolly banquet in San Francisco given in the Embassy's honor, Muragaki quietly records his reaction: "As a ceremonial expression of friendship, the dinner was perhaps sincere, but looked at critically, it was just like what I imagine to go on in an Edo restaurant when construction laborers have their drinking bouts."[1] His samurai contempt for common people, and the Americans, is only slightly qualified by a lame addition that what happens in an unfamiliar country is indeed as different from his wont as a dream from reality. The tune seldom varies. Except for his general admiration for the achievements in modern technology, America is for him *iteki* or *kokoku,* both meaning a "country of barbarians." If he feels compelled sometimes to respond emotionally to an alien situation, he finds a way of escaping it all by writing a highly unoriginal, unexciting *waka* as if he needed to compose himself. At the palace of King Kamehameha IV in Honolulu, where he was impressed by the charms of the court and the lush green of tropical plants, he organized his feelings into two *waka,* comparing in one his experience to that of a legendary fisherman meeting the sea-fairy at a submarine palace, and dismissing in the other the royal couple as a joke. What moves him must be either dream or joke, an unreality.[2]

The Vice-Ambassador's low opinion of the Western barbarians is not widely shared. Most others on the Mission are appreciative, at times enthusiastic. Nonomura Ichinoshin Tadazane, Muragaki's personal servant, is typical: "For the most part, the people of this country are extremely generous, honest, and sincere. They do not despise foreigners. They trust even those whom they have never seen before. They are also somewhat naive like our provincials who have never been to a big city."[3] If the patronizing tone is audible, that, too, is typical. After all, the Japanese visitors tended to be both approbatory and defensive, as people unsure in a foreign environment often are.

Fukushima Keisaburō Yoshikoto, at eighteen one of the youngest in the Embassy, is more liberal in his praise:

In my opinion, seventy to eighty percent of the Japanese believe the Westerners are little better than beasts. There are even those who went as far as to attack them with swords. Although we have not come to that extreme yet, [if we persist in such xenophobia] we shall be reduced to the same condition as the Chinese are now in. We should learn from the history of China. The Westerners are different, being hospitable and

friendly to foreigners as though we were all one race. Especially because
America is a new country, its people are gentle. Although their real
intention is not easily fathomable, they seem to be honest at first glance
... Of all the seventy-seven people in this Embassy, most were full of
anger and hatred toward the Americans, but as we have come to know
these people better, we are now regretting our previous error ... What we
should do is understand them precisely, and without being seduced by
their merits treat them with love and justice. Then they, too, will respect
us and abandon their intention of plunder.[4]

In his enthusiasm, he seems to have overlooked the fact that it was
these very Westerners, "hospitable and friendly to foreigners," who
were playing havoc with China and threatening the same in his own
country. Nagao Kōsaku, who was hospitalized in San Francisco and
was overwhelmed by the American doctors' care and friendliness, is
even more enchanted with the strange, new land: "The American
barbarians are better than the Asians. Because America is a new
country, its people are honest, friendly, and sincere. This is not just
my personal view. The entire world agrees on this: since Asia is an old
culture, its people are cold-hearted."[5] If Nagao's argument is less than
persuasive, his conversion at this time seems convincing enough.

*old
versus
New*

True, the Americans lavished money and hospitality on the Embassy. And these men were completely bedazzled by the sumptuous
display everywhere as they traveled. But were they really so charmed
as to believe that Americans were pure of heart, and the American
foreign policy sheer good will? Possibly. People forget much in mo-
ments of enthusiasm. To take a counter-example, the worldly-wise
Laurence Oliphant was certain that Japan was a veritable Paradise
Regained in her full splendor of innocence, beauty, and sensuality
when he wrote the *Narrative of the Earl of Elgin's Mission* after a
two-week stay in Edo. So enamored was he that he volunteered to
serve in the British legation in Japan three years later. But then, soon
after arriving for his second visit, samurai desperadoes broke into the
legation and nearly severed the young diplomat's head and left arm
from his body.[6]

Among the members of the 1860 Mission, the ever phlegmatic
Muragaki was the only one who speculated about the Americans'
motives for this wild welcome (the newness of the Japanese in the
world scene; the uniqueness of Japanese culture; and the unusually
large entourage of the Embassy).[7] Did the rest simply take the hospitality at face value? They had long known what had happened to
China at the hands of the Europeans. They also saw Chinese immi-

grants poor and mistreated in San Francisco. Didn't such observations
lead to any critical reserve? Kimura Tetsuta Takanao from the south-
ern fief of Kumamoto had a lengthy "conversation" with a Chinese
emigré in Honolulu, as did Tamamushi. Among other things, they
talked about the political situations of China, Japan, and the United
States.[8] Fukushima noticed that "the Westerners despised the Chinese
even worse than they did the black devils from Africa."[9] And yet
such knowledge is never developed into any analysis of the relationships between the West and Asia. China is China, Japan is Japan; and
the only connection made is Fukushima's pleas for self-restraint,
which is quite oblivious to the aggressive policies of the Western
nations.

In order to understand this Japanese reaction, we should perhaps
first look at their encounters with various races throughout the trip.
The Embassy group that voyaged around the globe had the unique
chance of meeting many representative human races. They met the
Polynesians in Hawaii; the Central Americans in Panama; the whites,
blacks, native Americans, and Chinese in the United States; the
Africans in Luanda, Angola; the Indonesians in the Dutch Indies; and
the Chinese again in Hong Kong. Everywhere they went the whites
dominated, and the colored majority of humanity were subjected
either to slavery or colonization. How did the Japanese of 1860, just
barely released from the total closure of their island country, see this
situation, and what was their reaction to the white supremacy?

We might briefly pause here and recall the traditional Japanese
idea of their place in the world. They had learned long ago from the
Chinese that the center of the world was China, a nation surrounded
by barbarians on all four sides. In those early days, when Japan was
sending tributary envoys and exchange students to T'ang China from
the seventh to the ninth century, they seem to have only occasionally resisted the status of a satellite, or the "Eastern barbarian" (tōi). As
time went on, however, insular introspection won out, and they
proudly remembered Prince Shōtoku's challenge to the Chinese Emperor in 607. According to the Prince, the relationship of the two
nations was not China, the Middle Flower, and its eastern vassal, but
the country of the rising sun (Japan) and the sunset country.[10]

Although during the Tokugawa era the Japanese were accustomed to thinking of their feudal domains as autonomous, independent "countries," there were occasions when they saw Japan as a
whole, particularly in its relation to the outside world. And as long as

Japan was regarded as a comprehensive unit, it was the "divine state" (*shinkoku*) as against the "barbarians" (*iteki, ikoku, ketō, banjin*).[11] The very physical absence of foreigners nurtured such ethnocentricity. To add to these circumstances, the orthodox Chu Hsi school of Confucianism (which encouraged Sinophilism) was being attacked with increasing fervor by the restless students of *kokugaku* ("national studies"), the Mito nationalists, and others. The influence of Kamo Mabuchi, Motoori Norinaga, Hirata Atsutane, and Lord Tokugawa Nariaki was rapidly spreading among scholars and students. Their theory of emperor worship, as we have already seen, converged with other forces into ideological justification for the restoration of imperial rule in 1867. What evolved along with such reassessment—against the background of Western military threats—was an intensely passionate and mythical nationalism. When stripped of its paraphernalia of ideology and myth such exultation of state is, of course, no other than unalloyed racism—especially in the context of Japan's later domination in Asia.

The members of the 1860 Embassy are nearly unanimous in rejecting all races except for themselves and the whites. Yanagawa Kenzaburō Masakiyo, Ambassador Shimmi's twenty-four-year-old attendant, calls the Hawaiians "by nature unintelligent, but quite honest" and describes their appearance as "like demons in paintings."[12] The first entry in Morita Okatarō Kiyoyuki's record in Hawaii bluntly asserts, "The Hawaiian sailors are all black and ugly like devils, [but] their bodies look strong and muscular."[13] Kahachi, the boilerman of the *Kanrin Maru*, talks about the native women, who are "very dark":

Their dresses are in printed cotton, with tight sleeves. They seem to cut a hole in a large piece of cloth and slip it over their shoulders. They wear a big comb in their hair, and put on a red and white necklace. They swim in the ocean without undressing. They seem to fish or catch something in the water—always in a large group with no men around. The native women are very lewd and don't mind sexual intercourse even during the day. When they see a Japanese, they silently come close and, paying little attention to what others might see, try to drag him along. Men and women walk barefoot. Occasionally we see some with shoes, but they seem to belong to the higher ranks. Until forty years ago, neither men nor women wore any clothes except for patches in the front.[14]

Such observations are repeated with minimal variation by all diarists who made any reference to Hawaiians.

And when confronted with the Africans in Luanda, they give full rein to their contempt:

Both sexes have kinky hair, and their faces are black and ugly. As I have said earlier, the men are slightly covered with something resembling short undershirts, and the women shield themselves with a piece of square cloth. The grotesque way they shuffle around in the sand reminds me of the painted images of devils. They are curious about us and look at us from front and rear. Some of them believe the Japanese are cannibals and run away in fright.[15]

All the remarks about the Africans are more or less the same, sneering at the bare bodies and black skin, occasionally adding further details concerning their body odor and movement, their tattoos and ornaments. Some describe the chain gangs of slaves, but none expresses any sympathy for the captives; nor do they deplore the inhuman treatment by the Portuguese. The possible exceptions are the comments made by Tamamushi, Masuzu Shunjirō, and Namura Gohachirō. Tamamushi is slightly more reflective as an observer: when he calls the Africans "pitiably stupid," he at least gives reasons

A chain gang at Luanda, overseen by a Portuguese slave-master. A drawing by Kimura Tetsuta.

for the harsh judgment, and his tone is generally saddened and sober. But even he seems to accept the shackling of slaves as inevitable.[16] Masuzu, an assistant treasurer, found the black men's misery "unbearable to watch," but he half excuses the brutality on the ground that the natives are "unruly and unmannered" (*kisoku kore naku, reigi no meigi mo korenaku*). His endlessly run-on sentence, however, seems to revert once again toward some sympathy for the slaves.[17] As for Namura, the principal Dutch interpreter, he condemns the sale of slaves as an "evil custom," briefly describing the English and American efforts to stop the trade. Namura, however, blames the Africans themselves for slavery: "The Africans' industry has been for many years the sale of their children and relatives to other countries."[18] The predominant Japanese indifference to the wretchedness of the Africans is of course due in large measure to their ignorance about this culture's history and circumstances, and yet their ethnocentricity must have dulled their compassion a little as well.

How about their reaction to the American racial situation just, as it so happens, on the eve of the Civil War? (Abraham Lincoln was nominated by the Republican party on May 18, while the Embassy was in Washington, D.C.) Did they have any inkling of the enormity of the events that were soon to follow? Do we see anything that might suggest some reaction—however aloof—on the part of the Japanese visitors? For Yanagawa, the racial separation is a simple fact: "The blacks are inferior as human beings and extremely stupid. They are segregated from the whites, and no blacks are wealthy. They work only as servants for the whites, and are forbidden to enter any gathering-places for the whites such as our hotel, churches, restaurants, exhibitions, or theatres."[19] Kimura Tetsuta, an attendant for Inspector Oguri, similarly rationalizes the black and white situation: "The laws of the land separate the blacks. They are just like our *eta* caste. But they [the whites] employ the blacks as their servants. The whites are of course intelligent, and the blacks stupid. Thus the seeds of intelligence and unintelligence are not allowed to mix together."[20] Even Sano Kanae, whose diary is packed with unbiased and factual information gleaned from geography textbooks, deviates for once and dismisses the black race, while maintaining his usual matter-of-fact tone.[21]

Most seem unable even to distinguish between the blacks and native Americans. Satō Tsunezō Hidenaga, a servant cook, divides the Americans into whites and blacks, calling the latter "the natives of

this land, an imbecile race."[22] Tamamushi, too, makes the same
error, although his comments are, unlike most others', moderated by
sympathy:

Of all the people the blacks number one-sixth. Among them there are
those who are like blacks but not blacks and like whites but not whites.
They come from the mixing of the whites and blacks. All these people are
not permitted to participate in the politics of the country. They are
employed as servants for the whites or in humble and menial work. But
the blacks are the indigenous race of America, and the whites are the
English race. It is sad that the guest should usurp the place of the host. Yet
the difference between intelligence and idiocy is undeniable. Thus there
appears to be something unalterable about the race of a man.[23]

Most men in the Embassy, in short, took the race and slavery question for granted, as though the blacks as a people did not really exist.
There are, however, a few cases where some actual contact seems
to have occurred. Morita Kiyoyuki tells a story that is unique among
these documents. As the fourth-highest ranking officer on the Mission, he was assigned a personal escort by the State Department when
the envoys were received by the President at the White House on
May 19. Morita traveled in a carriage with a William Preston, of
Louisville, Kentucky, who had been the U.S. Minister to Spain:

Preston was a big man, around thirty-eight or thirty-nine years of age. He
was proud as he pointed out the flags of the Rising Sun to me, saying "very
good." As he singled out black women, he said they were the same color as
the black wool suit he had on, and sneered at them, calling them ugly. He
seemed very pleased with the white people and, whenever he saw white
women, said "very good," and pointed them out to me.[24]

Preston's crude remarks on the blacks addressed to a Japanese guest
raise a few questions. Does this mean the diplomat felt that the
Japanese stood on the white side of the unpassable color line and,
further, that his Japanese guest would of course concur with him? Or
was he being cynically nonchalant as to the relative racial position of
his listener—an attitude that was as contemptuous as that shown
toward the blacks? Isn't his boorish behavior itself an expression of
supercilious disregard for the Japanese? Morita says nothing about his
reaction, but one does suspect that he might not have recorded this
episode unless he felt something more tangled and murky under-
neath.

The same Morita relates yet another experience, this time directly involving a Japanese encounter with a black:

Ever since our arrival here, all of us had been giving presents (like fans, pictures, and toys) to children, hotel employees, waiters, and waitresses who had been attending us. Almost everyone had been provided with something by now, and those Americans who owned no Japanese gifts looked almost embarrassed. But it seems that those who had received our presents turned out to be mostly white and attractive people. One day a black woman approached one of our servants who spoke some English, tearfully confiding to him that since Nature had given her a black exterior, she was scorned by everyone and was not lucky enough to be given presents from anybody, and that she hated herself. She also said white people — even children — were getting presents from the Japanese, but she and her people who had such an ugly look received nothing. He felt so sorry for her that he gave her a fan, and she was very grateful. It seems that the whites are beautiful and shrewd and intelligent; and the blacks are ugly and stupid. So the whites always despise the blacks. There are some white-and-black marriages, and their children are between white and black in complexion.[25]

Morita's own sympathy with the black woman is only faintly suggested through his reference to the servant's feelings and through the rather incoherent narrative itself. He is repetitive as though he is not in control. The sentiment he must have felt for the woman is then forcibly pushed aside with a hard, crude judgment, as if he needed to tidy up his confusion with a self-assuring cliché.

The Japanese callousness to the miseries of the blacks is inseparable from their eagerness to overhaul their contempt of Westerners with respect bordering on worship. Hirose Kakuzō Kaneaki is deeply impressed by the marked difference between white women and Hawaiian, calling the former "extremely beautiful."[26] Katō Somō describes the children's dance at Willard's Hotel in Washington: "About one hundred boys and girls ranging from five to nine years of age were dressed in beautiful clothes. The boys smaller than seven or eight had ribbons hanging from their shoulders, and the girls had bracelets and hair ornaments in gold, silver, and coral. They had neither powder nor rouge, but their natural, beautiful complexion was whiter than snow, and more resplendent than jewels. They looked like goddesses [*tennyo*] in Paradise [*shinsenkyō*]."[27] Katō's likening of the dancing girls to heavenly goddesses whose "complexion was whiter than snow"—a phrase that recurs in several diaries— reveals something more than an innocent admiration for lovely children. Metamorphosis is afoot. The whites who were no better than animals only a few weeks ago are now, for some men at least, turning into divinities. In their enchantment with the advanced technology, these men in the Embassy are on the verge of accepting the West even

May Festival Ball of the Children in honor of the Embassy at Willard's Hotel, Washington, D.C., on May 23, 1860.

to the extent of seeing white as beautiful, and its converse, colored as ugly. *The Japanese desire to become "White" someday*

To return to the initial question, the Embassy men were all too eager to accept the American welcome as genuine. As they once wanted to believe that Japan was China's equal, so they now wanted to regard Japan and the United States as on a similar footing.[28] In their identification with the white Americans, they were prepared to reject any people the white Americans scorned. Thus American racism did not bother them much, nor did white supremacy, since the Japanese would be like the whites some day. It takes a few more decades before the Japanese racial consciousness becomes glaring, but their identification with the whites and their resultant self-hatred are soon to take the form of wild swings between pro-Western and anti-Western national policies. And the gradually intensifying disdain for their fellow Asians is inseparably linked with it. The Japanese encounter with the blacks—or the whites, for that matter—is admittedly not fully realized at this stage. Still, at this first contact with the outside world, their future course is foreshadowed by their nearly inarticulate responses to the race situation.[29]

The American attitude toward the Japanese is almost as sugges-

Americans welcomed the Japanese Visitors (handwritten)

tive. There is no doubt that the official welcome was both well-meant
and overwhelming. Throughout the seclusion period Japan had excited a good deal of curiosity, and the Americans were truly interested. Second, to be visited by the most exclusive nation in the world
flattered American citizens. Third, the Ambassadors, reported as we
have seen to be the highest-ranking hereditary princes and nobles of
the empire, powerfully appealed to the snobbery of the democratic
people. Fourth, the territorial ambition of the United States having
been temporarily satisfied with the annexation of Texas and California, that nation could better afford disinterest in Asia than could the
European nations at the time, and this pacifist stand pleased the
American pride. Fifth, there was an actual need of Japanese ports for
the supply of provisions for the fast increasing whaling fleets (a $17-
million investment by 1850) and cargo ships. Last, Japan's wealth was
overestimated by the traders, who believed there might be as great a
market in Japan as in China. Money meant civilization, civilization
meant democracy, democracy meant freedom, freedom meant Christianity, and Christianity meant, of course, civilization and all else.
Through this absolutely unbreakable circular logic, the Manifest
Destiny decreed that the Japanese Embassy be treated with pomp and
extravagance, and America indeed hearkened.[30]

(handwritten margin note: The Manifest Destiny)

  Reflecting the offical policy, the press is generally effusive about
the occasion. From the *Daily Alta California* of San Francisco and the
Washington *National Intelligencer* to *Harper's Weekly* and *Frank
Leslie's Illustrated Newspaper,* major newspapers and magazines carried lengthy gossip about the Embassy, editorializing now and then
on the momentous significance of the visit. However, among the
typically jovial and banal accounts, one comes across from time to
time reports that are rather chilling, if not shocking, in racial terms.
Unpleasant incidents occurred along the way throughout the Embassy's itinerary. As the envoys arrived at Washington, "each carriage
was surrounded by a mob, who thrust their heads into the carriage,
and passed all sorts of comments among themselves upon the appearance of the stranger. One burly fellow swore that all they wanted
was to have a little more crinoline and be right out decent looking
nigger wenches."[31] In Baltimore,

(handwritten margin note: mob)

It was not long before a party of firemen mounted to the balcony with
scaling ladders, and, bringing their hose with them, invited some of the
Japanese to take hold. This brought out the under officers, and among
them Tommy, who "played away" for a time with much glee. But this did

not satisfy the bold flame-quenchers. What they wanted was a turn with the Japanese nobility, and nothing else would do. At last one of them was introduced to an Ambassador, and immediately gave characteristic expression to his feelings by pulling off his wet and heavy hat and clapping it on the head of his new acquaintance. This bit of jocosity took so well among the Baltimore gentlemen, that similar pleasantries were straightway indulged in; and the last glimpse I caught of Simmi, Prince of Boojsen, revealed him struggling beneath a military cap which some creature had shoved over his eyes, and pressed tightly down.[32]

And in Philadelphia,

The most disgusting and brutal language was unsparingly used by the crowd while the procession was passing over the route. This was especially the case in the lower portion of the city where the "governing classes" most do congregate. For instance, at one point, a Naval Commissioner was greeted with the cry of "Say, you man with the epaulets, is that your monkey you have got with you?" And this is but one in a hundred of the humors of the crowd.[33]

An interpreter in the Embassy, who clearly understood the verbal abuse, complained to the protocol officers, Captain DuPont and Lieutenant Porter. He must have assumed that the American government could control the public's behavior toward the Japanese envoys, as Townsend Harris had always expected the Shogunate to do for him. The difference between a democracy and a feudal authoritarianism most certainly did not occur to the Japanese.

Unpalatable as these incidents were, they were not as disturbing as the more subtle displays of contempt. A writer for *Frank Leslie's Illustrated Newspaper* reports that when the Japanese appeared for their first dinner at Willard's Hotel in Washington, the "impertinent and vulgar intruders" were completely disappointed because "the Japanese took wine and used knives and forks like any other well-bred people."[34] The same sense of frustration was noticed even at the Presidential reception of the Embassy at the White House: "The interview, far from being absurd or amusing, as was anticipated, was of a solemn and serious character."[35] In the following week, the same paper has this to say about the Embassy members' visit to Congress: "They were led over the building and shown the splendid ceiling, but, to the astonishment of those introduced, they manifested much more interest in the mode of conducting the legislative proceedings than in any other part of the show. They remained but a short time and then retired, followed, of course, by a loud laugh from the representatives and by a wild mob rush of men and women from the galleries, which were left nearly empty."[36] Everywhere they went, the fun-loving

Americans expected to have an amusing entertainment, something really droll. Disappointment at times ensued.

If these reports at times frown on the behavior they describe, there are others that are much less self-conscious. A reporter from the *New York Illustrated News,* apparently considering it amusing enough, wrote at length of his own hilarity as the envoys were ushered into the reception room at the White House:

> To speak honestly, they looked a comical group, and nothing but the remembrance that they were strangers and persons of mark in their own country, unused to western manners and habits, and that they had come here as the representatives of a great civilized nation — on a mission of amity and good will to us — nothing but this remembrance kept me from laughing heartily at their appearance. I know it would have been very wicked and very uncourteous — nay, downright barbarous — in me to have given way thus to the excessive titillations which agitated my diaphragm; but I very nearly did it, notwithstanding, and came well nigh killing myself with internal convulsions, because I did not do it.[37]

The rhetoric used in the American press, too, is interesting. The approval of the Japanese as a race was usually expressed in one of two ways, either by identifying the Japanese with the Americans or by separating them from the races they, the Americans, despised. Thus, *Harper's Weekly* calls the Japanese "the British of Asia."[38] Similarly, the *Washington Evening Star* asserts, "No nation possesses so many elements of the Anglo-Saxon mind as the Japanese."[39] To appeal to the popular acclamation of Tommy, the *Philadelphia Press* refers to the teenager as "almost Caucasian in his complexion."[40] And to deliver the Japanese from the lowly esteem in which they placed the Chinese, or "Celestials" as they called them, papers are nearly unanimous in emphasizing the differences between the Asian neighbors. The San Francisco *Daily Alta California* declares, "The countenance of these people wore a far more intelligent look than any Chinese that we have seen."[41] Another San Francisco paper, the *Daily Evening Bulletin,* endorses its local rival: "Their dress bears some resemblance to that of the richer Chinese, but exhibits a taste more in harmony with our own."[42] While the *Daily Alta California* keeps hammering, "The Admiral was dressed richly, but with none of the Chinese flashiness,"[43] the *San Francisco Herald* is even more categorical: "The distinction between the Japanese and Chinese is very marked, the former being a superior race, intellectually."[44] The east coast equivalent of the Chinese on the west coast receives a milder but similar jab from *Harper's Weekly:* contrasting the magnificent hospitality of "the rich and influential men—such as William H. Aspinwall,

Moses H. Grinnell, James Gordon Bennett, Charles Hecksber, Thomas Richardson, David D. Field, and others who have fine country places" with the "grossièretés which may be expected from the O'Tooles, and O'Booles, and O'Gradys, and O'Bradys of the Common Council,"[45] it urges the Japanese to forget quickly the Irish boors. People all over indeed seem to be enamored with themselves.

It would of course be convenient to blame the uneducated masses for their crude conduct as did a turn-of-the-century book that tried to link the American reception of the 1860 Embassy with the later treatment of Japanese immigrants on the west coast.[46] But such explanation is quite inadequate. Racial bias may have been more visible among the poor and uneducated, but it in fact stretches across all class lines, rich and poor, educated and ignorant. And if the ugly feelings were indeed characteristic of the lower strata of the society, why should that be surprising? Why should the Irish in New York in the mid-nineteenth century treat the peculiar-looking heathen visitors with affection and respect when they themselves are brutalized? Likewise, the blacks? In view of the Japanese visitors' own feelings about racial matters, one should perhaps conclude that it is pointless to wish for a more fraternal and humane racial situation in pre-Civil War America. The mid-nineteenth-century racial picture was a bleak one the world over. Even in libertarian England, almost no one among the literary leaders of the time (like Carlyle, Ruskin, Dickens, or Tennyson) spoke up for the cause of the black race (although radicals and scientists like Mill and Huxley, Darwin and Lyell did) in the Governor Eyre controversy of 1865–1868.[47] Dickens was passionate about slavery in *American Notes* after his visit in 1842. But his outrage did not grow out of any belief in racial equality, but rather of the observation everywhere of the sheer inhuman living conditions of the slaves. The twentieth century may not have progressed much beyond in this—or in any other—aspect, but peoples and races are at least more aware of each other.

One of the most striking differences between Japan and the United States at the time was, as it still is, the place of women in society. The liberty enjoyed by the Man'yō women and even by the ladies of the Heian imperial court had largely vanished by the time the essentially military Tokugawa government was established in the early seventeenth century.[48] In principle at least, it was a puritanic and masculine regime, confining the women to the kitchen, bedroom, and nursery. Among the poor, the inequality was somewhat

NATURAL MISTAKES.

Gentleman. "Hi! Here, you Nigger, come here!"
Colored Gentleman. "Nigger! — no Nigger, Sar; me Japanese, Sar!"
Tommy (*a little how-came-you-so*). "One of dem (*hic*) is my Hat me know; but me be (*hic*) if me can tell which him is."

mitigated by the job of remaining alive that involved men and women alike without discrimination. Among the baronial classes, the halls and offices (called *omotemuki*, frontal quarters) where serious business transpired were off limits to all women. Harem-like, the ladies of palaces and castles stayed sequestered in the interiors (called *ō-oku*, great depths), spending their time entirely among themselves awaiting the lord and master's return after dusk.*

In such circumstances, the most influential moral guide for women was *Onna daigaku* (Book for women), a popularized version of the fifth volume of the aptly entitled *Wazoku dōjiki*, which means "The lessons for children in vulgate Japanese," by the great seventeenth-century neo-Confucian scholar Kaibara Ekken. According to Ekken, the whole purpose and function of a woman's life lay in

---

*The life of women in the deepest interiors of Edo Castle was unique. Their living quarters were sealed off from the rest of the world, and the ladies and maids were allowed to venture out only on rare occasions. The court ladies — numbering in the hundreds — were at the beck and call of the Shogun, although obviously some Shoguns were more vigorous than others in chamber activities. Women over thirty (including the Shogun's official wife) were withdrawn from

service and sacrifice. While young, she serves her father; once married, she obeys her husband; in widowhood, she attends her son. She always stays at home and seeks to nurture feminine virtues. An amazingly one-sided document, it defines, for instance, the seven grounds for divorce.

A woman can be guilty of seven vices, any one of which is considered a sufficient ground for her husband to divorce her. The decree, being an ancient law, is called the "Seven Grounds for Departure." 1. She leaves if she disobeys her husband's parents. 2. She leaves if she is barren. 3. She leaves if she is lewd. 4. She leaves if she is jealous. 5. She leaves if she is seriously ill. 6. She leaves if she is talkative. 7. She leaves if she steals.[49]

Following a precept in the Confucian *Rei ki* (or *Li-chi,* in Chinese), one of the Five Classics, Ekken stipulated that separation of men and women after the age of seven be absolute. The sexes mix thereafter only in matrimony; any other relationship is illegitimate.[50]

Men, on the other hand, were free, being heroically dedicated to the welfare of their families, their domains, and their nation. So preoccupied, they deserved diversion. An elaborate system of sexual entertainment was devised, ranging from the geisha quarters to the institution of concubines and mistresses that always threatened to turn into full-fledged polygamy. For the samurai, in short, women were not worth serious consideration.

Most members of the Embassy had seen at least a few Western men before they left Japan. But very few in the Embassy, if any, had seen a Western woman before.[51] They were keenly curious, and generally defensive. Vice-Ambassador Muragaki was disturbed on his first visit to Secretary of State Lewis Cass by the presence of ladies in

this service. The Shogun could bestow a favor on anyone from the humblest bathroom attendant to the loftiest lady-in-waiting *(chūrō)* in his wife's court *(midaidokoro).* He never slept alone with the favored lady, since security demanded that several people be constantly awake in the immediate proximity. A second lady lay on the left side of the Shogun and still another on the right side of his bedmate or in the next chamber — though they were expected to keep their backs discreetly to whatever was (or was not) in progress. The second lady in the chamber was required to report next morning in detail about the night to her superior, one of the governesses of the immense premises. Many women who came to serve in the castle chambers, as could be expected, died virgins in their selfless observance of the virtues of faith and loyalty. The 1860 Embassy members could not have known much about this, since everything concerning the Shogun's personal life was kept in the strictest secrecy. Still, this is what they were vaguely anticipating to see — or not to see — in the White House! For the macabre life of women in Edo Castle, see Nagashima Konshirō and Ōta Takeo, eds., *Teihon: Edojō ō-oku;* Mitamura Engyo, *Goten jochū;* Murai Masuo, *Edojō;* and Ōta Kyōson, *Chiyoda-jō no ō-oku.* Some of these books are almost by nature salacious rather than enlightening, or even entertaining.

the State Department offices, although on this particular occasion he may have been more offended by not receiving any ceremony or refreshment, which he at once proceeded to characterize as a symptom of American barbarism.[52] At Secretary Cass's ball in the Embassy's honor, Muragaki had ample opportunity to observe American women:

We arrived at Cass's residence. I wondered about the nature of the ceremony we were going to perform on this occasion, since it was an invitation from the Prime Minister. To our great surprise, however, we found that the hall, passages, and rooms were all packed with hundreds of men and women. Innumerable gas lamps were hanging from the ceilings, and the glass chandeliers decorated with gold and silver were reflected in the mirrors. It was as brilliant and dazzling as day. Though we did not know what was happening, we somehow managed to make our way through the crowd to the room where Cass and his family stood, and were greeted by them. Even his grandchildren and daughters came to shake hands with us. Although we sat on chairs, everyone in the room also came to shake our hands. Since there was no interpreter around, I did not understand at all what was being said. The crowd was extremely dense. DuPont took my hand and led me to an adjoining room, where a large table was laid with gold and silver ware. At the center of the table were the Japanese and American flags to express friendship. We had some drinks and food at the table. Soon we were led away to another large room; its floor was covered with smooth boards. In one corner, there was a band playing something called "music" on instruments that looked like Chinese lutes. Men were in uniform with epaulets and swords, and women with bare shoulders were dressed in thin white clothes. They had those wide skirts around their waists. Men and women moved round the room couple by couple, walking on tiptoe to the tune of the music. It was just like a number of mice running around and around. There was neither taste nor charm. It was quite amusing to watch women's huge skirts spread wider and wider like balloons as they turned. Apparently, high officials and older women, as well as young people, are very fond of this pastime. The men and women went to the table for refreshments, then coming back for another dance. This, we were told, would continue all night. As for myself, I was astonished by the sight, and wondered whether this was a dream or reality. We asked DuPont to say good-night to the host for us, and left for the hotel. Admittedly, this is a nation with no order or ceremony [*rei*], but it is indeed odd that the Prime Minister should invite an ambassador of another country to an event of this sort! My sense of displeasure is boundless: there is no respect for order and ceremony or obligation [*gi*]. The only way to exonerate them is by recognizing that all this absence of ceremony issues from their feeling of friendship.

    All is strange,
        Appearance and language,
            I must be in a dream-land.
Women are white and beautiful, and they are handsomely dressed with

Presentation of an American lady to the Ambassadors at Willard's Hotel,
Washington, D.C.

gold and silver decorations. Although I am becoming accustomed to their
appearance, I find their reddish hair unattractive, and their eyes look like
those of dogs. Now and then, though, I see a black-haired woman who also
has black eyes. They must be descendants of some Asian race. Naturally
they look very attractive.[53]

One notes in this passage that our Ambassador is not quite so sure of
himself as usual. He is visibly tense, not knowing the nature of the
occasion. In his own country, a foreign ambassador—or any other
high official—would be received with a dignified ceremony undefiled
by the presence of women (like, say, the reception of a visiting cardi-
nal at the Vatican). Of course, there might be a banquet later on, and
even the company of women might not be altogether unlikely then,
but those women would be professionals trained to entertain men.
For the warriors and officials of higher ranks and their wives and
daughters to mingle together and dance and enjoy themselves in self-
abandon is an outrage in decorum that no self-respecting samurai
would ever tolerate. Muragaki is indeed distressed by these strange
women, but also fascinated, as his detailed observation testifies. But
before he admits their attractiveness to himself, his samurai sense of

aloofness must intervene. And as is usually the case with him, he writes a *waka* which, again typically, tries to remove his experience as a dream, a remote experience. The poem having cleansed his fears, he is now ready to be a little more honest with himself. So he calls the women "white and beautiful." He is even willing to face the sexual threat he feels vaguely in these women (the "eyes of dogs," or bitches?).[54] Then he re-collects himself with the image of the women of his own kind which was projected on the darkhaired women he saw at the ball.

The dance party was, understandably, a subject for several men of the Embassy. They had been utterly unprepared for such a form of entertainment. Morita Kiyoyuki, who went to the party at Cass's, calls it "indescribably noisy." He too is nervous: "Although there was very little that was licentious or lewd, it was unbearable to watch."[55] Ono Tomogorō, forty-three years old, is not amused either. Although he was quite comfortable with his American hosts at the Mare Island Naval Shipyard and was sufficiently interested in the American women to write about them at fair length, their dance was nothing but a "bore that annoyingly dragged on and on," and their singing reminded him of the "gibberish scream of a bewitched woman."[56] Hidaka Keizaburō Tameyoshi, a twenty-seven-year-old *metsuke* officer, was also present at a party, where "women and maidens were nude from shoulders to arms, and they had various ornaments in their hair. The way men and women, both young and old, mixed in the dance, was simply insufferable to watch."[57] Even the eighteen-year-old Fukushima dismisses the dancing as no more than a lot of "bouncing and leaping," and the ball itself as "noisy and uninteresting."[58] The kindest remark by far on American dancing comes from Muragaki's aide Nonomura, who compares the "dazzling" dancers to "butterflies crazed by the sight of flowers."[59]

Ambassador Muragaki was at his gallant and diplomatic best when he dined at the presidential dinner:

The President sat at the center, while his niece Lane sat opposite to him, with Shimmi sitting on her right and I on her left ... Including the women and high-ranking officials sitting with us, there were about thirty people at the table. We had two interpreters standing behind us. Soon soup was served, followed by various kinds of meat, and of course champagne, and other drinks. Aware of the President's presence, we were very careful about our manners. It was rather amusing to watch and imitate the table manners of a woman sitting next to me. Lane was behaving like the head of the house, supervising everything during the dinner. Her power and dignity were so impressive that she might have been taken for the Queen,

Banquet given by the President for the Ambassadors at the White House, May 25, 1860.

and her uncle, the President, for her Prime Minister. She told us to have more wine, asking in the meantime questions about our country. Most of her questions were posed from the American point of view, and I found them hard to answer. I gave noncommittal replies as best I could to her questions like "how many court ladies does the Shogun keep?" or "what are their manners and customs like?" She also asked which women did I find superior, Japanese or American? — a question I found amusing, since it was, after all, so typically feminine. When I told her the American women are the more beautiful of the two with their fair complexion, she and her companions looked very pleased.[60]

Muragaki then snaps out his true feeling into his diary, "Stupid gullible women!" The reader, for once, finds himself in tune with the Vice-Ambassador's annoyance.

The courteous treatment of the female by the male in America was challenged by several men in the Embassy. Fukushima was astonished to see women respectfully waited on by men: "When there aren't enough chairs, men stand by and women sit down. When a wife is thirsty, she makes her husband bring her a glass."[61] Fukuzawa Yukichi, who later was to write one of the most important feminist books, *Shin onna daigaku* (New book for women), disputing the authority of the old *Onna daigaku*, was similarly bewildered during this visit by the sight of a husband serving his wife.[62] The male

Fukuzawa Yukichi with an American girl in San Francisco.

chivalry was noted by yet another, Yanagawa Kenzaburō Masakiyo, a twenty-four-year-old attendant to the Chief Ambassador: "In this country women are usually revered. When a man enters a room, he greets women first if there are women present, and men afterward. Also a man takes off his hat when he greets a woman, whereas he does not do so in greeting a man. If a man meets a woman in the street, he steps aside and lets her pass first. The way women are treated here is like the way the parents are respected in our country."[63] Men as warriors at the top of the social hierarchy should naturally command respect from women. Why women, being frail-bodied and frailer-headed, should assert themselves and men concede to their superior air is a question that the Japanese men could not at all comprehend then, and I suspect many cannot even now.

There were a few men willing to see women of America in a more favorable light. Masuzu Hisatoshi, a treasury officer, was impressed by the fact that women in America, even the younger ones, are generally less "bashful" and more "strong-willed" than Japanese women.[64] Yoshioka Ryōdayū Yūhei, too, thought most American women to be "intelligent, high-spirited, and faithful,"[65] although he neglected to mention the ground for reaching such judgment. Katō Somō (who was so delighted with the children's dance performance at Willard's) was also unprepared to find the American women at all attractive; he was even more surprised to find that they were not licentious, though at times they were indecent.[66] Quoting from a learned book he had recently read, he discusses his own observations. (If Katō's quotation and his own remarks read like a garbled Zen question, one should not be alarmed: leaps between statements are a result of his hasty condensation of his source book.)

According to the fourth book of the *Gyokuseki shirin* [Gems from the forest of history and geography, published in the early 1860s], which describes the manners and customs of the United States of America on the authority of Dutch magazine articles, "There are no lewd women in the United States. All the women in America have loud and high-pitched voices. Their dance is quite different from ours. No woman is punished for betraying the trust placed on her. When she is in love, she is as silent about her feelings as is the quiet of a grave (which means even when men and women live together in the same house, there is no immoral, ribald conduct leading to a scandal)." "Hotels are greater in the United States than anywhere else. Also, people love traveling, which costs very little there. Steam ships are quite sumptuous." In my opinion, obscenity may be inherent in the customs and manners of the country, but the women are actually much more chaste than their appearance might suggest. For example, this same volume of the same book mentions that "boarding houses where widows and spinsters reside, as in certain kind of nunneries, are actually pleasure-quarters frequented by men about town." But brothels are to be found in any country in the world, and their existence alone cannot prove the immorality of the United States.[67]

Katō's initial feeling that American women are more libidinous than Japanese is nothing unusual. People the world over seem to be suspicious about foreigners' sexual habits and, as a rule, regard them as lewd and obscene in contrast to their own.

Harris, for instance, was disgusted with the Magistrates of Shimoda and other Japanese:

American thought of Japanese as lewd

The conversation now took the usual Japanese turn. The lubricity of these people passes belief. The moment business is over, the one and only subject on which they dare converse comes up. I was asked a hundred different questions about American females, as whether single women dressed differently from the married ones, etc., etc.; but I will not soil my paper with the greater part of them, but I clearly perceived that there are particulars that enter into Japanese marriage contracts that are disgusting beyond belief. Bingo-no-Kami informed me that one of the Vice-Governors was specially charged with the duty of supplying me with female society, and said if I fancied any woman the Vice-Governor would procure her for me, etc., etc., etc.[68]

Puccini

Harris's journal, of course, does not mention that a few months later he availed himself of the service so reprehensibly offered. And if his fling with Okichi, the Shimoda village girl, did not last beyond a few days, the failure seems not entirely due to the girl's concupiscence.[69] Even the gentle Samuel Wells Williams, always happy to find merits in the Japanese, is pretty firm about their salaciousness:

Of all heathen nations I have ever heard described, I think this is the most lewd. Modesty, judging from what we see, might be said to be unknown, for the women make no attempt to hide the bosom, and every step shows the leg above the knee; while the men generally go with the merest bit of rag, and that not always carefully put on. Naked men and women have both been seen in the streets, and uniformly resort to the same bath house, regardless of all decency. Lewd motions, pictures and talk seem to be the common expression of the viler acts and thoughts of the people, and this to such a degree as to disgust everybody. Alas for the condition and excellence of a simple, heathen people, dreamed of by moralists who never saw what they prate of![70]

Williams' is the standard verdict: the one establishment in those days that no Western traveler ever failed to visit in Japan was the public bath-house where native men and women bathed together apparently without feeling any sexual impropriety. For the foreigners, the promiscuous bath was incontrovertible proof of Japanese debauchery

Public bath at Shimoda. This illustration appeared in the first edition of Hawks's *Narrative of the Expedition.* After a shocked reaction, it was withdrawn from the later editions.

which, be they diplomats, teachers, traders, or missionaries, they personally needed to verify from time to time. They never seem to have dreamt that some in the next century might judge them, the moralists, to be more perverse than the heathen mixed bathers, and in their own countries at that.

It is true that the Japanese did not think much of being nude in public places. In fact, several men in the Embassy took a bath in the open air in San Francisco to the great indignation of neighboring ladies, and had to have curtains hung around the tub to conform to the California notion of modesty.[71] At the same time, the Japanese visitors were scandalized by the bare shoulders of the American ladies, the nude sculptures and pictures in public buildings, and above all by the free mingling of sexes in formal ceremonies. In the earlier stage of the visit, the American press noticed the aloofness of the Japanese visitors toward American women.[72] Later on, however, they were reportedly "overcoming their repugnance to female society,"[73] and were said to be "quite smitten with the beautiful ladies that [were] staying at Willard's."[74] It was even reported that they were ogling "the splendid women of Washington."[75] We do know

Tommy's adventure fairly well. As to the rest of the entourage, their real reaction is not quite certain. At least we might imagine that just as most of them came to love champagne and ice cream as time went on, so they may well have come to look upon these white-skinned, red-haired, strong-willed ladies of the West with a little less guardedness, with a little more friendliness.

Fukuzawa Yukichi had been the head tutor (*jukuchō*) for several years in the Ogata School in Osaka, noted for its curriculum in Western learning. So he was not at all surprised, according to his reminiscence forty years later, when he saw in San Francisco the telegraph and other signs of advanced technology. But he had difficulty understanding the "social, political, and economical" makeup of the Americans:

> One day I felt curious about the whereabouts of George Washington's descendents, and asked someone about them. His answer was, "There should be a female descendant somewhere who married somebody, but I don't know exactly." He was so indifferent to the question that I was quite taken aback. It struck me as really strange. Of course, I knew thoroughly well that the United States was a republic with a new president elected every four years, but still I thought Washington's offspring were very important people. After all, I had in mind Lord Minamoto Yoritomo and Shogun Tokugawa Ieyasu. That's why I didn't understand his answer.[76]

Probably he was less familiar with the American social-political structure than this passage suggests; for a few pages later in the same autobiography, he confesses his ignorance more directly. When he went to England a few years later, he didn't even understand the function of Parliament.[77] And if Fukuzawa, one of the best "Western experts" of the time, knew so little, how much did the rest of the Embassy members comprehend?

It is true that by 1860 a good number of books had been published on the subject of world geography. Among the later and more conspicuous ones are *Anguria jinsei joshi* (English character and geography), published in 1862 by a Nagasaki interpreter, Yoshio Naganori; *Yochishi* (The world geography), 1827, sixty volumes, by Aoji Rinsō; and *Konyo zushiki* (Illustrated world geography), 1845, five volumes, by Mizukuri Seigo, all based on Dutch sources. Mizukuri's book was the most widely read of the three, and it describes the United States in about forty pages in the second half of the fourth book. Mizukuri supplements this meager information about America with a few more pages in *Konyo zushiki ho* (Supplement), but even then the description is much too brief and scanty to make America available to its readers.[78]

While Holland remained an important conduit of information, China was becoming increasingly interested in the West as a result of the Opium War. Thus, numerous books were being published in China in response to the military threat, many of which were introduced to Japan. The single most important study was *Kaikoku zushi* (World geography with maps, *Hai-kuo t'uchi* in Chinese) by Gi Gen (or Wei Yüan), translated from Hugh Murray's *Encyclopedia of Geography* (1834) with further contributions by an American missionary, Elijah Coleman Bridgman, and published in 1842. Sixty volumes altogether, the book was perhaps the most comprehensive of all such studies, and it was brought to Japan around 1854 after initial government suppression. *Kaikoku zushi* was considered so important that it was not only translated in toto, but also broken into several separate parts and published at times in translation and at other times in the annotated *kanbun* form. All those ideologue-activists (*shishi*) fascinated with the affairs of the West, like Yokoi Shōnan (1809–1869), Sakuma Shōzan (1811–1864), Yoshida Shōin (1830–1859), and Hashimoto Sanai (1834–1859), avidly read it in some form or other. (It was in fact no other than Kawaji Toshiakira who sponsored the publication of the translation of *Kaikoku zushi* in 1854. Kawaji, one might recall, is one of the prominent Commissioners for Foreign Affairs who played a role in the treaty negotiations with Harris and others.[79]) Many of the Mission, too, must have read at least the sections dealing with the United States. Tamamushi, for instance, quotes from *Kaikoku zushi,* as well as *Konyo zushiki,* when he comments on Washington, D.C.[80]

These efforts are indeed impressive, and were useful in providing the Japanese with some vocabulary for strange objects and concepts, as well as some vague idea about America. And yet the books as a whole would not pass the test either of accuracy or comprehensiveness. They are full of errors, the translation terms are often extremely obscure, much information is irrelevant and useless, and perhaps most important, the explanation is too cursory on any given topic. To take the example of *Kaikoku zushi,* it devotes three volumes to the United States, Volume 39 (140 pages) treating the country as a whole, while Volumes 40 (78 pages) and 41 (35 pages) describe, respectively, the eastern and western states under separate headings. Two hundred fifty pages on the United States may seem a fairly detailed presenta-

A Spanish samurai named "Koronbus" having an audience with Queen "Isaberla."

tion, but the fact is it tries to do too much, explaining the history and geography of the country as a whole, and then of each state. It further lists all the main mineral and agricultural products of each state, while mechanically enumerating the population of cities and states.[81] In short, *Kaikoku zushi* did not allow its reader even a hint of the American social and political systems. Other, shorter books like Mizukuri's *Konyo zushiki* were of course less satisfactory.

To take one last example, *Meriken shinshi* (A new book on America, 1855), a popularized version of *Konyo zushiki,* is a charmingly illustrated five-volume work. The United States proper is discussed in its first two volumes, totaling some forty pages plus a few more passages scattered in the last volume. The table of contents reads like this:

Volume One: 1. The Story of a Man Called Koron [Columbus] discovering the Land of America; 2. The General Survey of the United States [one and a half pages]; 3. The Life of Koron [7 pages]; 4. The Northern American States; 5. New Spain; 6. New Mexico.
Volume Two: 1. California; 2. The Origin of the Republic; 3. The Thirty-One Republican States; 4. Two Additional Republican States; 5. The Thirty-One Republican States [a list of states, a map, a description of

Washington, D.C., a single-page fantastic explanation of the presidency and Congress]; 6. The Number of American Warships; 7. The Life of Washington [9 pages]; 8. Nova Scotia; 9. Canada; 10. New Britannia; 11. Greenland; 12. American Russians [American Indians]; 13. South America; 14. New Granada.[82]

Even if the Embassy members had read these avant-garde studies with considerable care, they would have had to start all over from scratch in order to understand the country in any coherent or comprehensive fashion. Thus, their studies were less than functional.*

The realization came slowly. During the voyage, they were impressed by the absence of rigid hierarchic separation among the crew members. Still, the military structure of a warship at sea—with no civilians and no women—was the closest approximation to their own warrior society. When they were received in San Francisco by municipal officials, however, their puzzlement seems to have commenced in earnest. The city structure of Japan at the time was as follows:

We may take Ōsaka as an example of the city as a territorial unit. The commandant of Ōsaka castle, a Tokugawa appointee, was the over-all military officer. Two town magistrates appointed by the *bakufu* from among high-ranking *samurai* were the actual heads of the city. Under them was a numerous staff of *samurai* officials, judges, inspectors of commerce, inspectors of temples, inspectors of the family registers, etc.

There also existed a council of elders (at first 21, later 14 and finally 10 in number) composed of members of leading *chōnin* families on a hereditary basis. Its functions were to oversee trade, supervise the wards, manage assessment and payment of taxes, and appoint the heads of wards.[83]

What is the status of the San Francisco mayor? Is his office equivalent to that of a *bugyō* (magistrate) occupied by a high-ranking warrior bureaucrat? Or the humble position of *machi-doshiyori*, burgher elder? President Henry Frederick Teschemaker of San Francisco was a "merchant," and yet he was called "president," the San Francisco mayoralty then comprising the presidency of the Board of Super-

---

*To read all these handbooks on the United States in connection with the 1860 travelogues is a fascinating exercise. Their meager substance is so similar from one to another that the reader might be able to trace the content of these geography books back to the Chinese and finally to Western sources. Some of the 1860 travelogues—such as Sano Kanae's *Man'en gannen hō-Bei nikki,* (The diary of the 1860 travel to America) for instance—explicitly state that they are dependent on some geography book(s) whenever they make a long comment on a city or a country. In other words, the traveler's observation is very much influenced by the book(s) he has read. And even the figures and facts and data he quotes seem to have come from Japanese and Chinese reference books rather than directly from American sources. Thus, there seems to be a circular route of information: Murray's *Encyclopaedia of Geography* to Bridgman's *Mirika gas-*

visors. It was an arrangement the Japanese were not acquainted with, even if they knew the word "president." What exactly does the office mean?—compared with the one in Washington? For the members of the Embassy, the distinction between the samurai and all the rest was of crucial importance. The officials of the City of San Francisco did not fit in either category.

Lieutenant James D. Johnston of the *Powhatan* left the Navy when the ship arrived in San Francisco, and this resignation, too, was something not readily comprehensible to the Japanese. The rule was: once a samurai, always a samurai. Was there any particular reason for Johnston to resign, exchanging his "warrior" uniform for civilian dress? Morita seems nonplussed as he describes Johnston's departure.[84] Captain Katsu of the *Kanrin Maru* similarly conjectures that the mayor and the city supervisors would be carrying two swords if they were

---

sei-koku shiryaku to Gi Gen's *Kaikoku zushi* to the 1860 travelogues. In the last stage of this process, the travelers go back to the original source and observe America directly as Murray presumably did at first, but much of their observation is already formed by the secondary information.

The best bibliography of the geography books during the Tokugawa period is *Sakoku jidai no Nihonjin no kaigai chishiki,* eds. Ayuzawa Shintarō and Ōkubo Toshikane. See also Osatake Takeshi, *Ishin zengo ni okeru rikken-shisō* and *Kinsei Nihon no kokusai kannen no hattatsu.*

Among the true leaders of "Dutch learning" — Sakuma Shōzan and Yokoi Shōnan, for example — knowledge of the West would seem to have been far more advanced than suggested by these handbooks. And yet one needs to recall that their interest in the West was a function of their *domestic* programs (1) for the defense of Japan and (2) for the reaffirmation of the hierarchic political order. Sakuma Shōzan's famous slogan "Eastern morality, Western technology" *(Tōyō no dōtoku, seiyō no geijutsu)* meant utilization of Western technological information for the purpose of maintaining the Eastern (i.e., Confucian) social and political structure. Sakuma thus remained totally aloof to any social and political alternatives that might have been suggested by studies of the West. And he is most representative of these activist scholars.

As a political theorist, Yokoi Shōnan was a bit different. While his belief in the supremacy of Confucianism over Western values never wavered, he saw that the Way of the Sages was at the present time better revealed in the West than in China or in Japan. His proposal was thus to revive the Confucian principle of love of humanity *(jin,* or *jên* in Chinese) in Japan and, while establishing at home a sort of "inter-fief republicanism" *(Nihon-koku kyōwa itchi no go-seiji),* to spread abroad the *jin* principle in order to restore truly global peace and justice (he attacked, for instance, Western imperialism and colonialism). Although his analysis of the nineteenth-century geopolitical situation is not well informed, his idealism and universalism are indeed unique among the political thinkers of the time.

Both Sakuma Shōzan and Yokoi Shōnan were Captain Katsu Awa-no-Kami's friends (Katsu later married Shōzan's sister). Incidentally, both their lives ended at the hands of fanatically anti-Western assassins.

Japanese.[85] The officials' lack of pomp and dignity such as would be invested in their Japanese counterparts only heightened their confusion. When John G. Downey, Governor of the State of California, casually dropped in to meet the crew of the *Kanrin Maru* at a hotel, the Japanese almost refused to believe that this perfectly ordinary-looking man unaccompanied by any attendant was the *daimyō* of a large territory called a "state."[86] Not sure about what the "state" as a regional administrative unit meant, they applied various Japanese words to it ranging from *kuni* (country) and *shū* (the standard translation term now for the American state) to *fu* (prefecture) and *buraku* (settlement, village).[87]

More than anything else, the presidency of the United States baffled the Japanese. Before the visit most of them had been under the vague impression that the President was more or less identical with the Shogun. The letters from the Council of State, for instance, were always addressed to "Your Majesty, the President of the United States," as they must have copied from the American letters addressed to "Your Majesty the Tycoon, the Emperor of Japan." Although the books on the West that were largely based on Chinese sources used words like *taiseikan,* *saijōkan, shutōryō seitōryō, sōtōryō,* and *daitōryō* for "president," Nonomura calls Buchanan *kokuō* (king), as does Yanagawa.[88] James Buchanan, however, did not behave like a monarch. He was incomprehensibly "unassuming and simple."[89] When an entertainment was offered at Willard's in Washington, the President stopped by with his nieces, and, as was the custom in those happy days before the introduction of the Secret Service, he even walked home to the White House alone without a single guard in attendance.[90] The President's ordinary business suit at the reception was itself a source of ceaseless wonderment. The Ambassadors—who had had the chance to glimpse the Supreme Ruler of Japan before their departure—expected to see in the President a similarly mighty person, as elaborately dressed and as deferentially attended. Since the Shogun was practically a deity, no one dared to look at his divine person; likewise, they expected Americans to lie prostrate before their President, the Shogun of America. After the initial shock at the plebeian interview, various attempts were made to comprehend the republican system of kingship. Who becomes the president? How is he chosen? Yanagawa's version is fairly typical:

At the time of the expiration of a President's term, the Prime Minister and a few other high officials (who have distinguished themselves with their own talents) are considered. If the Prime Minister and these nobles all decline the offer, then they—together with the retired Presidents—hold an "auction" [*nyūsatsu*] and choose the highest bid. According to another theory, the virtuous men are "auctioned" from the entire population, except for the blacks. On public occasions, the officials wear ceremonial attire with splendor and dignity. In private life, however, they are no different from common people, and they engage in commerce and agriculture in plain clothes. The high officials including the President walk around the city without any attendant, and nobody greets him either by bowing or removing his hat. Once indoors, even the President takes off his hat.[91]

This observation is endorsed nearly verbatim by Fukushima and Nonomura (who may have kept close company and shared the same informant, or read the same geography textbooks, or just simply copied from one another's diaries).[92] In another connection, Yanagawa and Fukushima both subscribe to the theory of a presidential ceremony, which they both claim to have learned from the Captain of the *Niagara:* "The American President surrenders his office after four years to the Vice-President. At the changeover, the new President enters the White House from the front gate, as the old President withdraws from the rear."[93]

These are wide-eyed reports by those who are mostly non-committal in their political observations. There are others that are clearly for or against what was taken to be the American political structure. The hostile version comes, of course, from Vice-Ambassador Muragaki, while the approving one comes from Tamamushi Sadayū Yasushige.

Muragaki's attitude toward America as a country of barbarians is confirmed at every point by his observations. Notice, for instance, his negative reaction to the burial of two *Roanoke* sailors at sea:

Two sailors, who had fallen ill some time ago, died. Their bodies, each wrapped in canvas and weighted with shot, were brought on deck. The chaplain officiated at the funeral service, attended by the Commodore and other officers on the ship. While the music was being played, the bodies were thrown into the sea, each from either side of the ship. The crew were seriously worried over the many cases of illness among them, caused, as they told us, by staying too long at Aspinwal.

We are told that it is a rule in the United States Navy that the bodies of all officers, up to the captain's rank, are taken to the nearest port for funeral, and that in the case of a commodore or an officer of a higher rank, his body is encased in a glass coffin, and sent back to his home; in the case of sailors, their bodies are buried in the sea. We indeed feel sorry for the unfortunates who died on the high sea.

We were surprised, however, to see the Commodore himself attending the funeral of mere common sailors. My countrymen suspect that the Americans, having no sense of either ceremony [*reigi*] or true hierarchic distinction [jōge no betsu], are ruled by the expression of sincerity [shin-jitsu].[94]

Translated literally, the last paragraph is almost unintelligible. Even in Japanese Muragaki's statement is hard to understand unless one learns what the Vice-Ambassador meant by *rei* and *gi* (or their compound, *reigi*). Obviously very important terms for Muragaki, they are frequently in his vocabulary, and an examination of his use might throw some light on his ideas and values.

When he witnessed the Americans respectfully removing their hats as they passed George Washington's grave, he noted that "even in this barbaric country that knows no *rei,* people pay their respects to Washington in accordance with the laws of nature."[95] Secretary Cass's "mild and dignified" manner at their first interview did not satisfy the envoy because Cass treated him cordially as though they had been old friends "without the slightest etiquette [*rei*]."[96] We have already seen his reaction to the ball at Cass's residence. Finally, his response to the presidential reception at the White House runs as follows:

We gathered together and talked of our experience on this memorable day. The President is a silver-haired man of over seventy years of age, and he has a most genial manner without losing noble dignity. He wore a simple black costume of coat and trousers in the same fashion as any merchant, and had no decoration or sword on him. All the high-ranking officials were dressed in the same way as the President, whereas the army and navy officers wore epaulets (the gold tassels attached to the shoulders, of which the length marked the rank), and gold stripes on the sleeves of their costumes (of which the number represented the rank, three stripes signifying the highest); and they carried a sword at their side. It seemed to us a most curious custom to permit the presence of women on such a ceremonious occasion as today. We remembered how we were received at the Sandwich Islands by the women alone — after the main event of our presentation — with somewhat greater formalities; this difference, we attributed, although we were not well acquainted with Western customs and manners, to the fact that the Sandwich Islands constituted a monarchy. The United States is one of the greatest countries in the world, but the President is only a governor voted in [nyūsatsu] every four years. (There will be a changeover on October 1 this year. We heard them suggest a certain man; when we asked how they could tell before the "auction," they answered that this man would be the President, because he was related to the present one. Judging from such remarks, I don't believe that the fundamental laws of this country will last much longer.) The President is thus not a king. Nevertheless, since the Shogun's letter was addressed to him, we adopted such manners of etiquette [rei] as were appropriate to a monarch. It was pointless, however, to put on the formal *kariginu* robe in his honor, since the Americans attach little importance to hierarchic distinction, and dispense with all ceremony [*reigi*]. We were, however, exceedingly happy and satisfied to have attained the goal of our mission here, an achievement worthy of any man's ambition, when we learned that the President was highly appreciative and took pride in receiving the first mission from Japan in his country before any other. We were told that he was letting the newspapers show our party dressed in *kariginu*.[97]

Rei (or *li*, in Chinese), which is often combined with *gi* (*i* in Chinese) without altering the meaning substantially as in *girei* or *reigi*, is usually translated into good manners, propriety, ceremony, ritual, rite, courtesy, decorum, etiquette, politeness, gratitude, or honorarium. The word means all these, and much more. One of the most fundamental Confucian terms, it points to the social order from which such ceremonial expressions emanate. In Mencius, *rei* is taught as "a way whereby one enters into communion with others," a "process of humanization," human relatedness.[98] In Hsün Tzu, however, such relatedness is more specifically defined in terms of hierarchy. *Rei* is "politicized."[99] And the concept of *rei* as the Tokugawa men understood it is hardly touched by any concern with human relationship except within the context of the political structure, that is, the meticulously formulated vertical hierarchy. The inferior bows to his superior in a prescribed fashion, because this bow confirms the order in which the two understand how to relate. The Ambassadors are dressed in a certain formal attire, because the particular habiliments so chosen define precisely the nature of the occasion as well as the relative positions of the participants. (Hence, Muragaki's obsession with epaulets and uniforms and *eboshi* and *kariginu*.) In fact, the Japanese language is itself impossible to speak without a precise grasp of *rei*, which operates in a strict and complex system of honorifics (*keigo*).[100] So viewed, rituals and ceremonies are expressions of the most essential values of Japan. In the great chain of being that—theoretically—connects the Emperor to the humblest laborers via the Shogun, lords, and myriad ranks of samurai, farmers, artisans, and merchants, all must perform ceremony so that order may be maintained and reaffirmed throughout.[101] (Toward the end of the Tokugawa era, the distinctions were somewhat relaxed, allowing for limited intermarriage, for instance, between the samurai and the merchant classes. But the job of bureaucrats like Muragaki was to maintain the status quo as much as possible.) For Muragaki a society lacking this ritual expression of hierarchic distinction, as well as such distinction itself (*meibun*), was doomed to anarchy and demise.

Likewise, Muragaki's response to the U.S. Congress as he saw it in session is, again, highly critical:

We were shown to a large hall where affairs of state were being discussed. The hall itself was some twenty *ken* by ten, and had a board flooring and panels all around, with a gallery built above it . . . On an elevated platform in front sat the Vice-President, with two clerks on the slightly lower platform before him. The members' seats were arranged in semicircle facing the platform where there were forty or fifty people, with files and documents on their tables. One of the members was on his feet, screaming at the top of his voice and gesticulating wildly like a madman. When he sat down, his example was followed by another, and yet another. Upon our inquiring what it was all about, we were informed that all the affairs of state were thus publicly discussed, and that the Vice-President made his decision after he heard the opinion of every member. In the gallery, we saw a number of men and women listening eagerly to the debate. We, too, listened but refrained from asking any more questions—despite the invitations to do so—since we didn't understand a word of the debate, nor did we have any reason for asking questions. As we left the hall, we were invited to go up to the gallery. We took our seats there and had a good view of the hall below where a heated debate was taking place. Even when discussing the most important problems facing the country, they wore their usual narrow-sleeved black coat and trousers, and cursed and swore in the loudest voices. The way they behaved, with the Vice-President presiding on the elevated platform, the whole scene reminded us, we whispered among ourselves, of our fishmarket at Nihonbashi.[102]

To assert an opinion, as to express one's sincere feelings, is regarded as disruptive of the cohesive social order. The ideal mode of giving an opinion would be to suggest it tentatively and unobtrusively so that it will subtly harmonize itself with the consensus that all are expected to do their utmost to bring about. Discussion is conducted in such a way that the highest in rank would represent the consensus. Congressional debate in Washington struck Muragaki as ill-bred and uncouth, thus dangerous and barbaric.

The strict adherence of the Japanese to the minutest etiquette was widely noticed by both Western visitors to Japan and American reporters observing the Embassy, very few ever guessing how fundamental their decorum and ceremony were to the entire social and political makeup of Japan. For Ivan Goncharov, who visited Japan in 1853, for instance, the Japanese passion for rituals was at first an absurd joke:

In Europe people are worrying at this moment about whether to be or not to be, but we argued for whole days about whether to sit or not to sit, to stand or not to stand, and later on about how we should sit and what we should sit on and so on. The Japanese suggested that we should sit on our heels on the floor in their fashion. If you kneel down and then sit on your heels, that is what sitting means to a Japanese. Try it and you will see what a knack there is about it. But you will not be able to go on sitting like that for five minutes, whereas the Japanese sit for several hours at a stretch. We declared that we could not sit like that and asked whether the governor would not sit in an arm-chair as we do. But the Japanese also do not know how to sit in our way and yet apparently nothing could be simpler. When they try, not being used to it, their legs grow numb. Remember how the crane and the fox entertained one another; we and the Japanese are in the same position.

Next day the Japanese appeared early in the morning, again at midday and once more in the evening. Their long, broad boat with a silken tail on its prow and an open stern is constantly arriving. First the junior interpreters come to say that the senior interpreters are just about to arrive and then the senior interpreters in their turn announce the arrival of the *gokenin*.

"What is all this about?"

"It's about the ceremonial."

"Again?"

"They have brought the governor's views."

"Well?"

"The governor asks whether you cannot sit on the floor," began Kichibe, laughing and grimacing.

"Good God, what people you are! You know we told you that we do not sit on the floor. We cannot, our clothes are not made for it, and sitting on our heels hurts us."

"Well then, sit down on the floor, but not on your heels and tuck your legs in somewhere beside you."

"Shouldn't we leave them on the frigate?" our people muttered, and ended by getting annoyed. We announced that we would bring our arm-chairs and chairs and would sit on them and that the governor might sit how and on what he pleased.

Kichibe, L'oda and Sadagora all hung their heads, but then agreed. This argument took place in the captain's cabin. The admiral announced his answer to them in the morning, and when he learnt that they had come again in the evening, with trifling explanations of the way to sit, he did not receive them but charged us to talk to them.[103]

Even Goncharov, however, soon realized this was no laughing matter. For "yielding to their insistence over trifles could give them grounds for demanding concessions in serious matters, too."[104] Ceremony was symbolic of the whole hierarchic relationship: if the Russians accept the Japanese form, that will be proof that the Japanese are receiving a tributary envoy; if the Japanese concede to the Russian form, it will be an acknowledgment of their inferior position. This is, one recalls, the most crucial lesson Perry had learned before coming to Japan. His success, and Harris's after his, in dealing with the Japanese is largely due to their shrewd mastery of ceremony and ritual.

The American newspapers were all impressed by the Embassy's "refinement" and "politeness," but they were less perceptive than Goncharov. There may be a reason for the inadequacy of their observation. For in the social context of the United States, characterized largely by the absence of rigid code and formal ritual, the Japanese *rei* and *reigi* could not realize their political potential, as we will soon see. At the same time, one does notice that within the Embassy itself the problems of protocol were continually raised and incessantly discussed. They fretted not only over their terms relative to the Americans but among themselves. While the job of maintaining social order within the group itself seems to have been left to Oguri, the Inspector, questions regarding rank or who would be permitted to ride as against who should walk were debated with dead seriousness, as is recorded in confidential notebooks kept by Morita Kiyoyuki.[105]

To Muragaki's traditional hierarchic views, Tamamushi's ideas stand in sharp contrast. Observing the American crew, whom his master dismissed as "disorderly," he makes the following comments:

Their discipline is very strict. But the sailors do not kneel down even before the captain, although they do take off their hats when they meet him. Actually, they make no distinctions between the captain and the other officers, or the officers and the common sailors. The high and low mix freely, and even the common sailors do not especially seem to worship their captain. The captain too does not seem to insist on his high rank, and behaves like their colleague. Their friendship is extremely close, and in case of a crisis they do their best to help each other. When faced with a calamity, they mourn together. These are things so diametrically opposite to what goes on in our country. The moon was brilliant tonight.

In our country the ceremonial rules [*reihō*] are very strict, and we are not easily granted an audience with the ruler, who is feared like a demonic god. Following his example, anyone with the slightest rank behaves pompously and insultingly to his inferiors. The friendship is so negligible that when a misfortune hits us there is no expression of sympathy. We are greatly different from them. This being the case, who would ever do his best when calamity strikes? Perhaps this is a result of long-lasting peace that has spoiled and softened us dangerously. Deplorable. Should we then prefer a society with no ceremonial rules [*reihō usuku*] but with intimate personal relations to a society with strict ceremonial rules but no intimate personal relations? I am not necessarily setting a high value on the barbarians' customs, but in view of the recent developments, the answer should be obvious.[106]

The same absence of *rei* is, in this view, not something to condemn, but to respect, even admire—although the ambiguous concluding statement reveals Tamamushi's uneasiness toward open acknowledgment of his feelings. For him, the lack of *rei* is even a military advantage, whereas for Muragaki it remains the decisive flaw in the United States military system.

Tamamushi was present at the White House reception of the Ambassadors, and was likewise impressed by the unassuming dignity of the President. He was neither upset by the presence of women nor bothered by the absence of elaborate etiquette.[107] His visit to the Capitol, too, was quite differently described from Muragaki's:

After about 200 yards, we came to the Congress Building called "Captain [Capitol] House." This is the most immense building in Washington and stands three or four storeys high. There is an entrance in every one of the four sides, and the perimeter is almost half a mile long ... When they discuss things, the officials and their secretaries sit at the center on the lowest level, and all the people involved in the matters discussed sit on the higher levels. Thus the officials are clearly seen and scrutinized by people, and no one will suspect those in office, who might otherwise secretly mix the public and private [*kōshi*] interests.[108]

To notice a conflict between the Vice-Ambassador and a menial servant is not to cast the former into the role of an aristocrat of the *ancien regime,* nor to call the latter a bourgeois revolutionary.[109] As we will see later on, Tamamushi's background is as Confucian as anybody else's, and in his later life, too, he leaned toward the feudal Tokugawa rule. At the same time, one notes in Tamamushi's record an articulate challenge to the dominant values.[110] It is even possible to see here a loosening of the vertical ties of loyalty. If it is right that the Meiji Restoration was achieved by lower-ranking samurai seeking effective execution of their program through association of like-minded samurai across the fief lines (thus replacing the feudal loyalty with an inter-fief, "national" fidelity),[111] Tamamushi's feeling is inseparable from such development. However modest his skepticism may be, he is one of the very few who discovered in an utterly different culture something he had seriously missed in his own.

I must end this discussion with an episode in the climactic ceremony that fulfilled the central purpose of the Embassy's round-the-world voyage, the audience with the Shogun of the United States. Before their departure, the Council of State as well as the envoys themselves were quite worried about whether the President was willing to grant them an interview. In Japanese diplomacy, giving a ceremonial reception for Townsend Harris had been thought an acknowledgment of their weakness. Ideally, an aloof rejection of any approach should have been the answer. Now in the reverse position, they suspected that the Americans might react in the same fashion: the President would try to avoid meeting the Ambassadors. Should they request an audience? But wouldn't they lose face if, asking for one, they were refused? The Council of State finally decided that the Ambassadors should not request an interview.[112] Thus, upon their arrival in Washington the Ambassadors wrote Lewis Cass asking him to see them, but they sidestepped proposing a meeting with the President.[113] Their matter-of-fact conference with the Secretary of State was both surprising and upsetting. But then they were informed that the Emperor of the United States was happy to receive them in person.

The day before the grave event, the two Ambassadors and the Inspector met to smooth out details of protocol with Captain DuPont and the Dutch interpreter Portman. The Ambassadors had not forgotten what they had heard about the negotiations of 1857 between the Commissioners for Foreign Affairs and the American Consul General Townsend Harris concerning his audience with the Shogun. Whether the foreigner should take off his shoes, whether he should bow, remain standing, what he should wear, at what point he should leave his palanquin (*norimono*)—such questions were endlessly assessed and argued, as usual. As the Shogunate officials did their best to hold the hairy barbarians down to the lowest possible protocol status, Harris, a brilliant student of the Oriental art of status language, firmly insisted that as the representative of the President of the United States he deserved a recognition and respect nearly equal to the Shogun's. Now the tables were turned. As emissaries of the Shogun, the Barbarian-Subduing Generalissimo of the Divine Empire of Japan, the envoys had to wrest out protocol concessions from the Americans. They would not remove their *zōri* sandals; they would bow no more than three times just as Harris did; they would alight from their carriages at the gate of the palace. The trouble was, the Americans in Washington knew nothing of the extraordinary importance the Japanese placed on such details in their symbolic language of politics. Harris had certainly written nothing about such peculiarities. Thus, for them the Ambassadors were like any other foreign diplomats—no more, no less.

Captain DuPont and his interpreter were pressed with numbers of minute—and what must have seemed to them fussy—questions. Where should the envoys leave their carriages? At the steps of the White House, DuPont replied. Could the ceremony be rehearsed? It was not an American custom, said DuPont, but it could be arranged. The Japanese said that they made much of etiquette (*keirei*) and practiced all important ceremonies. DuPont said all right, he would talk to the President about it. Then the Ambassadors told the Captain how the three would stand in a line, bow once, take a few steps, bow once again, step forward toward the President, and bow yet again, at which time the Chief Foreign Affairs Officer would pass forward the box containing the Shogun's honorable epistle, the Chief Ambassador receiving it and bowing once, coming to the center and bowing again, retreating to the original post and bowing once again, bowing altogether three times each way, and so on and so forth, and would this meet with American approval? Overwhelmed, DuPont said he could not follow the interpreter. So the envoys stood up and performed the whole procedure for him; DuPont said it was fine. The rehearsal did not materialize, as the President and the Ambassadors could not agree on a time. At the actual ceremony, the envoys expected the Americans to understand that they were exactly reproducing the precedent set by the Harris meeting in Edo, which of course was not at all the case: the Americans were utterly ignorant of this sophisticated choreography of politics.[114] *The choreography of politics*

Buchanan was amicable, thus offending Muragaki; he was dignified, but certainly no Shogun, thus disappointing the Japanese. Besides, of all American Presidents, James Buchanan, ironically enough, was among those least interested in pomp and ceremony: when he was Ambassador to the Court of King James, he insisted on appearing on state occasions in a simple business suit, refusing to dress in the diplomatic court uniform.[115] Why did I go to the trouble of wearing formal attire, what a waste of time and effort! confided the Vice-Ambassador in his diary.[116] That the Japanese could not perform their regular ceremony in a tit-for-tat fashion understood as such was ironic enough. After all, the dispatch of the Embassy was itself part of a grand tit-for-tat initiated by the newly budding Japanese diplomacy: you sent us Harris, we'll send you three ambassadors; you sent us a flotilla of warships, we'll send along one, too. Unfortunately, it is fairly certain that no American, perhaps not even Harris himself, was aware that that was the game the Japanese were playing. There was

The presidential reception of the Embassy in the East Room of the White House on May 17, 1860.

still another irony in that the high priests of ceremony, on this most solemn and grave occasion, made a public gaffe. As soon as Shimmi Buzen-no-Kami Masaoki sonorously recited his liege sovereign's airy tidings to President Buchanan and bowed the planned number of times, the envoys all walked out into the next room without waiting for the President's greeting in response, thus forcing a perplexed Captain DuPont to chase after them and fetch his wayward "princes" back to the East Room. Throughout, the Americans remained under the impression that this abrupt ambassadorial retreat was a part of their guests' mysterious protocol.[117] Quite understandably, none of the diaries mentions their error in performance, which if made known to the Council of State might conceivably have necessitated the "happy dispatch" of at least the Chief Ambassador, if not of all three principals.[118]

The tragedy of Japan is not that she borrowed so much from the West, but that many of the finer things which she studied have been trampled underfoot by the Japanese authorities and chiefly those techniques which serve the end of aggression and cynical diplomacy are being fostered and further developed.

— E. H. Norman

In Japan, McDonald's [hamburger chain] faced charges of imperialism and also ran into unscrupulous competition from homegrown chains. Den Fujita, McDonald's Japanese proconsul was, however, dauntless. "If," he said in an interview, "we eat hamburgers for a thousand years, we will become blond. And when we become blond—we can conquer the world."

— *New York Times Book Review,* April 4, 1976

If you want to know who we are,
    We are gentlemen of Japan;
On many a vase and jar—
    On many a screen and fan,
        We figure in lively paint:
        Our attitude's queer and quaint—
        You're wrong if you think it ain't, oh!

If you think we are worked by strings,
    Like a Japanese marionette,
You don't understand these things:
    It is simply Court etiquette.
        Perhaps you suppose this throng
        Can't keep it up all day long?
        If that's your idea, you're wrong, oh!

— W. S. Gilbert, *The Mikado*

Chapter Three

Minds

As I travelled hither through the land,
I find the people strangely fantasied,
Possessed with rumors, full of idle dreams . . .
King John

For it is a certain maxim, no man sees what things are,
that knows not what they ought to be.
—JONATHAN RICHARDSON,
quoted by E. H. Gombrich, *Art and Illusion*

The extant travelogues and memoirs left by members of the 1860
Embassy proper and the *Kanrin Maru* escort group number about
forty altogether. Although one of them, Hirose Kakuzō Kaneaki's
Kankai kōro nikki (The diary across the oceans), appeared in print
shortly after the adventure in 1862, for the most part the travelogues
were not intended for immediate publication. The decade of the
1860s, especially its first half, was a dangerous and bloody period both
for foreign residents and those Japanese who had dealings with them.
Any diarist trying to publish such a manuscript would do so only at
great risk. Having applied to the authorities for a permit to publish his
travelogue, a member of the 1862 Mission to Europe soon withdrew
his request in fear of retaliation.[1] Hirose's travelogue was an exception and seems to have made no visible impact.[2]

The absence of contemporary printing does not mean, however,
that these manuscripts were not read. Most works existed in several
copies. As many as thirty or more remain, for example, of Tamamushi's journal.[3] His specific instructions, "Not to be read by any-

97

one," on the cover of Book Eight (of the copy transcribed by him) seem to imply that other sections of that copy plus all other copies (all of which omit the subversive Book Eight) were indeed for circulation. Furthermore, most of the surviving copies in the authors' own hands had clearly been rewritten and revised after the journey was over. In fact, only a very few works were left in the initial diary form showing day-by-day entries during the voyage.[4] It certainly appears then that the writers were interested in showing their records to others and not merely in copying them as a mnemonic exercise. There are instances where the author either lectured or dictated, from memory and notes, to an interested audience (as in the case of Katō Somō and Kimura Tetsuta).[5] In short, the manuscripts were read quietly but eagerly despite the general hostility toward everything Western.

Among the documents, a few were simply intended to serve as technical logs and account books: Midshipman Akamatsu Daisaburō's *Amerika yuki kōkai nikki* (Diary of the voyage to America) and Kosugi Masanoshin's "Akoku jōge sonohoka nikki" (Diary of north and south America . . .) diligently record navigational operations aboard the *Kanrin Maru* to the exclusion of everything else; likewise, Chief Treasurer Morita Kiyoyuki's several volumes register expenditures and official memoranda. There is also a huge unpublished official record of the Embassy in six volumes.[6] Still others, like Katsu's and Fukuzawa's, look back from a safe distance of several decades after the fact to view the experience as a nostalgic episode of their youth. Finally, the work left by the Chief Ambassador, Shimmi Buzen-no-Kami Masaoki, is a series of *waka* (short poems) in the convention of *uta nikki* (poetic diary) intended more as a literary effort than a travel record.

It should be emphatically stated here, however, that the great majority are essentially personal travelogues, the writers' reports of their encounters with a strange people aimed at an audience who knew little about either the people or the country.

Most works are now available in print, the few that are still in manuscript form being of small interest. The most important modern collections are the first two volumes of the *Kengai shisetsu nikki sanshū* (*KSNS*) (Selection of embassy diaries) and the seven-volume set, *Man'en gannen ken-Bei shisetsu shiryō shūsei* (*SS*) (Collection of the historical materials of the 1860 Embassy to the United States). Some, like Muragaki's *Ken-Bei-shi nikki* (Diary of the Ambassadors to the United States) and Yanagawa Masakiyo's *Kōkai nikki* (Diary of the voyage), have been translated into English, but these renderings are quite unreliable, being inaccurate and unidiomatic throughout, as well as deceptive. (Apparently the translators—who all seem to have been motivated by some program or other for promoting "friendship" between the United States and Japan—simply laundered out any comments they felt might prove insulting to Americans, thus making the travelers appear markedly banal and unsophisticated.) Aside from the question of editions, a number of identical phrases and descriptions recur among the works. I have already remarked on several cases, and there is no doubt that some writers, eager to leave a memorial, but having little original to say for themselves, in certain situations simply lifted whole passages from their colleagues. One unidentified writer complains that more than a few diaries were copied from various records, especially from the single most important source, Tamamushi's *Kō-Bei nichiroku* (Chronicle of the voyage to America), which indeed shares a considerable number of phrases and descriptions with many of the journals.[7] However, this does not discount the possibility that Tamamushi and others may have had common sources of information rather than intending to plagiarize.[8]

Finally, these documents written by such a diverse assembly of men from all stations of life—from high Tokugawa bureaucrats like Shimmi and Muragaki and brilliant minds trained in Dutch learning like Fukuzawa and Katsu to members of "outside" domains like Tamamushi, even down to non-samurai menials like Kahachi—project a good representation of the Tokugawa mind as it encountered the mysterious West, just at the dawn of modern Japan. Being so convinced, I would like to examine the form and style of the travelogues, with the hope of more closely observing the contours of that mind.

One of the most striking features of the 1860 Embassy travelogues is the uniformity among them in both substance and form, that is, in what they wrote and how they wrote. Of course, some degree of stylistic difference and divergence of opinion does exist as we have already seen. And yet, in perceptual and formal aspects—the way they observed and commented, the style of their entries, the degree of abstraction or specificity, the personal involvement or disengagement from their own experience, even regarding the realm of opinion and attitude, and the subject matter they typically chose to write about— their uniformity is as palpable as is the diversity prevailing among, say, the travelogues left by contemporary Western visitors to Japan, such as Goncharov and Golownin, Harris and Heusken, Alcock, Osborn, and Oliphant.

I would first like to discuss the documents as *travelogues*, mainly focusing on the spatial sense revealed in the accounts. Obviously, both the ship's passage and the Embassy's tour through the states are essential to the narrative progression of the travelogues, which progress as the travelers voyage forth. And yet travelogues often seem characterized by a tension between the descriptive impulse to follow closely the route itself and the imaginative energy to reorganize the mere facts of the voyage into a more personal meaning. In the course of narration a tourist's actual itinerary, the basis of his travelogue, is continually mediated by such energy. Thus, the travelogue as a form always vacillates between a close account of the trip and an imaginative interpretation of it, which in the extreme case amounts to fiction. When this happens, the actual itinerary recedes to function as mere metaphor; on the other hand, when a travelogue tries to eliminate this fiction altogether, it becomes a record serving some purpose other than simply telling a story. Most travelogues, in other words, fall somewhere between *Gulliver's Travels, Pilgrim's Progress*, and the picaresque novel at one extreme and a mechanical naval log or routine flight record at the other.

By the normative travelogue I do not mean only literary travelogues such as Goethe's *Travel to Italy*, Dickens's *American Notes*, James's *The American Scenes*, and Lawrence's *Twilight in Italy*, but include also the nonliterary travelogues of C. Pemberton Hodgson, J. R. Black, Lieutenant James D. Johnston, and George Henry Preble, as well as those of the now familiar Heusken and Harris, Goncharov and Oliphant. I likewise refer to the long tradition of literary travelogue-diaries (*tabi-nikki* and *kikō bun*) descending from the Heian period to the Tokugawa, including *Tosa nikki* (935), *Kaidōki* (1223), *Tōkan kikō* (1242), *Izayoi nikki* (1282), and *Towazugatari* (1306), down to Bashō's masterpieces like *Oku no hosomichi* (1702) and *Oi no kobumi* (1709). Even in the more purely documentary travelogues—such as Ennin's ninth-century chronicle of his travels in T'ang China—the organizing impulse is often discernible to a degree scarcely evident in most of the 1860 accounts, which sometimes perilously approach the form of the log.[9]

Where does this inclination toward mechanical bookkeeping come from? Why is there so little evidence in most of these records of any will to interpret, or impose any imaginative structure on raw experience? Let us take one of the most common types of entry in the 1860 documents. While at sea, almost every voyager seems fascinated with the ship's changing location, which is recorded daily in a great majority of the travelogues. In many journals, a single notation marking the ship's latitude and longitude—plus at times a brief mention of weather or temperature—constitutes the entire record for a given day. To take just one example:

The 14th day, the fifth month; clear, rain in the afternoon; thermometer 70°. Day's run (from two yesterday to noon today) 181 *ri*.
Latitude N. 40''0'   Longitude W. 70° 0' 10

One is curious also why the ship's position was so important to them. Were nautical details always so interesting, especially to the ambassadorial members on the *Powhatan?* Did they really feel it essential that their readers know their geographical coordinates on a given day? Was there nothing more provocative to write about aboard the *Powhatan* and the *Kanrin Maru*, where they were after all living at close quarters with the barbarians for the first time? Answers to such questions must necessarily be fairly detailed.

For the Japanese, landlocked for generations in their island country, the ocean vastness without landmarks and bounded only by the horizon on all sides was a totally new environment. Back in Japan, by contrast, the space they inhabited was always distinctly defined in terms of fiefs and domains. The ordinary samurai dwelt either in his lord's castle-town (*jōka-machi*) or in Edo, where the Shogunate law of hostages (*sankin kōtai*) required that the lord reside every other half-year. The direct Tokugawa vassal (*hatamoto*), too, lived either in Edo, in a provincial Tokugawa territory (*tenryō*), or in his own domain assigned by the Shogunate. The common people—farmers, artisans, and merchants—also ventured out of their native towns and villages occasionally for purposes of pilgrimage, peddling, or recreation. When they did, however, they—everyone—had to secure a passport, for along the major highways there were checkpoints (*sekisho*) controlled either by the central Tokugawa regime or the local fief government to prohibit unauthorized movement. Thus, despite increasing traffic along the highways during this period, any individual's whereabouts was still a jealously watched aspect of feudal life.[11] People were always expected to account for being out anywhere away from home. A geographic curfew of this sort nonetheless produced compensating benefits, enabling samurai and lords alike to experience a deeper relationship to the immediate environment. Each person had his own niche in the local space. It appears that the neo-Confucian insistence on identifying lord-vassal loyalty (*chū*) with filial piety (*kō*) played a significant role here, for we see that the fief, or political space, was identified with the familial space. In addition, everywhere in this small island country, local historical and poetic associations (*utamakura,* poetic pillow) abounded, and there were numerous scenic places and historical sites (*meisho*) familiar to all since earliest childhood.

As a result, the space persons occupied at home was a world bound by the nexus of values and myths, where people and the immediate locale had real meaning and relationship within a religious and psychological scheme. For most Japanese at the time, their country (*kuni*) meant their fief (*han*) and not Japan as a whole; to the extent that Japan as a nation amounted to anything at all—as it must have to these first international travelers—it did so in an extension of the tribal and familial concept (as did their fief); in other words, it was only a larger unit presided over by the Tokugawa Shogunate (or, increasingly in the last Tokugawa years, by the emperor above him).[12] Whether referring to the fief in particular or the "divine country" (*shinshū,* or *shinkoku*) as a whole, this space was a mythical territory such as Mircea Eliade has called the "sacred space."[13]

The sea, however, was "outside space," annihilating all such meaning and myth as it does all local boundaries. As much as half a century later, even a serious student and teacher of English, Natsume Sōseki, sailing to England for a two-year stay, felt the same power of the sea as it threatened to wash over all the familiar distinctions and meanings. He wrote a long essay in his somewhat eccentric but charming English about the "nothingness" of the ocean, and of life itself, as though using the foreign language would somehow talismanically restore his confidence:

> The sea is lazily calm and I am dull to the core, lying in my long chair on deck. The leaden sky overhead seems as devoid of life as the dark expanse of waters around, blending their dullness together beyond the distant horizon as if in sympathetic stolidity. While I gaze at them, I gradually lose myself in the lifeless tranquility which surrounds me and seem to grow out of myself on the wings of contemplation to be conveyed to a realm of *vision* which is neither aethereal nor earthly, with no houses, trees, birds, and human beings. Neither heaven nor hell, nor that intermediate stage of human existence which is called by the name of *this* world, but of vacancy, of nothingness where infinity and eternity seem to swallow one in the oneness of existence, and defies in its vastness any attempt of description.[14]

The samurai of 1860 knew much less of course about such ways of responding to this experience of "outside space," and they must have found the American navigators' provision of a daily announcement of the ship's coordinates comforting. By its clarity, regularity, and authority, they were in a way redeemed each day from floating nameless, unlocated, and without discernible destination in a sea of what Eliade calls "profane space."*

It is true that one could find the log-like form in a few documentary diary-travelogues of Tokugawa Japan. *Hokuyūki* (1807), written by two Mito samurai about their intelligence tour in Hokkaidō, is a good example.[15] And yet, in Kaibara Ekken's *Kisoji no ki* (1685), Shiba Kōkan's *Saiyū nikki* (1815), Motoori Norinaga's *Sugegasa nikki* (1772), Tachibana Nankei's *Tōyūki, Seiyūki* (1795–1805), or Kiyokawa Hachirō's *Saiyūsō* (1855), the entries are—though often impersonal and unspeculative—structured, detailed, and informed with the sense of ease and intimacy with the spaces visited. In the 1860 records, on the other hand, the writers do not seem fully able to comprehend what they see and experience, the log-like entry of the ship's position being one instance of this general attitude toward profane space. Thus, they tend to describe geographic movement only, and that often in unadorned numerical terms: today we left Washington and came to Baltimore; today we left Baltimore and traveled ninety-eight miles to Philadelphia, stayed at a hotel called the Continental with seven storeys occupying about a hundred *ken* square of land, having crossed on the way three rivers, two of which had iron bridges with railroad tracks on them.

Only in a few exceptional cases is there an apparent desire to encompass and schematize this alien space rather than just paratactically run on in it. Tateishi Tokujūrō, Sano Kanae, and Tamamushi

---

*This experience might be made clearer when compared with the experience of the European immigrant in America finding himself away from home, from civilization, his "sacred space," and in the middle of the American desert or wilderness, the Americans' "profane space." Here, too, nothing in sight seemed to hold meaning: unlike Europe, raw Nature in America is innocent of history and tradition. The descendants of Euclid, Pythagoras, and Descartes, however, would not bow to any such passive documenting of their helpless situation in the world. They tend instead to push onward, aggressively searching out a habitable environ for themselves, and in the process projecting the structure of their own minds onto the vast seeming nothingness—which nature in America is. One result is the towns and cities carved out of the wilderness in which streets run in Euclidean lines crossing at clean ninety-degree angles. American spaces are a mirror image of the European mind, profane space here redeemed by the miracle of man's inner territory. No wonder America periodically uproots or paves over its settlements as often as possible. It is important that time-suffused, history-smeared spaces be born anew from time to time, fathered by the pure interior of the human mind.

divide their travelogues into separate units, each devoted to a city, in which they discuss in turn "geography," "people and culture" (*fūzoku*), "weather," "agriculture," "animals," "currency," and "commodity prices." Although their way of looking at each city as a separate territory derives partly from their long-accustomed view of fiefs as autonomous demarcated spaces, their format also reflects a borrowing from geography textbooks read before their departure (or after their return).[16] In fact, Sano and Tateishi explicitly state that their general surveys of cities are based on geography books (*chirishi, chirisho, chiri jiten,* and so on). While these few diaries do show an effort on the part of the writers to structure and interpret unfamiliar environments so as to make some sense of them, this is a rare phenomenon, most of the diarists almost hypnotically yielding to the rolling expanse which bears them forward.

It is similar with landscape description. From the Heian period to the Tokugawa, travelogues are not distinguished by elaborate verbal descriptiveness. For instance, the creative energy of even the major literary travelogues seems to find expression mainly in the composition of poems as the foci of the works, and any meditative or observational impulses that surface are held in check by various restrictive conventions. In short, one might say that the traveler's imagination is always redirected away from the actual landscape by poetic memory and association (*utamakura*). In works like *Sarashina nikki, Towazugatari,* and *Oku no hosomichi,* however, there are occasional passages which sensitively portray nature. Hills and trees, birds and flowers, ripples on the surface of a lake, the shadows of clouds moving across a meadow, the flash of sunlight in the distance—such particularized scenes, though carefully ensconced in an elaborate convention, take the reader quite by surprise with their sensuous immediacy. In the Embassy records as a whole, there is much evidence of the writers' wonder at the beauty of the places they visit, but they seem unconcerned with verbalizing their observations in detail. Take, for example, the two most descriptive accounts of San Francisco Bay, a splendor which all the members of the Embassy seem to have admired, and compare them with Heusken's exhilaration when sighting Mt. Fuji. Here is Muragaki on San Francisco Bay:

As the smoke from the guns drifted away, there emerged from behind it, a lively city, with houses stretching along the foot of the hills, and the dock crowded with men and women. The city was far superior to the Sandwich Islands, and the houses, built four or five storeys high, looked beautiful.

A street of San Francisco. A drawing by Kimura Tetsuta.

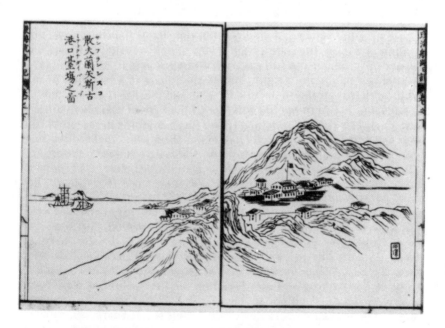

A view of San Francisco Bay. A drawing by Hirose Kakuzō Kaneaki.

After a short while, the *Powhatan* weighed anchor, and slowly steamed into the Bay, which, from four to five miles across at the entrance, became narrower, surrounded by smoothly outlined hills on both sides. There were no woods in sight, but herds of cattle or sheep grazing on the hillside, looking as small as so many black ants. The presence of curiously shaped rocks in the Bay, some of reddish hues and others black, made the scenery quite beautiful.[17]

And Morita, the chief finance officer:

I was told this place was San Francisco. In the morning we sailed over the rough waters between two protruding hills. There was a battery with two cannons. There were many brick buildings with four or five storeys. Their chimneys were as high as the watch-towers in Edo, towering over the house roofs. On both sides of the ship, all the hills bore the colors of spring, and the blue grass and green trees were as in a painting. Sheep and cattle and horses were idling on the hillsides. The hills jutting out into the waters were faintly visible, and the reflections of the distant sailboats were as quiet as though sitting on the surface of the water. There were mountains in the rain, there were mountains in the sun, and the beauty of the scene was amazing to see.[18]

And here is Heusken, Harris's interpreter, on Mt. Fuji:

As we near the valley and emerge from the clouds that hover over the summit of Amagi, the countryside begins to unfold; valleys of ravishing beauty upon which the sun casts a gentle glow appear before our eyes. Rounding a mountain, I sight through the foliage of a few pine trees a white peak that gleams in the sun. In an instant I realize that I am looking at Fujiyama. Never in my life will I forget the sight of that mountain as I saw it today for the first time, and I don't think anything in the world will ever equal its beauty. There are mountains three times higher than Fuji; the glaciers of Switzerland are, no doubt, impressive and magnificent; the summit of the Himalayas, the sublime Dawalaquiri, raises its venerable brow to immeasurable heights, but one cannot see it until one has climbed other mountains that hide it from sight in the plains; one sees but ice and glaciers; snows surround you wherever you may turn your eyes. But here, in the midst of a smiling countryside covered with abundant crops — with pine groves and giant camphor trees that seem to vie in longevity with the very soil where they were born, making shade with their majestic foliage for some *miya* or chapel, dedicated to the ancient Gods of the Empire, and as a backdrop for this theatre of plenty and serenity — the pure outline of the unique Fujiyama rises like two symmetrical lines toward the sky, whose pale blue seemed dark, compared to the immaculate snows of the mountain that reflected, like another Kohinoor, the rays of the setting sun.

  In spite of myself I pulled the reins of my horse and, carried away by an outburst of enthusiasm, I took off my hat and cried: "Great, glorious Fujiyama!" Glory forever to the mountain of mountains of the Pacific Sea, which alone raises its venerable brow covered with eternal snow amidst the verdant countryside of Nippon! Jealous of its beauty, it will not suffer a rival which might lessen its splendor. Its crown of snow stands out alone above the highest mountains of Nippon, and Amagi, which we have just passed after a most difficult day, seems only a small hill, hardly worth mentioning.

Ah! Why don't I have about twenty of the friends of my younger days around me! The surrounding hills would soon repeat the echo of a thrice repeated *hip, hip, hip, hurrah* in honor of the sublime Fujiyama.[19]

Heusken's description is not only detailed and comparative, but he insists that he himself be a dramatic character in the scene. He is placed stage-center in the space he is viewing: Mt. Fuji and the boyishly exuberant Heusken stand face to face, as it were. On the other hand, Muragaki and Morita hover like pale shadows in the wings; their San Francisco Bay sketches are detached and the observers themselves distant—if not absent altogether. The numerous conventional terms (mainly *kambun* epithets and phrases) that abound in the imagery remind one of some modest scrolls. Comparative references are, naturally, limited: as against Heusken's Alps, Himalayas, and Dhaulagiri, Morita offers the homely "Edo watch-towers." Heusken is relaxed, fully absorbed in discovering the grandeur of Fuji, while Muragaki and Morita are aloof to an unfamiliar loveliness. And as if to avoid the challenge of the unknown, they seek protection in clichés and numbers and measurements ("four or five storeys," "four to five miles," "two cannons,"). The Japanese travelers clearly feel out of place, and dare not allow themselves to be at ease with nature in America.

Another way of looking at this perceptual and formal passivity is to think of it in temporal terms. Read as diaries, the 1860 Embassy records reveal certain significant features. In the sense that practically all of them have a day-to-day format, they are diaries. But again these particular diaries do not have narrative characteristics of the form as are generally understood. Following the pattern of my discussion of the travelogue form, I would like to place the 1860 documents in the contexts of both literary and non-literary *diary* traditions of Japan and the West.

The diary by definition follows the days and months in the natural flow of time, and yet most diaries reveal a counter-impulse at work to transcend the temporal determination, very much as we saw was typical of the travelogue form. In real life, things happen all the time one after another; in a diary, the recordings are bound to be selective, and arranged in a sequence to yield projected meaning. One might readily think of Western literary diaries—like Samuel Pepys' *Diary* or Defoe's *The Journal of the Plague-Year*—to see how these "diurnal" records radically approach being works of art. Or, take Thoreau's *Walden*, a diary account of the writer's stay near Walden Pond for two years, two months, and two days. The diary is basically a redemptive form beginning with the winter of spiritual death and ending with the spring of resurrection. So organized, it turns into an interpretation, or fiction. As with *The Pilgrim's Progress* and *Gulliver's Travels* for the travelogue, so with *Wuthering Heights* and *The Sorrows of Young Werther* for the diary, where, despite the fact that these works have a carefully wrought temporal delineation, the fictive imagination breaks chronometric events into a new arrangement which is in itself a shape, or meaning.

Works in the Japanese literary tradition of the *nikki*, too, are almost always battlegrounds between the habit of staying in step and the impulse to mold the sequential experiences into some significance. Take the numerous "search for the way" (*gudō*) and "pilgrimage record" (*sankeiki*) type travelogue-diaries—*Kaidōki, Tōkan kikō, Tsukuski-michi no ki,* and so on and on—where the actual chronology is universally adjusted to a conventional calendar: the seekers always leave home in the fall, for instance. Likewise in the great poet Bashō's travelogue-diaries, the facts or surface events of his trips are continually pitted against the interior, poetic journey through an imaginary time-space strictly defined by the conventions.

As against these literary diaries, one must of course mention here the immense and unbroken tradition of the documentary diary born before the ninth century and still alive in our own time. First written in Chinese characters (*kambun*), these journals were basically court chronicles. Unlike the literary diaries written in the Japanese syllabary (*kana*) by women, these chronicles merely recorded the public events and court ceremonies on a daily basis often with no personal comments at all. Some of them, written by extraordinarily determined men, spanned several decades: Fujiwara Michinaga's *Midō Kampaku-ki,* for instance, was written over twenty years (998–1021), *Gyokuyō* by Kujō Kanezane over thirty years (1164–1200), and Sanjōnishi Sanetaka's diary, *Sanetaka-kō-ki,* continued for a full sixty years (1474–1535).[20] In such massive diaries, control of the overall shape would obviously have been impossible. As their authors lived, grew old, and died, these works began, continued, and ended. The diaries were co-authored, as it were, by individual men and by time itself.

By the Tokugawa period, most documentary diaries were no longer written in Chinese characters, nor were they so uniform in style, tone, and subject matter. Although many of the old conventions still survived (brief, public, impersonal entries; compulsive attention to the weather; general lack of interest in overall form), there were signs of greater diversity. If Arai Hakuseki's entries (1693–1717) were brief (the famous Chūshingura—the Forty-Seven Rōnin—vendetta receives a mere three lines!), Umezu Masakage's (1612–1633) were comparatively long. While public, official diaries still flourished in this period, those by Yamashina Kototsune (1576–1601), Matsudaira Ietada (1577–1594), or Kawai Koume (1849–1885), to take random examples, were private and personal. Also, whereas many were *either* private *or* official, Matsuzaki Kōdō's *Kōdō nichireki* (1823–1844) contained a mixture of personal experiences, social events, lecture notes, and comments on books. And Motoori Norinaga left many diaries each quite different from the others: his 1763–1767 entries are no more than page after page of daily weather reports, while his *Zai-Kyō nikki* (1752–1757) shifts from a brief and Chinese-character style to an elaborate record written in the Japanese syllabary. In short, the early conventions were loosened enough by this time to allow wide divergence in format. And there is no reason to believe that the 1860 Embassy members had only one model in mind while composing their daily entries.

Unlike those extremely long diaries, however, the 1860 Embassy documents detail a single trip of relatively short duration. As such they could readily have been molded into narrative form, had the writers felt any desire to impose some interpretation on their experience. Yet one finds among the forty-odd records not one with a narrative framework. Almost without exception, the 1860 diaries fall under the complete sway of the day-to-day progress of time. Many begin with the first day of the trip and close with the last, between which all descriptions and comments are ascribed to definite dates— in some cases without the omission of a single day. That is, the travelers do not organize experience into a structure that counteracts or supplements the flow of time. As they live through time, their accounts of their experiences, like the minutes of a committee meeting, follow a chronometric sequence, and this seems to provide adequate expression for them. What I wish to argue here is that these diaries assumed a daily log form, not because the writers felt more natural clinging to the old official diary convention but because they were for some reason inhibited from interpreting their unique experiences. As the trip begins, the diary begins; the travel ends, and so concludes the diary. The trip *is* in itself the whole meaning of the writing.

Now to compare the 1860 Embassy diaries with the documentary, non-literary accounts of voyages to Japan by contemporary Westerners: first of all, there are very few Western works left in the form of diaries—Townsend Harris's, George Henry Preble's, Edward Yorke McCauley's, Samuel Wells Williams's, and Dr. James Morrow's. Of these five, the last four, which record the Perry expedition, were forced to remain in the (unpublished) diary form by the Commodore's ban on keeping any private record of the adventure. (Heusken's journal does not belong with these, since his unexpected death gave him no chance to consider its possible final form, nor does Hawks's *Narrative of the Expedition,* which is an official chronicle written by a third party.) All the rest—by J. W. Spalding, Edward De Fonblanque, Robert Fortune, Sherard Osborn, James D. Johnston, and Bayard Taylor, as well as Alcock, Satow, Hodgson, Golownin, Oliphant, and Goncharov—are set in a narrative mode with a beginning, a middle, and an end, consequentiality, and structure. To point out this difference is not simply to refer to the relative socio-literary roles the diary form plays in the two cultures. The difference is quite important. Western travelers, unwilling to leave everyday events discrete and uninterpreted in the flow of time, were determined to impose some meaning by lifting them out of the strictly chronological order. Second, individual entries in diaries by Harris and others show a continual struggle against all-powerful time. They seldom let stand a mere account of activities without analysis; they reminisce, compare, speculate, generalize, and dramatize, to an extent nowhere evident in the 1860 diaries. We shall see more on this later when an extended comparison is made between Harris's style and Muragaki's.

This impression that the writers simply allowed the force of time to carry them along is reinforced by the circumstance that written Japanese at the time had no paragraph structure, or even a distinct sentence form. A sentence typically runs on and on, until a new sentence imperceptibly materializes, growing out of the previous one. Descriptions and comments continue without a break until a new subject is introduced or a new date entered. The absence of punctuation and paragraphing alerts one to the fact that ideas are not propositional. That is, the will to organize perceptions into words, words into sentences, and sentences into arguments is weakened by the passive acceptance of the diurnal and nocturnal cycle which, in controlling so much about the shape and contents of the diaries, apparently satisfies the writer's need for form.

Even the calendar used on the voyage posed a minor dilemma. The Japanese of those years used a lunar calendar which was not abandoned until 1873. Thus, while aboard American ships and in the United States, whenever they discussed their plans or itinerary with the Americans, their chronometric system had to be adjusted to an alien time scheme. For example, one of the ambassadorial letters written in English in Washington, D.C., to the Secretary of State is dated "the 25th day of the second-thirth [*sic;* intercalary third] month of seventh year of Ansei,"[21] which translated means May 14, 1860. The hours of the day, too, were numbered off differently. The result was that a sort of capsule of time, a protective bubble, was formed around the Japanese travelers, as though they were carrying a bit of Japan along, a sacred time-space precluding their being plunked directly into the middle of the American reality.

In this respect, Western travelers in Japan fared quite differently. While they could not readily participate in the time of their strange environment either, they had the white man's confidence that their chronometric system was nearly universal in the world outside this eccentric island. In their view, Japanese time was a quaint and inconvenient residue from the past, whereas theirs flowed throughout the world.

If the Japanese Ambassadors were both spatially and temporally alienated—unable to feel at ease in American places or to refer freely forward and backward during their tour—it may be interesting to surmise their attitude toward their own experience. How did they see and relate to their actions and observations? This question brings us to the second, and perhaps most important, feature of the diary as a form: the first-person narrator whose daily experience presumably provides the basis for the narration. The diary as understood in the modern West is by definition a record of one's personal experience/observation, intended in some cases to remain closed to all but the author himself, but in others to be made public while retaining the appearance of privacy. Either way, the form is fundamentally first-person. What is remarkable about the 1860 Embassy records—and the ancient and extensive Japanese diary tradition as a whole—is the general absence of the first-person narrative feature.

Granted, there are a few among them that employ the first-person narrative voice as well as various first-person pronouns. Let me, however, concern myself at present with the overwhelming majority that are narrated throughout with hardly any first-person pronouns, leaving those exceptional works for later discussion.

The lack of first-person pronouns in a Japanese narrative does not by itself indicate a third-person narrative, since the Japanese sentence regularly omits the pronouns, especially in the nominative case, unless clarification is particularly needed. In addition, the verb conjugation has no reference to the person of the subject and thus no bearing on the determination of the narrative person. To be sure, the system of honorifics, defining as it does the relative status positions of narrator, reference, and listener, helps clarify the identity of the omitted subject. And there are other grammatical features that suggest the narrative voice. Still, many sentences remain quite unclear as regards the identity of the narrator and the omitted subject. The Japanese equivalent of "took a walk around nine o'clock" can, theoretically, be in either the first, second, or third person, depending on the narrative context.*

There is also the case of "ambiguous" pronouns that might be

---

*This passage is perhaps unintelligible to those who are unfamiliar with Japanese. In Japanese there are no pronouns equivalent to the English I/we, you/you, he-she-it/they. Instead, there are a good number of pronominal words for each of these English personal pronouns, from which selection is made in accordance with the relative or absolute social positions of the speaker, listener, and referent. It is possible to argue that the Japanese language lacks the category of personal pronoun, although what this means philosophically, or even culturally, is not at all easy to explain precisely. On the one hand, it seems quite possible that the absence in Japanese of an equivalent of the word "I" has some bearing on the Japanese concept of the self (or the lack thereof); it is also possible, on the other hand, to argue that the Japanese grammar has compensatory features (honorifics, various *joshi*, *jodōshi*, etc.) that subtly indicate the person of the narrator without the specific use of a personal pronoun. See S.-Y. Kuroda's brilliant articles, "Where Epistemology, Style, and Grammar Meet" and "Reflections on the Foundations of Narrative Theory." Also see a series of conversations *(taidan)* that Ōno Susumu had with writers in various disciplines, collected in *Taidan: Nihon-go o kangaeru.* Ōno appears somewhat undecided on the issue in several passages in the book that touch on this particular subject (pp. 135–137, 203–204, 214–218, 222–223). It is irrefutable, at any rate, that there are frequent cases in Japanese where the narrator of a sentence and the agent of an action described in a sentence are simply impossible to determine.

construed as either first- or third-person. Take an example from *Ikoku no koto no ha*, written by Kahachi, the humble stokers' foreman on the *Kanrin Maru*. Throughout, the dominant pronominal term he uses is *ichidō*, "altogether," which can mean all of us, all of you, or all of them. While the context clearly rejects the second person, it is sometimes impossible to determine whether Kahachi numbers himself as one in the "altogether" (thus marking the narration as first-person) or not (thus marking it as third-person). In fact, the overwhelming impression is that Kahachi, like many others, did not much care whether the story he told included himself or not. It is only on the basis of the content and context of the narrative along with various grammatical features that one can ascribe the third person to most of the 1860 Embassy accounts, and that only in a very general sense. The diaries by Murayama, Masuzu, Namura, Morita, Nonomura, Sano, Fukushima, Kosugi, Yoshioka, Hirose, Katō, Kimura, Ono, and *Amerika tokai nikki* (Diary of the voyage to America), by an unidentified writer, all belong in this category, the first-person pronominal terms (such as: singular *yo*, *ware*, *sessha*, *boku*; and plural *warera*, *bokura*) occurring but rarely in these documents.

Confronting something so totally new as these men were, why was it, then, that they didn't talk about it in the terms of *personal experience*? Why were they only interested in describing people, events, and things, like faucets and call bells, horse carriages and fire engines external to themselves? What is the meaning of such thorough impersonality? First, we can say that as, by and large, second- and lower-echelon officers, they were in no position to make any important choices or decisions—particularly during the voyage. This meant that they were necessarily quite passive as regards action and movement. While they did not figure much in the picture, what was seen and heard did, and had to be recorded. Second, and concomitant with the first point, their sense of self was different from the Western, which tends to particularize and individualize any experience. Kahachi's report is a good example of this, but others, too, demonstrate indifference to their own feeling and response, even to their personal condition.

Take, for instance, a section of Murayama Hakugen's *Hōshi nichiroku* (The embassy chronicle). His entries from February 15 through 18 (according to the envoys' lunar calendar, the twenty-fourth through the twenty-seventh day of the first month) read as follows:

Western particularization & individualizing the self.

24th. Fine, cloudy, windy. [My] countrymen were without exception seasick; some vomited; fortunately, I did not go so far as to throw up; but felt nauseated and lay in bed eating nothing all day.
25th. Fine, cloudy.
26th. Fine.
27th. Drizzled. Stormy; great waves; [my] countrymen all took to bed and could not walk around; the ship rocking greatly; could not get to sleep throughout the night; [an] American voyaging for twenty years says [he has] never encountered a storm like this; [my] countrymen quite exhausted.[22]

He does talk about his own seasickness once, referring to himself as *yo*; but any interest in talking about his own condition is continually deflected so as to describe it in terms of the group *(hōjin, countrymen)* of whom he is only one member. The analysis here might have to be slightly qualified by the fact that Murayama was a physician attached to the Embassy and his interest in others might thus be interpreted as appropriately professional. But such is not the case, this being but one of many examples and chosen simply for its brevity.

Nonomura Tadazane's entry for March 29 (in the lunar system the eighth day of the third month) likewise deemphasizes his presence in the scene:

The 8th day, third month. Between three (half past eight [Japanese time]) and four (seven [Japanese time]) this dawn the heaven in the direction of the north shone like a flame; [my] countryman [countrymen?] saw this, and says [said?] land must be near, [it] must be a brush-fire; and [he? I? they? we?] asked an American; [the American answered that he had] seen this before, but [he] didn't know the reason; [a] Dutch book explains it merely as the northern light; southeastern wind; the ship sailed in the ox-tiger [northeastern] direction; thermometer 60 degrees; before noon 270 *ri*.
Latitude N. 36°57′ 25″
Longitude W. 135°26′ 14″[23]

To Murayama, his own experience is not of vital interest; and as for Nonomura, whether he personally saw the "northern light" (aurora borealis) is not at all clear and is insignificant as well. In both entries, one has the impression that things happen to them all, and these shared experiences *are* what interest them individually.

In fact, this sighting of the "northern light" is also reported in the works of Katō, Sano, Kimura Tetsuta, Hirose, and Tamamushi.[24] But with the exception of Tamamushi's *Kō-Bei nichiroku*, no book specifies the narrator as having the experience by the unmistakable "I saw" or "we saw." Only by the context—detailed description, illustration, declarative tone—can the reader surmise that the writers were most probably among those witnessing the phenomenon, but it is still perfectly possible to argue on the other hand that they may indeed not have seen it personally.

Related to this ambiguity of perspective is the curious fact that it is impossible to establish authorship of several of the 1860 journals. True, there is nothing surprising about people leaving their diaries anonymous: some writers felt no reason to sign manuscripts while they were being privately circulated. At the same time, what is odd is that some, like *Kanrin Maru kō-Bei nisshi* (Chronicle of the voyage of the *Kanrin Maru* to America) or *Amerika tokai nikki* (Diary of the voyage to America), can pretty well be attributed to one man or one of a few (on the basis of external evidence and the content and style of the remarks themselves), and yet these diary authors describe (what is probably their own) actions without once relating the writer to the self written about. Here again, the official documents—say, the minutes of a committee meeting—could be said to have the same impersonal style. But the 1860 Embassy diaries are, as I have established earlier, *not* official records. Further, they are hardly devoid of signs of the authors' involvement. Indeed, anonymous diarists' personal responses—contempt, dissatisfaction, admiration—are just as freely expressed (or unexpressed) as in other, author-identified diaries of the group. It appears that the interest in the *who*, who viewed, did, and felt, is characteristically ignored for the *what*, what was viewed, done, and sensed, as though personality were of little importance to either reader or writer.

Now for the few exceptional travelogue-diaries that do make fairly regular use of I-pronouns. The most conspicuous is Vice-Ambassador Muragaki's work. Surely his being the second in command of the group must have required the "I." Although quite passive as a diplomat, still he could not evade the authority vested in his office. His inferiors looked to him for leadership; the Chief Ambassador asked his counsel; and the Americans talked to him and expected discussion, planning, decisions. Thus, when making diary entries, he could not easily avoid the first-person singular pronoun *(onore,* self, is the word he chose probably for its slightly tough, mock-boorish connotation, rather than *yo,* the neutral, dignified pronoun most commonly used in the 1860 records). Psychologically, too, Muragaki was, as we have seen, rather a self-important man. He always considered himself a cut above his subordinates, and this attitude is quite salient in his diary. (He calls them *gesu,* menials, rascals.) Muragaki seems then to view America from a separate individual perspective, and not

from a position of group identities. At the same time, his encounter
was finally not at all personal. There is little engagement of his
personality, sense and emotion, thought and feeling, as we will examine in greater length later on. If this sounds somewhat paradoxical,
one should recall that his isolation was itself part of the hierarchic
structure, and his consciousness thus largely socially defined.

Kimura Settsu-no-Kami Yoshitake, Commodore of the *Kanrin
Maru*, was very much in the same position. As leader of the escort
group he had to assume authority and responsibility, and consequently his *Hōshi Meriken kikō* (The ambassadorial travel to America) inevitably contains many first-person sentences. Kimura,
however, was a naval administrator trained by Dutch officers, and his
officers in turn were mostly cadets educated at the Nagasaki Naval
School. Further, he was for some time associated with his American
counterparts at the Mare Island Naval Shipyard. Finding himself in
this way among a congenial professional group, he was more relaxed
with Americans than diplomats like Muragaki, and, as we have seen,
there seems to have been a genuine exchange of visiting and friendship between the Americans and Kimura's crew. Reflecting this, his
writing, too, is far less guarded and dislocated than Muragaki's. Just as
Midshipman Ishikawa's navigational log is matter-of-fact and unself-
conscious, so is Commodore Kimura's. His is an objective and unob-
trusive "I," a merely functional and descriptive "I," inserted there
because his position required a separation of the "I" from the others.
While discrete, this "I" experiences no hierarchic alienation from his
inferiors or from the Americans as is evident in Muragaki's writing.
Nor does he seem concerned with his own particular experience.
Somehow one cannot help seeing here an early example of that
important by-product of technology: achievement, by circumventing
and supplanting ordinary language and personality, of a smooth and
efficient intercultural "communication" by professional and technical experts, not rivaled by diplomatic and cultural representatives.

The record of the head of the Embassy, Shimmi Buzen-no-Kami
Masaoki, similarly employs the first-person pronouns. It is unique in
consisting of a series of poems (*waka*) in the convention of the poetic
diary (*uta nikki*). It begins with *waka* commemorating the departure
and ends with those celebrating the return. Its literary value is not
impressive. Highly imitative, the poems are no more than the expression of social refinement, what must have passed among the
Tokugawa samurai for a measure of taste and sophistication. In
Hawaii, for instance, he exchanged a series of playful poems with an

officer in his retinue, expressing a mock-attachment to an American woman he chanced to see. One of them, a self-admitted imitation of Ki no Tsurayuki's famous *waka*, reads like this:

> To pick a flower
> From the shadow on the water.
> Gaze and gaze in vain.

> *Mizu no moni, utsuru hana o oru gotoku,*
> *Itazura ni nomi, miru zo haka naki.*[25]

He also wrote several verses toying with puns on the names of the Queen of Hawaii and President Buchanan's niece. If he shows any talent, it is for social manners, not poetry. Transcribed after his return, the poetic diary is nonetheless striking inasmuch as it reveals the Ambassador as totally poised, not at all ruffled by the exposure to the strange and the unaccustomed.

Tamamushi, who habitually employs an "I" pronoun (*yo* in this case) in his *Kō-Bei nichiroku*, is different. Ambassador Shimmi's manservant during the voyage, Tamamushi was born to a low-ranking samurai family in the Sendai domain in the north. During his early years, he was a brilliant student at the clan's official school. After running away to Edo, he worked for a time as a laborer for Hayashi Daigaku-no-Kami Fukusai (or Tosho), the hereditary Lord Rector of the official Tokugawa college, the Shōheikō Institute (comparable to, say, Oxford in its early days). Once recognized for his gifts, Tamamushi was quickly promoted to head tutor (*jukuchō*) at the school. It happened that Hayashi was the chief negotiator for the Commodore Perry talks in 1854, and Tamamushi's joining the Embassy was no doubt traceable to his master's influence. In fact, on their departure from Japan, it was no other than Iwase Tadanari, one of the initial planners of the Embassy back in 1858, who wrote Tamamushi a farewell poem in classical Chinese.[26] Now, while Tamamushi's scholarship was truly distinguished, there was nothing in his background to suggest any substantial exposure to "Dutch learning." The curriculum of the Shōheikō school was solidly Neo-Confucian and quite orthodox, and Hayashi was, if anything, known for his contempt for the new-fangled Western learning.[27] Tamamushi had toured in the north, and discussed the nature of the Russian threat in a nine-volume geographical study (which may have given him the opportunity to ponder the international situation of the time), and, as we have already noted, he had read *Kaikoku zushi* and other books on the West. But still, at the time of his departure from Japan, he was as dead set against the barbarians as anybody else in the Embassy.[28] Once, while on board the *Powhatan,* Tamamushi heard the crude men of the West playing musical instruments, and was profoundly irritated. And being constantly subjected, in such claustrophobic quarters, to the harsh, unfamiliar American gabble only further grated upon the aide's ragged nerves. Therefore, when visiting with a Chinese emigré in Honolulu, he declared himself a "dedicated student of the Way of the Sages [*seikyō,* or *seidō,* Confucianism], unlike many others on the Mission trained in Western learning."[29]

And yet Tamamushi was always fair, giving recognition where due. On the stormy crossing, it was not only his Japanese colleagues who offered him assistance and encouragement; several American sailors made clear, across the language barrier, that they were concerned with their passengers' welfare and comfort. He also appreciated the American officers' genuine camaraderie with their men, in marked contrast to their rank-conscious Japanese counterparts. Little by little, Tamamushi's evaluation of the Americans began to change. And as we saw earlier, his good feelings toward America gradually became more authentic than anyone else's on the Mission. As he mulled over the questions raised by America and its people, he had to disengage himself from the others, and use the first-person singular. Unlike Vice-Ambassador Muragaki's "I" necessitated by external authority, Tamamushi's developed as he assumed critical authority and intellectual responsibility for himself. His exceptional insight and commentary demanded that the first-person singular pronoun not be left implied, but made fully explicit. Thus, the subject of his sentences must be isolated from the generalized "we-they" by the singular, unambiguous, and explicit "I."

The Muragaki-Tamamushi contrast is intriguing. Both had been contemptuous toward the United States at first. However, Muragaki's attitudes remained essentially unaltered. If he did come to concede to the West superiority in weapons development and health care, his evaluation of America as an inferior and barbarous country never wavered. The voyage, then, was little more than a necessary aspect of his career in the Tokugawa regime, and the reward on his return— audiences with the Shogun, a promotion, and gifts such as an elaborately wrought hilt, fifty pieces of gold, four seasonal dresses, and 1,500 bushels of rice a year (300 *koku*)—was the acme of achievement he had all along striven for.[30] The rhetoric of the summary, toward his diary's end, reveals Muragaki as close-minded as ever, as though he had never taken any time off from his bureaucratic routine.

Tamamushi, on the other hand, underwent a serious reexamination of his beliefs. Intellectually caught short, he was nonetheless honest and alert to all he experienced, not allowing the inertia of prior convictions to interfere with personal observation. If there was any early sign of modern awareness in the 1860 Embassy records, it was surely most visible in Tamamushi's, whose first-person singular pronoun is a sign of the exceptional mind that harbored no fear of keeping one's distance from the others. It is noteworthy that this critically uncompromising book by Tamamushi was the one more modeled after and copied from than that of any other writer in the group, and it has survived in far more copies today than anyone else's.

Earlier (in Chapter I) I mentioned that the kind of information gathered by the Japanese travelers in 1860 was disconcertingly mechanical and uncoordinated, and pointed out two external factors contributing to such poor performance: linguistic incompetence and the severe restriction on personal movement. Here I would like to discuss what information meant in the context of Japanese intellectual life, and relate it back to the perceptual and formal features of the travelogues, especially to the absence of self-consciousness.

Many Western visitors to Japan in the 1850s recorded the puzzling and frustrating experience of not getting the simplest questions answered by officials. That master ironist Goncharov put it this way:

"What is the population of Nagasaki?" I once asked Baba Gorozaemon—through an interpreter, of course. He repeated the question in Japanese and looked at a second colleague, who looked at a third, who in turn looked at a junior *baniosi*; the junior *baniosi* looked at an interpreter, and so the question and the look came back to Baba again, though without an answer.

"Sometimes there are fewer," said Sadagora at last, "and sometimes there are more."

"Are all your houses one-storeyed, or do they sometimes have two storeys?" asked Pos'et.

"They sometimes have two storeys," said Kichibe and looked at L'oda.

"And sometimes three," said L'oda, looking at Sadagora.

"There are sometimes even five," said Sadagora.

We began to laugh.

"Do you often have earthquakes?" asked Pos'et.

"Yes, we do," answered Sadagora, looking at L'oda.

"How often? Once in ten years or once in twenty years?"

"We have them once in ten years and once in twenty years," said L'oda, glancing at Kichibe and at Sadagora.

"The mountains crack and the houses fall down," added Sadagora. And the whole conversation continued in this fashion.[31]

Townsend Harris's complaint is exasperated and humorless. Transmitting the U.S. Patent Office's request for information about Japanese cotton, he received next to no reply:

It is a beautiful specimen of Japanese craft, cunning and falsehood. Their great object appears to be to permit as little to be learned about their country as possible; and, to that end, all fraud, deceit, falsehood and even violence, is justifiable in their eyes. It is true that this is the most difficult country in the world to get information; no statistics exist; no publications are made on any subject connected with industry.[32]

There is no question that the functionaries were under strictest command not to reveal any information whatever about Japan to foreigners. But where, we ask, did this policy of noncommunication and secretiveness originate? A paranoiac worry over national security? A totalitarian structure depending for survival on rigid adherence to an official line? Of course. But underlying these in turn was a philosophical attitude toward knowledge which requires some explanation.

First of all, while the Japanese declined to answer the foreigners, that is not to say they kept their mouths shut or their minds closed. They asked numerous questions about the West, as has been mentioned by nearly every foreigner who came in contact with them around that time. Similarly, Harris's frustration and Goncharov's lampooning notwithstanding, the Japanese were not unacquainted with the system of keeping records. On the contrary, the records stored by the Tokugawa and domainal governments, towns, villages, and families are so immense that they now serve historians as a treasure house perhaps unparalleled in the world. There were also continual experimentation and innovation in agricultural skills and financial management.[33] When the Tokugawa officials faced Westerners, however, they were unwilling to share the knowledge with strangers. Information had to remain within the tribe.

Second, when the Japanese faced Westerners, they wanted only a particular kind of information. Very early on, Arai Hakuseki (1657–1725), an eminent Neo-Confucian scholar and high-ranking advisor to the Shogun, divided the realm of knowledge between the "metaphysical" (*keijijō*) and the "physical" (*keijika*), conceding to the West superiority in practical and technological knowledge while making no qualification whatever for the moral excellence of the Neo-Confucian world view.[34] Despite his considerable curiosity about the West, he peremptorily dismissed, for instance, Christianity as "irrational" and "immoral." Arai Hakuseki wanted to learn technology from the West, but not what had contributed to produce it, that is, the assumptions and values that had formed the whole culture. His attitude was more or less typical of the succeeding "Dutch scholars' " toward the Westerners: learn practical knowledge but as for moral and other values preserve what is already there—the indigenous Japanese, the earlier imports from China, and some Buddhism, however the blend may have been defined by individuals.

Quite obviously, the Tokugawa period was intellectually far from dormant over its two and a half centuries. From the very beginning, the Chu Hsi world view was challenged by Kaibara Ekken (1630–1714), Arai Hakuseki himself, Ogyū Sorai (1666–1728), and many others. Miura Baien (1723–1789), one of the greatest skeptics of Tokugawa Japan, for instance, raises in epistemological treatises such as *Taga Bokkyō kun ni kotaeru sho*, 1777 (In answer to Taga Bokkyō) fundamental questions concerning the ground for belief. What is interesting about these extremely difficult but fascinating books is, however, that Miura does not persist in calling *all* into doubt; instead, he questions the doubting self itself. Instead of finding the thinking self as the proof of being, Miura Baien eventually leaps back to the security of community, the Neo-Confucian political absolute as embodied in the Tokugawa structure.[35] And as for the ultimate acceptance of the Confucian categories of *chū* (loyalty), *kō* (filial piety), *jin* (charity), and *rei* (hierarchic distinction), even scholars in the *Ōyōmei (Wang Yang-ming)* school, critical of the Tokugawa administration, such as Nakae Tōju (1608–1648) and Kumazawa Banzan (1619–1691), strayed very little indeed.[36]

Even later "Dutch scholars" like Hiraga Gennai (1728–1779), Sugita Gempaku (1733–1817), Honda Toshiaki (1743–1820), or Sakuma Shōzan (1811–1864) were quite aloof to what we might call the "humanistic" aspects of Western culture which they might well have come across in their perusal of Western books and documents. As a matter of fact, even those ideologue activists in the mid-nineteenth century who were practically agitators for insurrection against the Shogunate—like Yoshida Shōin and Hashimoto Sanai—never thought of putting their Western knowledge to use for reexamining these traditional hierarchic values. They desired Western knowledge only because they considered it helpful to fell the Tokugawa House (though not the hierarchic structure itself), and paradoxically to expel the Westerners themselves. Sakuma Shōzan's slogan "Eastern morality, Western technology" (*Tōyō no dōtoku, seiyō no geijutsu*), was soon slightly abbreviated to "Japanese soul and Western technology" (*Wakon yōsai*), and this new version was to survive well into Meiji Japan and even, in several aspects, into present days.[37]

Their determination to keep the "metaphysical" (read moral, or cultural) tradition undisturbed was shared not only by ideologues, but also by actual rebels and rioters of the time who attempted armed rebellions against the authorities. Ōshio Heihachirō (1793–1837), who attacked the Magistrate of Ōsaka on behalf of the starved populace, nonetheless took it for granted that the direct imperial rule would cure the Tokugawa ills, in his *Gekibun* (Summons to insurrection, 1837).[38] Miura Meisuke, a leader in the great peasant riot of 1853, asked his relatives to remain loyal to their good lord in his prison letters.[39] In short, before the 1867 Restoration, there were extremely few men who were willing to seek, or even felt any need for, alternatives to the traditional principles of *chū, kō, jin,* and *rei.** For scholars and activists alike, knowledge still responded to the calls of an insular society requiring ever-renewed affirmation of inherited values, not systematic information for adapting to a new philosophy, nor a universalist perspective on the world mediated by an individual's unabridged life experience.

The information the 1860 Embassy members collected was certainly not of a type to spark any comprehensive "humanistic" confrontation with the tradition. So much of it consisted of separate (and more often than not, trivial) facts and data, and so little was organized toward any "theoretical" understanding of the new experience. Admittedly, the Western counterparts were not much better. Alcock's construction of Japanese grammar, Oliphant's pastoral myth built after a two-weeks' sojourn, and George Smith's theological verdict on the Japanese are all preposterous misunderstandings of Japanese culture as we conceive it now. Yet, in these wrong-headed books there is an awareness that facts and non-facts, data and non-data must be evaluated, selected, and coordinated before they are acceptable. With the exception of Tamamushi and Fukuzawa (whose memoir was written decades later), the Japanese diarists of 1860 were satisfied with accumulating large amounts of unrelated materials that would not significantly shake their convictions about the world outside.

*A quite different view is expressed by Tetsuo Najita in his book *Japan*, an excellent study of the intellectual history of the country (see esp. chaps. 2 and 3, pp. 16–68). Najita cogently analyzes the continually shifting philosophical status of categories like virtue, norm, utility, etc., thereby revealing Tokugawa

To put it differently, of these three main obstacles to information gathering, the first two were shared by visiting Westerners of the time as well; they could not speak the language of the host country, and their movement, too, was seriously limited (though in their case by the host government). And yet Alcock and Siebold, Hodgson and McCauley were all—whether aware of it or not—children of Copernicus and Descartes, Hamlet and Faust. Not only were they curious about their surroundings, but curiosity propelled their lives. They were adept—as the Japanese chose not to be—in modifying or simply abandoning established beliefs and dogmas in the face of new discoveries. The reader of an Occidental travelogue would at once be impressed by the qualitative difference between the texture and density of its analytic observation and that of its Japanese counterpart. What separates the two is their differing attitudes toward information and knowledge, insight and understanding, and, closely related to this, their essential difference in attitude toward the self.

Before modern analytic thinking emerged, the Westerner had to acquire the habit of speaking in the isolated first person, as did Descartes in his *Discourse*. Dependence on an implied first person and the resulting ambiguous subject in Japanese did not encourage a similar development. The "I" tended not to detach itself from the other "I's" and thus stayed immersed in the world. There was neither the joy nor the misery of the lonely self; instead, with the ambiguity of

Japan as far more intellectually volatile and various than I have. His conceptualization allows him also to see in many thinkers of the time an awareness of selfhood (the "spiritual self" in Nakae Tōju and Kumazawa Banzan; "personal autonomy" in Ōshio Heihachirō). For myself, however, Tokugawa thinkers seem almost totally circumscribed by a hierarchic world view, leaving little space for recognition of a separable self. (The only exceptions I could think of are: Shiba Kōkan [1748–1818], a painter heavily influenced by Western techniques, who wistfully talks about European countries and insists on the equality of men ["*hito to shite* hito o tōtomu" in *Wa-Ran tensetsu* [1795]; the anti-feudal egalitarianism of Andō Shōeki [1703–1762; see E. H. Norman, Maruyama Masao, and Noguchi Takehiko]; and Yokoi Shōnan's universalism as referred to earlier.)

Similarly, H. D. Harootunian, in his lucid and energetic book *Toward Restoration*, finds in the 1867 changeover far greater "revolutionary dimensions" (p. 409) than I do. I do agree that Sakuma and Yoshida, for instance, were potentially aware both of Japan's place "among the nations of The Five Continents" (p. 173) and of the need for a "transvaluation of values" (p. 407). To me, however, the two men's knowledge of and interest in the West seem neither deep nor wide enough to allow them so "radical [a] break with accepted usage" (p. 407) and with the past. In this respect I find helpful Uete Michiari's "Sakuma Shōzan ni okeru jugaku, bushiseishin, yōgaku," pp. 652–685, and Robert N. Bellah, "Continuity and Change in Japanese Society."

the subject allowing his action and being to be collective, man in Japan retained the security of community, however temporally and spatially circumscribed he may have been by the tribal mythology. If Maruyama Masao is right, as I believe he is, in diagnosing the conspicuous absence of the speculative habit (*shisō*) in the whole Japanese tradition, it is a price the culture has been willing to pay. It has chosen to forego universalist knowledge, skeptical observation, and individual reflection in order to sustain a close and coherent community inherited from the long past.[40]

For all its inclinations and preferences, Confucianism was by no means a deterrent to other kinds of learning. If it was not exactly charged with the humanistic spirit, it nonetheless taught a reverence for learning in general; if free inquiry was not the first principle of Confucian learning, it allowed the student to interpret the Way of the Sages as *he* saw it; and if group consciousness was dominant, it yet encouraged vigorous competition within the group. Besides, theirs was a largely pragmatic version of Confucianism. Thus was the Tokugawa mind prepared with a context of learning that would readily allow a new influence to begin its work. For instance, once the information brought back by the 1860 Mission was found to be overly random and mostly useless, this inadequacy was efficiently corrected. The next Tokugawa embassy, the 1862 Mission to Europe, was more pragmatically organized in accordance with that realization.[41] Actually, this ability to absorb vigorously what was only very recently encountered would be unthinkable without the system of basic education provided by the long Confucian tradition and the bureaucratic structure deeply rooted in it. Ronald Dore would defend it this way:

Knowledge was imparted by the teacher to be accepted, not to be improved upon. And this attitude, given the initial decision to learn from the West, produced a humble attentiveness and an assiduous thoroughness. Every detail went down into the notebook; every utterance of the foreign *sensei* was treated with solemn respect. Had the Tokugawa schools been mainly concerned to "teach people to think," had they encouraged the free play of ideas between teacher and pupil on a footing of near equality, many more steamships might have had their boilers ruined by men who thought they could run them by the light of pure reason before they got instructions in how to keep them filled with water.[42]

There are two accounts of diplomatic occasions that were very much alike, one by an American and the other by a Japanese. One is Harris's description of his audience with the Shogun in Edo Castle on

December 7, 1857, and the other is Muragaki's record of his reception by President Buchanan on May 19, 1860, in the White House. Of course, there were numerous differences, too, between the two situations. This was the first foreign envoy Japan had received for a very long time; for the United States, international diplomacy was routine. Harris had lived in Japan for over two years and thus had come to know the customs and manners of the people fairly well, whereas Muragaki had been in the United States only a few hectic weeks. Harris was accompanied by Heusken alone, the two comprising the entire American delegation; Muragaki, on the other hand, was surrounded by two additional envoys and numerous attendants. While Harris aggressively fought for this mission, Muragaki was merely given the assignment—and that not particularly for his talent or experience. In short, they were two individuals with differing talents and abilities. And finally, there remains the immense difference in the geopolitical situations of the two countries: one powerful and confident with its advanced technology and abundant resources, the other surrounded by menacing powers and just awakening to its absolute military and economic inferiority.

Against such disparities, the similarities might appear rather meager. The writers were both principal envoys and their interviews were both totally unfamiliar events. Both were in foreign environments and were provided lodgings and escorts by their host governments. Both ceremonies were brief and merely formal. Both accounts were written soon after the events. Japan was a place many Americans wanted to visit; so was America for an increasing number of Japanese. Despite the acknowledged paucity of similarities, however, the concrete situational likeness is compelling. I would like to compare how these basically similar diplomatic occasions were observed and recorded by the two men. My intention is to concentrate on the *formal* aspects of the narrative, avoiding in analysis the obvious differences in substance as much as possible. And my hope is that the result will show clearly and specifically the differing workings of the Japanese and American minds as the two cultures came in contact for the first time. In other words, I believe the comparison will support what has been argued thus far. The passages are somewhat long, perhaps, but they must be reproduced in their entirety. Here is Townsend Harris in Edo Castle:

Monday, December 7, 1857. I started for my audience about ten, with the same escort as on my visit to the Minister, but my guards all wore *camissimos* and breeches which only covered half the thigh, leaving all

Townsend Harris and Henry Heusken on their way to the audience with
the Shogun. The last man is Moriyama Takichirō, the interpreter.

the rest of the leg bare. My dress was a coat embroidered with gold after
the pattern furnished by the State Department: blue pantaloons with a
broad gold band running down each leg, cocked hat with gold tassels and a
pearl handled dress-sword.

   Mr. Heusken's dress was the undress navy uniform, regulation sword
and cocked hat. Our route was by the same street that I have mentioned
on my visit to the Minister, but we crossed the moat by a bridge that was
about half a mile from my house. The gateway with the quadrangular
building was precisely like those described in my *Journal* of the 4th inst.;
so also the appearance of the streets, buildings, people, etc., was exactly
the same. On arriving at the second moat all were required to leave their
norimons [palanquins] except the Prince of Shinano and myself. We
crossed the bridge, passed the gate and quadrangle, and pursued our
course, and everything was so exactly like what I then saw that nothing
but the assurances of Shinano could convince me that I was in a different
quarter. When we arrived within about three hundred yards of the last
bridge, Shinano also left his *norimon;* and our horses, his spears, etc., etc.,
with the ordinary attendants, all remained. I was carried up to the bridge
itself (and, as they say, further than any Japanese was ever carried before),
and here I dismounted, giving the President's letter, which I had brought
in my *norimon,* to Mr. Heusken to carry. We crossed this bridge through
the same quadrangle as before; and, at some one hundred and fifty to two
hundred yards from the gate, I entered the Audience Hall. Before entering, however, I put on the new shoes I had worn on my visit to the
Minister, and the Japanese did not even ask me to go in my stocking feet.
As I entered the vestibule I was met by two officers of the household. We
stopped, faced each other and then bowed. They then led me along a hall
to a room where, on entering, I found the "two chairs" and a comfortable
brazier. I should here note that tobacco is *not* served among the refresh-

ments of the Palace. I again drank the "tea gruel." The room in which I was seated was different from any I had seen before. The ceiling or *plafond* was divided into square compartments of some thirty inches, the ribs or divisions being about two inches wide and the same in thickness. It was either painted or covered with paper, — I could not determine which. The ground was a fine ultramarine, on which arabesque figures were drawn of various colors; the posts and beams were of unpainted wood; the usual height of Japanese rooms is from eleven to twelve feet. I thought these to be about thirteen to fourteen feet. I have already mentioned that a Japanese house is cut up into rooms by sliding doors or screens, and that in a short time a whole building may be converted into a single room by the removal of the screens; by this process what was hall becomes part or parts of the rooms. The height of these doors varies from five feet six inches to six feet six inches. Transverse beams are placed in those positions which are to serve as the division wall or partition of a room; a series of grooves is deeply cut in the under side of the beam [and] corresponds with shallow grooves cut in a beam of the floor placed directly under it.

When it is desired to remove a partition, the parts are lifted up until the foot is clear of the floor groove. It is then carried forward or back until the angle it forms will allow the upper part to be removed from the upper beam.

To construct a room the above process is simply reversed. The sliding doors are from four to four and a half feet wide, and they always slide past each other, so that of necessity there must be as many grooves as there are parts of the screen — four is the usual number. The part between the upper beam and the *plafond* is variously filled. Sometimes it is with frames resembling our window sashes on which paper is pasted, and it looks exactly like a sash that is glazed with rough ground glass. Another, and the most usual mode, is to fill the space with light and neatly made lattice work. At the Palace I saw another mode of filling this space. It was (apparently) carved openwork representing birds, fruits, flowers, and arabesque ornaments, all very highly colored and producing a tawdry effect, which was the more remarkable as the Japanese do not greatly affect violent contrasts or gaudy colors. They apparently prefer the neutral tints and have a good eye for the harmony of colors. The partitions, doors or screens, were painted with passable drawings of their favorite fir tree. This description is exact for every part of the Palace which I saw, and which was equal to some seven or eight of their ordinary rooms, but on this occasion a number of rooms were thrown into one. I was now conducted to another part of the Palace. As I passed along I saw some three hundred to four hundred of the *Daimyo* and high nobles sitting in exact rows, all facing in one direction. They were all clad in Court dresses, of which more anon.

The room to which I was conducted was a large one (but [the] screen [was] made of gilt paper; I have never seen a single expensive screen made of lacquered ormolu and mother-of-pearl since I have been in Japan; I think they were only made by the express orders of the Dutch); and here some of my Commissioners came to pay their respects to me in an informal manner, and some cheerful conversation passed between us. I should describe the Court dress, but to convey an intelligible idea of it is beyond the power of mere words. Drawings are indispensable to a clear understanding of it. The *camissimo,* or upper garment, differs from the ordinary one by coming down quite to the hips. The breeches are the great feature of the dress. They are made of yellow silk, and the legs are some six to seven feet long! Consequently, when the wearer walks, they stream out behind him and give him the appearance of walking on his knees, an illusion which is helped out by the short stature of the Japanese and the great width over the shoulders of their *camissimos.* The cap is also a great curiosity and defies description. It is made of a black varnished material and looks like a Scotch Kilmarnock cap which has been opened only some three inches wide, and is fantastically perched on the very apex of the head. The front comes just to the top edge of the forehead, but the back projects some distance behind the head. This extraordinary affair is kept in place by a light colored silk cord which, passing over the top of the "Coronet," passes down over the temples and is tied under the chin; a lashing runs horizontally across the forehead, and, being attached to the perpendicular cord, passes behind the head, where it is tied. The *camissimo* is without sleeves and is worn over the other garments. It is made of some highly gummed material which makes it quite stiff. Imagine a Van Dyke [collar] of two half diamonds or lozenges. The acute points project over each shoulder; from thence the line of its shape runs so as to strike the waist or girdle. The front and back are composed of box pleats, and the whole is secured by the waist girdle.

My description cannot be very intelligible, but it is the best I can give.

My friend Shinano was very anxious to have me enter the Audience Chamber and *rehearse my part.* This I declined as gently as I could, telling him that the general customs of all Courts were so similar that I had no fear of making any mistakes, particularly as he had kindly explained their part of the ceremony, while my part was to be done after our Western fashion. I really believe he was anxious that I should perform my part in such a manner as to make a favorable impression on those who would see me for the first time. I discovered, also, that I had purposely been brought to the Palace a good hour before the time, so that he might get through his rehearsal before the time for my actual audience. Finding I declined the rehearsal, I was again taken to the room that I first entered, which was comfortably warm and had chairs to sit on. Tea was again served to me. The servants in the Palace wore black dresses, and their heads are entirely shaved. They are either priests, or wear the dress of priests.

I here discovered that one of my Commissioners, Kawasi, Prince of Saiyemo, is brother to the Prince of Shinano, my host or keeper. He is a lively, cheerful person and was vastly pleased when I told [him] he looked younger than Shinano, although he is four years his senior.

He is the head of all the governors of cities and provinces, and all business from or to them passes through his office. At last I was informed that the time had arrived for my audience, and I passed down by the poor *Daimyo* who were still seated like so many statues in the same place; but, when I had got as far as their front rank, I passed in front of their line and halted on their right flank, towards which I faced. Shinano here threw himself on his hands and knees. I stood behind him, and Mr. Heusken was just behind me. On looking out I saw a small courtyard surrounded with wooden buildings one story high and covered with tiles. The audience chamber faced in the same manner as the room in which the great audience was seated, but separated from it by the usual sliding doors, so that, although they could see me pass and hear all that was said at the audience, they could not see into the chamber. At length, on a signal being made, the Prince of Shinano began to crawl along on his hands and knees; and when I half turned to the right and entered the audience chamber, a chamberlain called out in a loud voice, "Embassador Merrican!" I halted about six feet from the door and bowed, then proceeded nearly to the middle of the room, where I again halted and bowed; again proceeding, I stopped about ten feet from the end of the room exactly opposite to the Prince of Bittsu on my right hand, where he and the other five members of the Great Council were prostrate on their faces. On my left hand were three brothers of the Tykoon, prostrated in the same manner, and all of them being nearly "end on" towards me. After a pause of a few seconds I addressed the Tykoon as follows:

May it please Your Majesty:
In presenting my letters of credence from the President of the United States, I am directed to express to Your Majesty the sincere wishes of the President for your health and happiness and for the prosperity of your dominions. I consider it a great honor that I have been selected to fill the high and important place of Plenipotentiary of the United States at the Court of Your Majesty; and, as my earnest wishes are to unite the two countries more closely in the ties of enduring friendship, my constant exertions shall be directed to the attainment of that happy end.

Here I stopped and bowed. After a short silence the Tykoon began to jerk his head backward over his left shoulder, at the same time stamping with his right foot. This was repeated three or four times. After this he spoke audibly and in a pleasant and firm voice, what was interpreted as follows:

Pleased with the letter sent with the Ambassador from a far distant country, and likewise pleased with his discourse.
Intercourse shall be continued forever.

Mr. Heusken, who had been standing at the door of the Audience Chamber, now advanced with the President's letter, bowing three times. As he approached, the Minister for Foreign Affairs rose to his feet and stood by me. I removed the silk cover over the box, opened it, also raised the cover of the letter so that the Minister could see the writing. I then closed the box, replaced the silk covering (made of red and white stripes, six and seven), and handed the same to the Minister, who received it with both hands and placed it on a handsome lacquered stand which was placed a little above him. He then lay down again, and I turned toward the Tykoon, who gave me to understand my audience was at an end by making me a courteous bow. I bowed, retreated backward, halted, bowed, again retreated, again halted, and bowed again and for the last time. So ended my audience, when I was reconducted to my original room and served with more tea gruel. In order to see as much as I could, I asked to be shown to a water closet. On leaving the room I found myself in a small court surrounded by wooden buildings exactly like those described on the opposite side of the house. A good deal of negotiation had been used by the Japanese to get me to eat a dinner at the Palace, alone or with Mr. Heusken only. This I declined doing. I offered to partake of it provided one of the Royal Family or the Prime Minister would eat with me. I was told that their customs forbade either from doing so. I replied that the customs of my country forbade anyone to eat in a house where the host or his representative did not sit down to table with him. At last the matter was arranged by ordering the dinner to be sent to my lodgings. I had not been long in the room last mentioned before I was requested to meet the Council of State. I found them in the place where the *Daimyo* had been seated, but who had now left the room. Hotta, Prince of Bittsu, spoke and in the name of the Council congratulated me on my arrival and audience, and then said His Majesty had ordered a present to be offered to me, which was then in the room, at the same time pointing to three large trays each holding five silk *kabyas* thickly wadded with silk wadding. I thanked the Council for their kind inquiries and desired them to return my thanks to His Majesty for his present. After this, bows were exchanged and I turned and left the room going towards the vestibule; but a few yards from it I halted and turned, when the Council of State again formed line and took leave of me by a deep bow. At the vestibule I met the two officers who had first received me, and I exchanged bows with them, and then left the Palace, and proceeded to my *norimon* and returned home by the same route I had come by.

The Tykoon was seated in a *chair* placed on a platform raised about two feet from the floor, and from the ceiling in front of him a grass curtain was hung. When unrolled it would reach the floor, but it was now rolled up, and was kept in its place by large silk cords with heavy tassels. By an error in their calculation the curtain was not rolled up high enough to enable me to see his headdress, as the roll formed by the curtain cut through the centre of his forehead, so that I cannot fully describe his "crown," as the Japanese call it. I was afterwards told that this mistake arose from their not making a proper allowance for my height, as, had my eyes been three inches lower, I could have seen the whole of his headdress. This may, or may not be so. The dress of the Tykoon was made of silk, and the material had some little gold woven in with it. But it was as distant from anything like regal splendor as could be conceived. No rich jewels, no elaborate gold ornaments, no diamond hilted weapon appeared, and I can safely say that my dress was far more costly than his. The Japanese told me his crown is a black lacquered cap, of an inverted bell shape. The dress of the Tykoon was differently shaped from those of his courtiers and appeared like loose robes, while his breeches were of a reasonable length. The material was far inferior to the glorious "kincabs" of the Benares looms.

I did not see any gilding in any part, and all the wooden columns were unpainted.

Not an article of any kind appeared in any of the rooms, except the braziers and the chairs and tables brought for my use. At the right side of the last gate I entered, a square pagoda or tower of three stories was erected. There was the same absence of military display as on my visit to the Minister. Soon after reaching my quarters the dinner followed. It was very handsome according to Japanese rules, and the centerpieces were beautifully got up. Miniature fir trees, the tortoise and stork, emblems of longevity, with tokens of welcome and respect were prominently exhibited. I merely looked at it but was unable to eat a morsel, as I was seriously ill. I had taken a violent cold; had much inflammation of the lungs, and now a violent ague fit attacked me. I was glad to send for the doctor of the Prince of Shinano, a very intelligent man that I had frequently seen at Shimoda. Finding I had already taken cathartic medicine, he prescribed tisanes, feet in hot water, to drink freely of hot *cunju,* or rice gruel, and to put on as many clothes as I could pile on my bed, so as to promote perspiration.[43]

And here is Muragaki in the White House:

Intercalary third month 28th [May 19, 1860].

Cloudy. As the hour for our presentation to the President of the United States was appointed for twelve o'clock, we made all the necessary preparations with the utmost care. Masaoki (wearing a short sword with silk twined scabbard), I (with a short court sword with gold hilt), and Tadamasa (bearing a sword with scabbard twined in front), were dressed alike in *kariginu* and *eboshi* with light green braided cords, and wore sandals woven of silk threads. Both Morita and Naruse Masanori wore *horoginu,* while the two officers of superintendent's rank put on *su-ō,* and Namura Gorō, our official interpreter, was dressed in *kamishimo,* made of ramie cloth.

We drove off in open carriages-and-four, Masaoki with Captain Du-Pont riding in the first carriage, I with Captain Lee in the second, and Tadamasa with Mr. Ledyard in the third, followed by other members of the Embassy in carriages, and servants on foot. (The First and Second Ambassadors and the Censor each took with them three footmen, one spear-bearer and three retainers, while Morita and Naruse were each accompanied by two retainers, one spear-bearer and one sandal-carrier.) Our procession was headed by a score of men in grey uniform (probably city officials), immediately followed by a band of some thirty musicians, and several mounted cavaliers; then came a group of men, bearing upon their shoulders the despatch box with a red leather cover, and accompanied by the officer in charge, a foreman and an interpreter; these were followed by a long line of carriages in good order, on either side of which marched the guards to the accompaniment of music played by the band.

The ambassadorial procession to visit the President.

The wide main street was literally packed with vehicles, men and women who were eager to get a glimpse of our procession. We couldn't help smiling, finding ourselves feeling quite elated at representing Japan in such a grand style in the foreign land. I even forgot my limitations as I looked at the wonder registered in the faces of the crowd, as they pressed forward to see our party in strange costumes such as they had never seen nor could have ever imagined.

Through the iron gate of the President's official residence, we continued to drive some 140 yards, accompanied by the cavaliers, soldiers and our servants, up to the main entrance of the building. Having left our carriages there, we were conducted up a flight of stone steps and through several rooms, into the anteroom, prepared for the Ambassadors and the Censor. Morita and the rest of the Embassy members were shown into another room. We were ushered into a large oval-shaped room, measuring probably 7 *ken* by 4, with a carpet of beautiful designs in bright blue on the floor; draperies of similar pattern and color hung inside three large glass windows. There were large mirrors on all the walls, and before them, tables of various sizes, on which were placed Japanese lacquered writing boxes and other Japanese articles, which had been presented to Commodore Perry on his visit to Japan. General Lewis Cass came in and greeted us. After he left, Captains DuPont and Lee led us to the Audience Room; Naruse Masanori carried the despatch box, containing the Shogun's letter. (The imperial letter was written on gold-leafed Japanese paper with a picture of flowers and birds, and placed in a plain paulownia casket with a lining of silk brocade, which was tied in the middle with

Reception of the Ambassadors by President James Buchanan at the White House, May 17, 1860.

vermilion cords. Its cover was made of purple Chinese satin with tassels of similar color attached to its four corners. The box in which this was contained, was of black lacquer with scarlet silk cords tied in the middle; this box had been handed over to Captain DuPont before the ceremony.) As we approached the Audience Room, the doors to its entrance were swung open on both sides. In the center of the room, which measured approximately 6 *ken* by 13, stood President Buchanan, flanked by high-ranking civil and military officers; at his back were many ladies, young and old, all attired in beautiful dresses. Having entered the room and bowed, Masaoki, I, and Tadamasa advanced to the center of the room. We bowed once again and approached the President. Masaoki delivered a short address, conveying to him the imperial wishes, which was then interpreted by Namura. After his address, Masaoki took the Shogun's letter from the casket, held out by Naruse Masanori, and presented it to the President; the casket was handed over by Naruse to the Secretary of State Cass. We withdrew to the center of the room, whereupon, Morita and the rest of the Embassy were led to the President's seat. We then retired to the anteroom, having expressed our gratification for that occasion.

As we were resting in the anteroom, Captain DuPont came and asked us if the ceremony of presenting the imperial letter according to our customs was completed. We said yes. Thereupon, he conducted us once again to the Audience Room. This time, the President shook hands with each of us, and made a short speech to the effect that the President and the

entire American nation rejoiced in establishing friendly relations with
Japan for the first time since her declaration of seclusion, and particularly
in receiving her first Embassy to the United States, and that they were
exceedingly gratified to have received the Shogun's letter of goodwill. He
then presented us with a written copy of his address. After that, high-
ranking officials came forward and shook hands with us; as the greeting
seemed to go on forever, we took the first opportunity to withdraw to the
anteroom, after making our final bows. We drove through the same streets
back to our hotel.

At four P.M., Captain DuPont and Mr. Ledyard called on us, informing
us that it was a Western custom to pay visits to foreign ministers in
Washington. We told him that we would visit only ministers of those
nations with whom our country had concluded amicable treaties, but not
the others; they agreed to our condition. We changed into our travelling
costumes, and made a swift round of visits in carriages. When we arrived
in front of a minister's residence, we had our visiting cards (bearing our
names in both Japanese and English), sent in by our driver, so that we did
not even have to get out of our carriage. It was a most convenient custom.
We made a round of several residences, but did not even know which
minister's house we were visiting. At the British and Dutch ministers',
we were shown in and met their wives and children; theirs were beautiful
houses. It was already evening when we returned to our hotel.

We gathered together and talked of our experience on this memorable
day. The President is a silver-haired man of over seventy years of age, and
he has a most genial manner without losing noble dignity. He wore a
simple black costume of coat and trousers in the same fashion as any
merchant, and had no decoration or sword on him. All the high-ranking
officials were dressed in the same way as the President, whereas the army
and navy officers wore epaulets (the gold tassels attached to the shoulders,
of which the length marked the rank), and gold stripes on the sleeves of
their costumes (of which the number represented the rank, three stripes
signifying the highest); and they carried a sword at their side. It seemed to
us a most curious custom to permit the presence of women on such a
ceremonious occasion as today. We remembered how we were received at
the Sandwich Islands by the women alone—after the main event at our
presentation—with somewhat greater formalities; this difference, we attributed, although we were not well acquainted with Western customs
and manners, to the fact that the Sandwich Islands constituted a monarchy. The United States is one of the greatest countries in the world, but
the President is only a governor voted in [*nyūsatsu*] every four years.
(There will be a changeover on October 1 this year. We heard them
suggest a certain man; when we asked how they could tell before the
"auction," they answered that this man would be the President, because
he was related to the present one. Judging from such remarks, I don't
believe that the fundamental laws of this country will last much longer.)
The President is thus not a king. Nevertheless, since the Shogun's letter
was addressed to him, we adopted such manners of etiquette [*rei*] as were
appropriate to a monarch. It was pointless, however, to put on the formal

kariginu robe in his honor, since the Americans attach little importance to hierarchic distinction, and dispense with all ceremony [*reigi*]. We were, however, exceedingly happy and satisfied to have attained the goal of our mission here, an achievement worthy of any man's ambition, when we learned that the President was highly appreciative and took pride in receiving the first mission from Japan in his country before any other. We were told that he was letting the newspapers show our party dressed in *kariginu*.

> *Emishira mo aogitezo miyo higashi naru,*
> *Waga Hinomoto no kuni no hikari o.*
> Suffer the barbarians to look upon
>   This glory of our Eastern Empire of Japan.

> *Orokanaru mi omo wasure te kyō no kaku,*
> *Hokori-gao naru Hinomoto no Otodo.*
> Forgetting their meek ignorance, how proudly today
>   Shine the countenances of Japan's Embassy.[44]

First, as to sheer quantity, Harris's version is the lengthier of the two. And even Heusken's record, which falls short of Harris's, still exceeds the Vice-Ambassador's. Among all the 1860 Embassy records of this event, however, Muragaki's is by far the longest and most attentive to detail of all the works by this group, which mostly devote only a few words to this central event of the Mission to America. And thus it may be safe to assume that the Japanese travelers were not as interested as the Westerners were in giving an elaborate account of any and all events. A general indifference to details and aversion to words unquestionably characterize their reports.*

Muragaki, however, is not always impatient with minutiae. For instance, he describes the "light green braided cords" attached to his and Oguri's *eboshi* caps, a small enough detail almost matching Harris's concreteness in describing the same type of cap seen at Edo Castle ("It is made of a black varnished material . . . where it is tied"). The motives behind the descriptions seem different, however. Muragaki discusses particulars of the uniforms worn by members of the Embassy not out of interest or curiosity, but because he felt compelled to record how faithfully they all had followed prescribed ceremonial dress and protocol.[45] He is thorough and precise about the Japanese side, but much less so about the American. He is in fact hardly interested in the particulars of the Americans he observed such as the

---

*Many Embassy diaries are quite brief. Muragaki's—with Tamamushi's—is among the longest (over 200 modern pages), the rest averaging around 50 to 150 pages. Daily entries, similarly, are often limited to from several lines to a couple of pages, seldom exceeding three or four.

soldiers' uniforms and the dress of the officials and the women, his attention to them being more a function of meticulous observance of ceremonial rules (or the politics of ceremony, *rei*), not a developed skill in observation. Harris, on the other hand, seems fascinated with the particular. He too describes his own and Heusken's dress uniforms, but his interest ranges further. He not only explains the fine details of the *eboshi* caps, but also those of the ceilings, the sliding doors, and many other features of the palace interior, the *kamishimo* coats, the Shogun's outfit (not failing to notice Iesada's epileptic spasms), and above all the choreography of the ceremony. Though no book lover, he did read Bulwer, Kingsley, Disraeli, and Thackeray, and their increasing alertness around that time to the function of details in narrative texture is a trait Harris shared. Correlative as it is to the surface specificity of Romantic poetry, such particularism points to the whole post-Enlightenment development of subjective experientialism.[46]

Next, what about the two men's curiosity about unfamiliar things? Desirous of as much information as he could get, Harris asks to be taken to the water closet. Although he does not then describe what he saw (unlike the hotel-confined junior Japanese officials who were intrigued by the workings of the flush toilet), his inquisitiveness is very apparent. Vice-Ambassador Muragaki, on the other hand, is uninterested—almost apathetic in contrast. After being strongly encouraged by the protocol officers to visit other foreign diplomats in Washington, the envoys did so but insisted on severely limiting their visits and staying but the shortest possible time. The custom of leaving cards greatly pleased them. "It was a most convenient custom," writes Muragaki, satisfied with the relief it offered to the task of actually meeting great numbers of foreigners. Further, when they did visit, he and the other two Envoys did not even trouble themselves to find out whose residence they were visiting. Admittedly fearful of any possible protocol blunder, the Envoys shunned all unnecessary exposures to such danger. Still, their passivity and boredom remain part and parcel of their total dedication to the successful performance at the programmed ceremony.

Apathy is more often than not a result of helplessness. Knowing next to nothing about America, the Ambassadors depended on Captain DuPont and the other officers for nearly all of their physical arrangements. Yet here (for this ceremony), they seem not to have understood the nature of the occasion, and surely not procedural matters, as we saw in the last chapter. What is important, though, is their conviction that ceremony in America, or rather the lack of it, is an egregious transgression against taste and morality, in which they, the Japanese, have no inclination whatever to participate even for a short-term advantage. Rather, they will blindly adhere to the one right and natural form of ceremony, which is their own. Harris, too, is guilty of this same self-centeredness. Just as Muragaki and his associates were disappointed with the lack of presidential pomp ("no decoration, or sword"), so was Harris surprised by the absence of splendor in the proceedings ("But it was as distant from anything like regal splendor as could be conceived" and "I can safely say that my dress was far more costly than his"). Their letdown afterward is also quite similar. Yet Harris did understand the politics of ceremony, and knew how to manipulate it to his advantage. He knew why he was allowed to stay in the palanquin while others were not; he knew exactly what an invitation to dinner or any repast at the palace meant; he knew why he must insist on keeping his shoes on (though he did concede to wearing a new pair). He guessed his hosts' game, and played it well on their terms, as the Japanese would never have dreamed of doing in America.

Obviously, Harris's advantage was that he was an experienced traveler who had already visited many other countries. Aside from acquaintance with his own and several European governments, he had had the experience of signing a treaty with Siam before going to Japan. He thus had a context for comparison, which the Japanese lacked. We will note that this use of comparison as a mode of logic seldom occurs in Muragaki's writing, as it does in Harris's.

For instance, the Harris diary begins with a comparison of the scene along the route with that of his earlier visit to the Castle; he likens his treatment with that of others (rank itself is a comparative concept); he looks at the palace interior in the context of other Japanese buildings; he notices various types of ceremonial dress; and he evaluates the Shogun's sumptuousness next to that of other Asian potentates. To Harris the logic of comparison comes naturally; not so to Muragaki.

Muragaki does make some comparisons, certainly. But his terms are meager, being limited solely to those of Japan and America (although once he does refer to the Sandwich Islands monarch). He does not mention here his experience at the State Department a few days earlier, nor does he recall being entertained by the President of the Board of Supervisors in San Francisco.

More important, the absence of a comparative consciousness leads to several other descriptive and narrative features of Muragaki's work. One is his visible indifference to unfamiliar things for which he had no approximate Japanese terms ready at hand. He discusses the soldiers' uniform, calling it a grey wool "tight-sleeve coat" (*tsu-tsusode*). But this expression differs little from the one used to explain the President's business suit, "black wool tight-sleeve coat and tight *mamohiki* [pants worn by laborers]." In fact, Muragaki's unequal attention to the Japanese side of the whole event may be partly due to his discomfort in finding words for the unfamiliar Western things. Harris, on the other hand, can resort to more or less equivalent terms from the object vocabularies of other cultures ("a Scotch Kilmarnock cap" and "a Van Dyke [collar] of two half diamonds or lozenges"). And, despite the difficulty he, too, often felt in description ("to convey an intelligible idea of it is beyond the power of mere words"), he keeps trying.

Generalization is, of course, especially affected by comparative awareness. After drawing a general picture of the typical Japanese interior, Harris gives the particulars of the Palace decor. What he saw there he felt produced "a tawdry effect," which he then hastens to qualify: "[in general] the Japanese do not greatly affect violent contrasts or gaudy colors. They apparently prefer the natural tints and have a good eye for the harmony of colors." Muragaki's argument moves quite differently. Finding it unsettling that the commander-in-chief of the United States should be so plainly dressed, he goes on to accept an intriguing hearsay regarding the forthcoming presidential election, and then adds the even more intriguing prediction that a country so unprincipled will assuredly perish in the near future.

Among all the stylistic differences, however, their treatment of first-person pronouns is the most important. The narrator's consciousness of his own thought and action is different. Harris's entry begins: "I started for my audience about ten." The singular "I" and the strong active verb are conspicuous. This is an occasion Harris personally planned and fought for. Against a complete hierarchy of lords and warriors, he alone won the coveted role of representing his government and country. Harris the narrator is supremely confident about Harris the diplomat. He is thus, both personally and officially, an emphatically felt and presented individual. In the very first sentence, Harris the egotist describes the dress of his Japanese guards as if these men were merely an attachment to his official person. Likewise, his reference to Heusken in the second paragraph. In his "undress navy uniform" the interpreter figures as just another part of the scenery.

Harris is the actor, *he* is the dramatist, and it is *he*—and not the United States of America—who will be conducting this important audience with His Majesty the Tycoon. All the rest is stagecraft.

As significantly, Muragaki's diary begins with a routine Chinese character for "cloudy." The day is like any other, and the weather must be noted first in accordance with convention. This opening remark in Japanese is fairly well represented by its English counterpart. The implied subject being "we" (as in the translation), the "we" prepared for the interview which was scheduled by the American officials for twelve noon, American time. Neither Muragaki nor Shimmi the Chief Ambassador nor Oguri the Inspector, nor indeed any others of this Embassy, really desired this audience. Most were there because they were told to be there; and all were there because Perry forced Japan to open her ports. The verbs are most often in the passive voice, and sentences almost always begin with a plural first-person pronoun. Muragaki is only a small sausage (or *yakitori* shish kebab?) assigned to this unpleasant task, whereas the triumvirate as a whole—actually, the Council of State back in Edo, or more accurately the Americans before them—are pulling the strings for their every motion.

Muragaki's depiction of Japanese dress greatly contrasts with Harris's description of his and Heusken's uniforms. He begins with the Chief Ambassador's appearance, then goes down the line to his own, then the Inspector's, in an order strictly defined by rank and protocol. There is nothing personal in this description. The "I" Muragaki uses in the context is simply a physically distinguishing "I," a marker delineating the "I's" body from the others without at all implicating the personae of the "I" and the "they." Unlike Harris's "I," his is as void of official will and plan as it is of personal presence.

Throughout his narrative description, Muragaki never once uses an "I," the action invariably being recorded in the plural. He never singly initiates any action whatever. No matter what is done, it is a group effort, planned and carried out by the group as a whole.

But even Muragaki must stop to reflect at times, an activity necessarily in the singular. One such reflection concerns the pride he felt as he saw the immense crowd gathered to watch the Embassy along their route. "I [we?] had the feeling that the glory of our Empire was radiantly shining in this barbarians' country; and forgetful of my own humble station, [I] looked around with tremendous pride." The pride surely belongs to him, since in this matter he is unlikely to be speaking for Shimmi and Oguri. At the same time, the first-person quality of the experience is mediated by the public and impersonal nature of the man's pride. Muragaki felt "proud" only because he was a member of the collective group (*kōkoku*, divine country, empire) currently arousing so much interest in America.

Similarly, his summary comments on the occasion—disappointment with the "disorderliness" of the Americans and yet some sense of satisfaction with the day's event—hardly refer to his own feelings. Muragaki the individual is content because the Embassy as a whole accomplished something that day. The rhetoric is full of conventional terminology presumably shared by all in the situation. It is socially assumed he will feel happy, therefore he is. One can see the same rhetorical psycho-manipulation—an individual taking great pride in the welfare and success of his group—continuing full strength throughout the nineteenth century into the twentieth right up to the present.

The "emotions" Muragaki allows himself to express on this occasion are really public sentiments. Assuredly, he does participate, yet there is very little in this basically official response that is catalyzed into a fully personal experience, almost as if—aside from his ambassadorial role—there were no individual at all.

Compare this with Harris's self-confidence throughout his narrative. He too must have felt pride, but not just in the "glory" of the United States. Rather, his pride lay in his single-handed feat in establishing diplomatic relations between the two countries. He is only one unarmed American among the mightiest warriors of Japan. Yet he knows that he is constantly protected by the brute force of the East India Squadron and that this fact is ever-present in the mind of every Japanese official. Pride he need not mention; it goes without saying. In fact, Harris behaves in his normal, personable manner even while functioning as the official representative of the United States. He refers to Inoue Shinano-no-Kami Kiyonao as "my friend." The pleasantries exchanged with Kawaji Saemon-no-jō Toshiakira are good-natured and intimate. In short, the formality of the occasion does not overwhelm Harris to the extent of draining him of all emotion and response.

The endings of both of these accounts are telling. Harris has performed the ceremony in full persona. Though tense, he does not first discuss his personal state but focuses on the audience itself. Once his account of the event is finished, however, he faces his exhaustion quite matter-of-factly. Arriving home after the performance where so much was at stake internationally, he collapses from his chronic "lung congestion." His extraordinary exertion had been as much psychological as physical and there were severe consequences. The narrator describing this collapse is open and personal, almost the archetypal nineteenth-century white man, both ethnocentric and humanistic, struggling to confront each experience with the continuous personal existence that is the self.

How about Muragaki's close? He must also have been quite tense. But no matter what may be the stuff of his "personal experience" that day, his personal being is nowhere evident in his account. He needs but one mode of commenting on his own performance, that is, the nonpersonal, official mode. At the end of his entry for that day, Muragaki composes *waka*. Public and objective, sketchy and antilyrical, Muragaki's two *waka* are expressions of collective satisfaction with the ceremonial performance, not at all the kind of poetry written by the nineteenth-century Westerners. The groups performed smoothly today; the larger—and more elevated—group back home will approve when they hear of the day's performance. A fitting ritual ending to this ritual narrative. Ceremony was performed across the ocean by the "whole Japanese nation." The contrast between Harris's confession of bodily frailty and breakdown after facing solo the nobles of the whole Japanese Empire and Muragaki's celebrating the American event with stylized public *waka* constitutes perhaps the clearest of all such contrasts presented by the two cultures, then and now.

bodily frailty
v.s.
public waka

There is an urgent need for Japan to become strong enough militarily to take a stand against the Western powers. As long as our country is lacking · in military power, the law of nations is not to be trusted. When dealing with those who are weak, the strong nations often invoke public law but really calculate their own gain. Thus it seems to me that the law of nations is merely a tool for the conquest of the weak.

— Kido Kōin, *Diary*, December 1868

"The Chinaman's a native," I said. "That's the look on a native's face, but the Jap isn't a native, and he isn't a sahib either. What is it?" The Professor considered the surging street for a while.

"The Chinaman's an old man when he's young, just as a native is, but the Jap is a child all his life . . ."

— Rudyard Kipling, *From Sea to Sea*

After the Egyptian and Indian, the Greek and Roman, the Teuton and Mongolian, the Negro is a sort of seventh son, born with a veil, and gifted with second-sight in this American world — a world which yields him no true self-consciousness, but only lets him see himself through the revelation of the other world. It is a peculiar sensation, this double-consciousness, this sense of always looking at one's self through the eyes of others, of measuring one's soul by the tape of a world that looks on in amused contempt and pity. One ever feels his twoness — an American, a Negro; two souls, two thoughts, two unreconciled strivings; two warring ideals in one dark body, whose dogged strength alone keeps it from being torn asunder.

— W. E. B. Du Bois, *The Souls of Black Folk*

Chapter Four

Lives

Contemplation of my travels, in which my often rumination wraps me in a most humorous sadness.
As You Like It

This modern age, so full of freedom, independence, and our own egotistical selves.
Natsume Sōseki, *Kokoro*

The escort group on board the *Kanrin Maru* returned to Edo Bay on June 23. After over four months, the sailors were jubilant to be home again. As soon as the ship reached Uraga, the sailors were given a shore permit presumably for a warm bath and a toast of *sake*, with the blessing, in the form of generous tips, of Commodore Kimura and Captain Katsu.[1] According to Fukuzawa Yukichi's memoir, he was the first to step ashore. When challenged by a waiting friend to guess the greatest event to hit Japan in his absence, the shrewd Dutch scholar struck target: the assassination of pro-trade Regent Ii Kamon-no-Kami by xenophobic Mito warriors, an event that decidedly changed the course of Japan in the years to come.[2] The Japanese mood for the Westerners had turned yet a notch chiller.

The ambassadorial retinue aboard the *Niagara* cast anchor at Shinagawa on November 9, after the voyage around the globe. Their joy was even more intense as their sojourn had taken twice as long. The Shinagawa port that welcomed them back, however, was ominously still. The seventeen-gun salute fired from the American warship was not echoed by any from the Japanese coastguard.[3] The travelers were oblivious—at least for now—to such official details, or

145

rather the absence of them. Tamamushi reports that dozens of his friends, having learned of the ship's arrival, were waiting on shore to congratulate his safe return and exchange news. "A humble student like me received such a welcome," he records, "it is needless to say what it was like for the high officials."[4]

The ambassadorial triumvirate was given an audience with the Shogun himself next day; a few days later they visited Townsend Harris at Zempukuji Temple to report the success of their mission and thank him for the American hospitality. In the following weeks they had several opportunities to appear before the Shogun to talk about their experience abroad. The gifts from the United States to the Tokugawa ruler were unloaded, and the return gifts to the President of the United States and other American officials were transmitted to the *Niagara*. The officers from the American warship, together with Harris, were invited to a feast at the residence of Andō Tsushima-no-Kami Nobumasa, a member of the Council of State, where they received those mysterious presents mentioned earlier.[5] The San Francisco *Daily Evening Bulletin* reporter cannot have been wholly inaccurate in describing the Americans' dismay at the noticeably cool reception:

Before the return of the Commissioners, public opinion [among the Westerners in Japan] was divided as to the effect of their visit to the United States. The worst fears have been realized. The reception given to the Japanese Commissioners in the United States has only had the effect to increase their self-importance and superiority over the western nations. In any country claiming to be civilized in the least degree, the Commissioners would have been welcomed back with some *eclat*—with procession, triumphal arches, fire-works, salutes. At least, there would have been a large gathering of people (if but out of curiosity) to behold these renowned travelers, the first that have left Japan authoritatively for some 250 years. Not so, however. This would have shown too much deference to America, and would to a certain extent appear to have acknowledged their superiority. So the Commissioners were ordered to leave the *Niagara* in as quiet a way as possible, in the ordinary garb of their country, so that they could not be distinguished from the common herd in the streets. It now turns out that there was not a single man of distinction among them. All were third- and fourth-rate men, with a sprinkling of the lower order.

The glorious reception given these fellows in the United States—feasting, dancing, showing up, lionizing—must have been most gratifying to them. What precious fools they must have thought us! How degraded we must have appeared to them as compared to the privileged classes in Japan! And, then, our women! Do they want to know who their darling Tommy was before he joined the commission? I will post them up:

Tommy was a third-rate interpreter in the Custom House, who used to bore us for *stumps of cigars*. If we wanted anything done quickly, it was but to offer a stump or two, and it worked like a charm.

Much to the astonishment and chagrin of the officers of the *Niagara*, they found these same Commissioners, with few exceptions, at a dinner given by the Prime Minister crouched down on their knees around the room, motionless for hours, and were left in that degrading position when the officers retired. Others acted as waiters on the Ministers and guests. The renowned Tommy was not honored even to that extent—he was not permitted to be present at all. It is the general belief among the Japanese merchants that the Commissioners will be put out of the ways altogether, or employed in distant islands, where they cannot endanger the Government by enlightening the people.[6]

If the officers managed to suppress their annoyance and disappointment, their men were less discreet: the sailors are said to have got drunk, had many fights, and sworn terrible blasphemies. The rampage lasted right up until their ship weighed anchor on November 19.[7]

On January 11, the Ambassadors and the principal officers of the *Kanrin Maru* were received in Edo Castle by the Shogun, all to be formally rewarded with promotions. Shimmi Buzen-no-Kami was given the raise of three hundred *koku* of rice annually, Muragaki Awaji-no-Kami likewise three hundred *koku*, and Oguri Bungo-no-Kami an increase of two hundred *koku*—decent bonuses by any estimate, one or two *koku* (about five bushels) of rice being considered adequate to sustain a peasant for a year. Commodore Kimura, Captain Katsu, and others, too, were awarded prizes, though on a smaller scale.[8]

All was not to remain well for long. Exactly four days later, on January 15, 1861, Harris's young interpreter, Henry Heusken, was slaughtered. He was riding home on a dark rainy night from the Prussian Legation to Zempukuji Temple, when seven assassins suddenly leaped on him and his Japanese guards. Fatally wounded, Heusken was carried back by his surviving attendants to the Harris residence, where he died shortly after midnight. It was four days before his twenty-ninth birthday, and he had spent four and a half years in Japan. Harris's shock and grief were understandable: Heusken had been not only his indispensable interpreter, secretary, nurse, and assistant, but also his sole companion, a "son," as Harris's official dispatch described him.[9] It is not unlikely that his resignation submitted six months later to President Lincoln was—aside from his poor health—at least partly the result of this unexpected loss. The

Japanese, too, lost with Heusken's death one of their warmest-hearted friends and supporters.

It fell upon the former Ambassadors to carry a message of condolence from the Tokugawa government to the American Minister a few days later; it was also their task to represent their government in Heusken's cortege from Zempukuji Temple where he had lived to Kōrinji Temple where he was to be buried. The day of the funeral was charged with grief, anger, and fear. Rumors blazed throughout the city of a renewed attack on the procession, and Shimmi Buzen-no-Kami advised Harris to avoid the ceremony. Characteristically, Harris took the risk. The entire Western diplomatic corps formed the procession, plus scores of Prussian and Dutch marines and officers and a large train of Japanese guards. The roads were lined with tens of thousands of onlookers, but nothing untoward, at least on that day, took place to thicken the gloom. Later, the Tokugawa government contributed the sum of $10,000 to the support of Heusken's mother living in Holland.[10]

The slaying of Henry Heusken was neither the first nor the most momentous of the anti-Western assaults. As soon as the port of Yokohama was opened in August 1859—long before the Embassy's departure—a Russian officer and two sailors were cut down. Ever since then, there had been a number of bloody attacks on Western visitors and their Japanese associates, including the assassination of Regent Ii. After the Heusken incident, however, the political repercussions became quite serious. The Mito retainers' attack on the British Legation at Tōzenji Temple (that nearly killed Laurence Oliphant[11]) in July 1861; the assassination attempt on Andō Tsushima-no-Kami, considered pro-Western, in January 1862; and the Satsuma warriors' deliberately planned assault on some English merchants and their female compatriot (called the Namamugi Affair, or the Richardson Incident) in September 1862—such outbursts, among many others, were growing both extremely menacing for Westerners and costly for the Shogunate on account of the indemnity payments. The pro-trade faction in the government could number fewer and fewer supporters among the lords and vassals, or even within the administration itself.

The Western representatives, on the other hand, were insistent on expanding their profitable trade with Japan, and were ready to suggest the use of force to their home governments. Finding the Shogunate both unwilling and unable to punish the Satsuma domain for the

The attack on the British Legation in July 1861. The wounded Oliphant is seen inside the left room.

Richardson murder, the British Minister finally deployed a squadron of seven ships to bombard Kagoshima, its castle town, in August 1863. The result was unexpected. Once the Satsuma men realized the English naval force held the upper hand, peace was rapidly restored, and the fief's leaders eagerly tried to establish a direct trade and diplomatic relationship with the British Legation, in contravention of the Tokugawa regulations governing domestic security. In the meantime, the Shogunate had been kept under intense pressure to "Expel the Barbarians!" by the imperial court, which was more and more guided by the young samurai, especially from the Chōshū and other southwestern domains. On June 25, 1863, the date imposed by the Kyoto court on the Tokugawa administration for execution of the expulsion policy, the Chōshū men opened fire on an American ship passing through the Shimonoseki Straits. Soon afterward the French and Dutch ships were also attacked. The Western retaliation was now peremptory. The allied fleet of seventeen British, American, French, and Dutch warships with a total of 305 cannons sailed into Shimonoseki in September 1864 and demolished all the Chōshū fortresses. Chōshū had no choice but to capitulate. Here again, upon acknowledging the overwhelming military superiority of the West, the Chōshū leaders swiftly moved to enter a friendly relationship with the Westerners, especially with the British. One of the side effects of this confrontation was the rapprochement of Satsuma and Chōshū: steadily antagonistic till 1865, this alliance eventually proved to be the principal force behind the overthrow of the Tokugawa Shogunate.[12]

The Tokugawa government, half-hearted at best in opening Japan, had remained indecisive to the end, caught between demands for fulfillment of treaty obligations and the pervasive domestic opposition to the barbarians' presence. Actually, the leaders of the anti-Western forces soon realized the impossibility of expulsion, and yet they saw just as clearly the advantage of exploiting anti-Western feelings for the purpose of crushing the Tokugawa domination.[13] What emerged from this web of conflicts was the gradual assumption of hegemony by the adherents of the imperial court, which the Westerners, too, came to recognize before long. The pattern of the 1860s then was that of a steady shift of power in the country, and of Japan's increasing acceptance of its place among the nations of the world. Similarly, the leadership within each clan was rapidly moving down from the hereditary lord and his generally demoralized cohorts to the lower-echelon samurai who had been carrying on all along the actual daily governance. The so-called Restoration of imperial rule was achieved, in short, by the inter-fief alliance of low-ranking warrior-administrators with the emperor's sanction.

Throughout this internal development, foreign powers did not stand idly by. Admittedly, the American leadership waned after Harris's departure in 1862. His replacement, Robert H. Pruyn, lacked Harris's missionary zeal; besides, embroiled in the Civil War, the United States could little afford to pay serious attention to the affairs of a remote island country. The leadership among the Western powers soon shifted to Great Britain. Rutherford Alcock, Minister to Japan between 1859 and 1864, was among the first foreigners to sense the eventual demise of the Tokugawa rule. His aide, Ernest Satow, published "English Policy" in the spring of 1866 in the *Japan Times*, a small English paper in Yokohama. When it was translated into Japanese (as "Ei-kokusaku-ron"), the ideas presented in the small essay had a powerful impact on those Tokugawa challengers in providing them with the vision of a Japan governed by a confederation of

Tokugawa and other feudal families *(shokō rengō).*[14] Although Alcock's successor, Harry S. Parkes, took an officially neutral posture
toward the domestic power struggle, he was far from hostile toward
the foes of the Tokugawa House. He made clear by 1867 that he no
longer considered the Shogun the legitimate monarch of Japan, but
merely one of the three hundred lords, over whom the emperor in
Kyoto had the final sovereignty. And through various contacts in the
southwestern fiefs, Parkes and Satow quietly guided and advised those
who were engaged in political, and later military, struggles with the
Tokugawa government. The British munitions dealers, too, were active in trade with the Satsuma, Chōshū, and other domains to arm
them for the final showdown.

With its eyes on the British policy, France was determined to take
a contrary stand. Léon Roches, the French Minister since 1864,
adopted the strategy of staying close to the Tokugawas, offering them
various kinds of military and technical aid. There were many such
behind-the-scenes intrigues among the administration in power, the
rebellious clans, and the Western governments—again as has often
been the case with non-Western countries in turmoil, before and
since. Somehow the empire survived so many hands in the pot, and
when the last Shogun, Tokugawa Yoshinobu, finally resigned from
the office of "The Generalissimo for the Subjugation of Barbarians"
(Sei-i Tai-Shōgun), the new government, presumably directly ruled by
sixteen-year-old Emperor Meiji (Mutsuhito) but actually by men
from Chōshū and Satsuma, did not hesitate to ratify all the treaties
signed by the Tokugawa government. In the fall of the Tokugawas
and the restoration of the imperial rule—obviously far more complicated than this briefest synopsis might suggest—the later careers of
the ambassadorial members are inextricably enmeshed.

The 1860 travel to the United States was indisputably a major
event for everyone in the Mission; for many the journey was perhaps
the most important experience in their often gray, prosaic lives. Yet to
define precisely the effect of the occasion on each man's life is far
from easy. The direct knowledge of the outside world may have
changed the views and values of some; but then again it may have
reinforced whatever opinions they may have held prior to the voyage.
One can vaguely conjecture on the basis of what we know of their
later days, but such exercise is neither interesting nor profitable. It is
much too facile, after all, to reiterate that a Fukuzawa's fascination

Tokugawa Yoshinobu, the last Shogun.

Tokugawa Yoshinobu after the Restoration.

with the West was further intensified, or that a Muragaki's lethargic reaction seems to have stayed lethargic. But beyond that, to venture any general remark is a hazardous business. I would like, therefore, merely to present a pastiche of some of the careers that remained unforgotten, ignoring the explicit cause-and-effect readings of the voyage and the later lives.

To begin with Shimmi, the Chief Ambassador, there is really very little to be said about his later days. A dull bureaucrat's life can hardly be expected to turn at once into an impassioned one full of excitement. He continued as a Commissioner for Foreign Affairs till 1862, then served for two more years as a chamberlain/advisor *(sobashū)* in the Tokugawa Palace. In 1866, he retired because of ill health. Soon after the Restoration, he went home to the province and died in 1869 at forty-seven. His contribution to Japan's understanding of the West was nearly zero.[15]

Vice-Ambassador Muragaki Awaji-no-Kami, the author of the most loquacious diary, returned to his old office, continuing to climb the bureaucratic ladder as Magistrate of Hakodate, Commissioner for Foreign Affairs, Commissioner for Construction *(sakuji bugyō)*, and so forth. He too retreated from the public scene for health reasons in 1868. He died twelve years later, having achieved scarcely anything notable. Muragaki is best remembered for the travelogue and immense office memoranda he accumulated while Magistrate of Hakodate between 1854 and 1860 (which are now printed in 3,000 modern pages in six volumes).[16]

Commodore Kimura Yoshitake's life, too, was relatively eventless. Having been appointed to an advisory post in the military structure, Kimura advocated immediate naval expansion. His proposals were all ignored, however, and he briefly resigned from service in 1863. Back on active duty as rector of the Kaiseisho Institute (formerly the Institute for the Study of Barbarian Books) for a short time, he was then employed in the Inspector's Office *(metsuke)* mainly in charge of foreign affairs and defense. He served also as a top-ranking naval administrator before the fall of the regime. It was during these years that Kimura again met Captain McDougal of Mare Island, now in command of the U.S.S. *Wyoming.* He never joined the new government, despite several invitations. His name survives largely through his *Kanrin Maru* adventure, although he did publish several books including a diplomatic history of the thirty years before 1868. The *Thirty-Year History (Sanjū-nen-shi)* is prefaced by his good friend Fukuzawa Yukichi, the leading educator of the time and of course

Kimura's manservant during the voyage aboard the Tokugawa corvette.[17]

Against such unexciting lives that more or less petered out after the great trip abroad, the end of Oguri Kōzuke-no-suke (Bungo-no-Kami), the Embassy Inspector, is a bloody tale. Far more energetic than any of the above three, Oguri became a vigorous leader of Tokugawa loyalists during the last years of the regime. The year following the voyage, he was dispatched to Tsushima Island (between Kyūshū and Korea), where a Russian corvette under Captain Birilev was displaying all signs of preparations for an indefinite stay. Oguri's bargaining was utterly ineffective, failing to persuade the Russians to leave, but he learned an important lesson in international intrigue from this involvement. As Oguri found the situation to be out of Japan's military control, the Tokugawa government sought aid from the British navy, which was deeply interested, if not in Japan's territorial integrity, in maintaining Britain's domination over the Asian seas. The Tokugawas won: in the face of the greater force of the British Asia Squadron, the Russians swiftly sailed away.[18] To fight one force with the force of another is a technique Oguri was to rely on increasingly in his later career. Incidentally, Oguri built in Edo around that time a glass and brick house, one of the earliest "Western-style" residences ever owned by a Japanese.[19]

Oguri was appointed Commissioner of the Navy in December 1864, replacing Katsu Rintarō, who appeared, in the eyes of the Council, much too dangerously conciliatory to the challenging domains. Oguri was a staunch Tokugawa loyalist. He at once purchased warships from the United States, and then conceived a grand plan for constructing, with French aid, a Tokugawa Navy Shipyard near Edo, complete with various factories and an iron foundry. The plan was modeled after the Toulon Shipyard on a one-third scale. In the succeeding years, he further contracted a huge purchase of ships, cannons, and munitions, and accepted offers from French Minister Roches to supply the Shogunate with French officers to drill the troops. The costs of the whole defense plan loomed immense for the by then thoroughly impoverished Tokugawa government. The price of the shipyard alone was estimated at two and a half million dollars, and the loan negotiated in September 1866 between Oguri and the French Minister specified the amount as six million.[20] But Oguri was adamant. If these loans entailed a concession to France of some control of Japan's economy, Oguri was convinced they were justifiable for the sake of his liege lord. In some ways resembling many dictators of today's world, Oguri would doggedly pursue the course of rebuilding the Tokugawa hegemony—unperturbed by the thought that his interests and those of Japan as a whole might not coincide.

During these last years of the regime, Oguri held a number of important positions—City Magistrate (*machi bugyō*), Army Commissioner, and later Treasury Commissioner. In the last capacity, he was indefatigable in trying to raise revenues for the empty tills of the Tokugawa regime: he tightened the budget, hiked the foreign exchange rate of *koban* and *ichibu* coins, imposed new taxes and issued bonds, minted cheap coins, schemed many complicated deals with powerful merchants like the Mitsuis—in short, he played with finesse all the tricks that are played by treasurers of a fiscally ruined government. And like all other tax men, Oguri was universally disliked. That he was resourceful and inventive there is no doubt; as to whether he had sufficient imagination to read the inevitable advance of history in the 1860s is quite something else.

In retrospect, at any rate, it was too late for the Shogunate by the time he became the central policy maker. A Tokugawa absolutist to his end, he advocated—although the Restoration had already been proclaimed and the office of the Shogunate was surrendered—an all-out battle against the combined forces of the southwestern fiefs that were marching with the imperial sanction. Even Tokugawa Yoshinobu, the last Shogun, who had always depended on Oguri in his numerous schemes for the sustenance of Tokugawa supremacy, rejected the advice, and perhaps to protect himself dismissed Oguri. Oguri had to run for cover to his home village. In the spring of 1868, one thousand troops, sent by the new imperial army, came to arrest Oguri Tadamasa, and a few days later he and his son were both decapitated at the nearby river bank. Tsukamoto Mahiko and Ebata Yūzō, his personal servants, who accompanied him to Washington, were also beheaded.[21] Oguri was only forty years old.

Captain Katsu Awa-no-Kami Rintarō (Kaishū) of the *Kanrin Maru*, too, had a turbulent life after his return.[22] He was appointed before long to the assistant directorship of the Institute for the Study of Barbarian Books. But research administration hardly suited his restless temperament, and Katsu soon found compensation in the intrigue-ridden Tokugawa politics. In 1862 he was made director of the Naval Academy, and was then promoted to Acting Commissioner of the Navy. His interpretation of the time was diametrically opposite to Oguri's. Although Katsu and Oguri agreed to the opening of the ports, Katsu was, unlike Oguri, no longer convinced that the

Tokugawa House could or should maintain the Shogunate as the de facto ruler. Sooner or later, the emerging alliance of the southwestern fiefs would establish a new order under the imperial throne. The program for Katsu was, then, that of saving the Tokugawa House at least as one of the active participants in the new coalition government by persuading the Shogun to resign from office. An adroit maneuverer, he fully exploited his position as a naval expert: he was the head of the Kobe Naval Academy (Sōrenjo), an official institution he had personally founded in 1863 to train talented samurai from all over Japan regardless of their domainal affiliations. One of his students, for instance, was Sakamoto Ryōma, an important Tosa activist in creating the Chōshū-Satsuma coalition;[23] and another, Yokoi Saheita, was a nephew of Yokoi Shōnan, one of the most progressive thinkers of the time. He knew everyone (Sakuma Shōzan, for instance, was his brother-in-law), and thrived on peddling his influence. Because of his extensive connections outside the Tokugawa government, however, he was looked upon with suspicion within the administration itself. In 1864 he was dismissed from the office of Commissioner of the Navy and succeeded by the loyalist Oguri.

Katsu was much too talented and needed by the Tokugawas to be banned from active duty for long. Besides, as he had envisioned, Japan was progressing—at least for a brief while—toward a confederacy government. After a year and a half of unemployment, he was restored to his former post, although his actual duties consisted of a series of negotiations with the Chōshū-Satsuma alliance. The anti-Tokugawa faction, however, was by 1866 determined to destroy not only the Shogunate, but the Tokugawa House as a feudal power as well. Tokugawa Yoshinobu, the last Shogun, was a peculiarly complex person, never quite decisive, or straightforward, and he did not trust Katsu. Although at the final stage Katsu Awa-no-Kami was virtually prime minister of the Shogunate, he managed little more than to salvage Edo from a devastating battle that might have been waged between the imperial coalition forces marching eastward and the Tokugawa loyalist forces staying behind to defend their lord's castle. Because of the famous meeting between Katsu and Saigō Takamori, a Satsuma man who was among the most powerful in the early years of the imperial government, the Shogun's capital escaped fire and destruction. Katsu's deft manipulation of the influence of British Minister Harry Parkes and his fleet of warships on the imperial forces was undeniably important in averting the holocaust.[24]

After the Restoration, Katsu Kaishū briefly held a series of high

Katsu Awa-no-Kami as Commissioner of the Navy in the Tokugawa government.

offices in the imperial navy. But his role as a political wizard and a supportive critic of the government was far more important. Advising his old Tokugawa friends and needling his new Meiji government associates, he was widely respected. To his house in Shiba, Tokyo, visitors are said to have flocked in hordes.[25] Although he remained a free-spirited and sharp-tongued critic, he was delighted with the lofty title of count conferred on him in 1887. If he was among the first to foresee the end of the Tokugawa feudalism, he was among the last to recognize the inevitability of the abolition of the privileged samurai class. Throughout his long and lively career, he displayed no interest whatever in the people's rights (*minken*) movements.[26] The contradiction of the Tokugawa defender who did his best to dismantle the regime is shown in one more aspect: soon after the death of his Annapolis-trained son in 1892, he adopted the last Shogun's youngest son (by one of his mistresses) as his heir by marriage to his granddaughter. His declared purpose was to restore the eminent title to the fallen Tokugawa family, an intervention of mystifying logic.[27] Perhaps the union with the most powerful family of the land was a dream he had never forgotten since his humble beginning as the son of a nearly starved, half-vagabond samurai.[28] He lived till 1899, and died an illustrious subject of the empire at seventy-six.

These five men were luminaries. Which means that not only remarkable men like Katsu and Oguri, but also undistinguished ones like Shimmi and Muragaki are, despite their meager achievements, still remembered fairly well. The same, of course, does not apply to the vast majority of the humbler members of the Embassy. Many disappeared quietly into the shadows, leaving not even the faintest trace, once their mission was over. The graves of the three deckhands who died in San Francisco are all recovered now, and a monument celebrating the centenary of the *Kanrin Maru* visit stands outside the San Francisco Presidio against the magnificent view of the Golden Gate. But most sailors who made it back to their homes can hardly be expected to have left any sizable ripples.

It is quite surprising then that we should know something, though very little, about as many as forty out of sixty-seven boilermen and deckhands aboard the *Kanrin Maru*.[29] Most of these men continued to earn a living from the sea. Several became successful captains, while others prospered as ship mechanics and engineers. Many seem to have enjoyed old age, treasuring some odds and ends they preserved from the memorable voyage. Luckily—or unluckily—all were not dull model burghers. At least one, Ishikawa

Daisuke, a brother of Ishikawa Masatarō (who left the detailed navigation log), seems to have lived dangerously. He is said to have converted all the bonuses given at the end of the mission into small coins, gone all dressed up to a brothel, and showered the *ichibu* silver coins among the crowd of admiring whores. Nemesis, even in remote Japan, was swift as usual in catching up with such an act of extravagance. When he embarked on a long voyage next time, he could not even walk from the pain of syphilitic chancres. Fearless man as he was, Daisuke heated a pair of iron tongs red hot and cauterized his sores, thus valiantly defying the vengeful goddess.[30] There was one other high liver. Wakabayashi Kakunojō was not so lucky in his combat with the goddess, however; tortured with pain of advanced syphilis, he was carried up to a doctor's office on a hill in Ogasawara-jima. His moaning and groaning was so pitiful on the way up that his sailor friends named the hill "Aita-zaka" (It-hurts-it-hurts hill) after his cries. Presumably the hill is still so called.[31]

The fates of the middle-rank men, lower samurai, followed a similar course. Some, like Morita Kiyoyuki, the treasurer, died soon after,[32] but most lived on, remaining in the Tokugawa or domainal structures until the Restoration. After the power turnover in 1868, they either retired to vanish thereafter from the public eye or served in the new Meiji government, climbing up the new, but similar, bureaucratic ladder for a few more decades. Hidaka Tameyoshi, who wrote the *Bei-kō nisshi*, is fairly typical. He joined the 1862 Mission to Europe and wrote one more travelogue. Upon his return he acted in various capacities in munitions manufacture for the Shogunate, and following the Restoration he worked for the new government as an engineer. After a long and uneventful life, he died in 1919.[33] As for "Tommy" (Tateishi Onojirō), the darling of the American press, he was formally recruited as an interpreter by the Tokugawa government and later opened a school of his own in Edo. He moved to Kusatsu, where Ernest Satow apparently encountered him (see chapter 20 of Satow's book). "Tommy's" name now changed to Nagano Keijirō, he participated in the Iwakura Mission of 1871. No fuss was made this time either in America or Europe. A pretty boy at sixteen, Tateishi-Nagano was by now a diminutive man of twenty-eight, undistinguishable from any other samurai official. Still, he apparently persisted in his role as a ladies' man. For, according to one record, a complaint charging lewd advances was filed against him by one of the female students traveling with the mission. Not much is known about his later life, but he is said to have held various lower-middle-rank jobs in the Ministry of Foreign Affairs during the Meiji era.[34]

This pattern of smooth transition holds for a surprising number of the *Kanrin Maru* members especially. Their long service in a well-structured bureaucracy may account for the surprisingly easy move from one regime to another. The fact that these particular samurai were also forerunners of professionals and engineers better explains the trend. They were trained to navigate and build ships—for whom and for what purpose were matters that did not vitally concern them. I can count nearly a dozen whose naval careers remained constant before and after the Restoration: Ban Tetsutarō, Okada Seizō, Nezu Kinjirō, Kosugi Masanoshin, Akamatsu Daisaburō, Sasakura Kiritarō, Ono Tomogorō, Hida Hamagorō, Hamaguchi Kōemon, Makiyama Shūkei.[35]

Akamatsu Daisaburō, the most successful in this group, might serve as a fair model. The author of *Amerika-yuki kōkai nikki* (Diary of the voyage to America), Akamatsu was a "Dutch scholar" and a graduate of the Nagasaki Naval Academy before the voyage. In 1861 he was given an instructorship in the Academy, and the following year was sent to Holland to study shipbuilding techniques. Six years later he returned, only to find the Tokugawa regime thoroughly demolished. Now unemployed, he taught at the Numazu Military School founded by the Tokugawa men who were forced to move from Edo to the Shizuoka province. On Katsu's urging, however, he quit the school in 1870 and joined the imperial army (Heibu-shō). From then on, Akamatsu's career spiraled steadily upward. An important officer in the imperial navy within years, he accompanied the expeditionary forces to Formosa in 1874. He held a number of high administrative positions, rising at the end to the rank of Vice-Admiral. In 1887 he received the title of baronet, and even became a member of the House of Peers. His wife, who bore him twelve children, was a sister to both a surgeon general of the imperial army and a count. Akamatsu lived to a ripe seventy-nine years and died in 1920 after a long, respectable, and uninteresting career.[36]

There are many who either chose not to or could not join the new government after 1868. Masuzu Shunjirō, who wrote *A-kō kōkai nikki* (Diary of the voyage to America), is one who comes to mind. He toured Europe as a member of the Embassy under Takeuchi Shimotsuke-no-Kami Yasunori in 1862, authoring another travelogue, *Ō-kō-ki* (Diary of the voyage to Europe). He, too, pursued his career in the Treasury Department of the Shogunate, but he did not continue in public service after 1868. After this the man virtually disappears from the record, though his death is known to have occurred around 1900.[37] A similar circumstance attends Namura Motonori, the chief interpreter for the Embassy. That he kept interpreting and teaching languages under Magistrate Muragaki Awaji-no-Kami in Hakodate is certain. We also have hard proof that in 1866 he traveled to Russia with Ambassador Koide Yamato-no-Kami Hidezane to bargain on the Sakhalin border. But he hovered outside the Meiji government, and consequently not much is known about him before his death in 1876.[38]

If Namura at least produced a number of language students, Murayama Hakugen, the physician attached to the Embassy, could not even boast of this achievement in his own field. He was born too late, or too early, depending on how one evaluates Confucian (or Chinese) medicine. A health practice consisting largely of the use of herbs and acupuncture and moxacautery and massage was roundly discredited in the ensuing "enlightened" Meiji era. No longer able to survive on the proceeds of his profession, he had to look elsewhere for income and so began to work as an editor and compiler of records for various public offices, an employment he pursued until his death in 1893.[39] Hirose Kakuzō (Hōan) Kaneaki, the author of *Kankai kōro nikki* (Diary across the oceans), was also trained in medicine, although his capacity on the Mission was merely that of attendant to Morita Kiyoyuki, the treasurer. After his return, he talked about his experience in America in addition to publishing the book. No one in his hometown believed him, suspecting that he was bewitched by the "Christian magicians." His medical practice was ruined, and he died a lonely old man in 1865.[40]

The demise of the Tokugawa regime meant unemployment for hundreds of thousands of its vassals, retainers, and servants. There were three hundred feudalities, too, that were radically reduced in stipends, and then replaced with prefectural structures controlled by the centralized government. This in turn created even greater unemployment among the samurai, who were generally unskilled in any practical work. Many were forced to seek a trade, an option despised by the gentlemen-warriors far more vehemently than by their Victorian counterparts who similarly were faced with the ignoble task of making ends meet. Nonomura Tadazane, the author of *Kōkai nichiroku* (Chronicle of the voyage) is one of those samurai-turned-businessmen. After the Restoration, he sold his belongings including

samurai-turned-businessmen

his two swords to raise enough capital for a "Western clothing" store (*yōhinten*), an enterprise no doubt helped by his observation of the Americans. Business prospered, and before his death in 1884 he expanded the store to include kimono fabrics as well. His biographer hits a dead end after these meager details.[41]

Nakahama Manjirō (John Mung), the greatest English interpreter of Japan at the time, continued to work as an interpreter and language instructor. The memory of his youthful adventures far from perished in the erstwhile shipwreck. Eager to return to the rough ocean waves, he became in 1862 captain of a whaling vessel, fulfilling the dream he had never relinquished since his Fairhaven days. The career abruptly terminated after catching only two whales. Apparently the English sailors he had hired were soon identified as dangerous criminals (nonetheless totally indispensable for the operation of the boat), and thus had to be arrested and subsequently fired. In 1864 Manjirō moved to the Satsuma fief to teach navigation and English, traveling twice during this period to Shanghai to purchase ships for his home fief of Tosa. After the fall of the Tokugawa regime, he was offered a professorship at Kaisei College by the new government, and he joined the 1870 delegation to Europe for the purpose of observing the Franco-Prussian War for the new government. On the way he left his group for an overnight visit to Captain Whitfield of New Bedford, who had rescued him in the Pacific some twenty years earlier. Later on, he taught English in Tokyo, as Edo was by then called, occasionally visiting his village home in Nakanohama, Tosa. He enjoyed a life of leisurely retirement for the last thirty years until his death in 1898 at seventy-one.[42]

In the middle of these more or less orderly lives, there were a few that ended in bloody chaos. Hideshima Tōnosuke progressed well for a while. A samurai from the Saga domain, he was allowed by his lord to pursue his English studies in Nagasaki; he also trained himself in navigation and military science with the Dutch officers stationed in the port city. When ordered to inspect a corvette bought by the Saga fief from Thomas B. Glover, something went amiss. He became involved in a fight and slaughtered a Tanaka Giemon and his son. The reason is given merely as "madness" (*ranshin*) in the *Saga han kaigun-shi* (The naval history of the Saga fief). Further details are unknown.[43]

If the Hideshima incident is likely to be personal and psychological, the four other violent ends are clearly political events. Suzufuji Yūjirō, the author of "Kō-A nikki" (Diary of the voyage to America), whose painting of the *Kanrin Maru* in the storm (see the frontispiece) is the best known of all the ship portraits, successfully resumed his career in the Tokugawa navy. When the Shogunate fell, he was eager to sign up with the loyalist fleet led by Enomoto Takeaki, who escaped in 1868 to the north with the best Tokugawa warships. His plan was to build a Tokugawa state in the sparsely populated Hokkaidō in defiance of the new regime. Suzufuji, however, was prevented by an illness from departing in time. In total despair and chagrin, he disemboweled himself.[44]

Matsuoka Bankichi was more fortunate. After a smooth Tokugawa career, he could safely join the Enomoto squadron, and participated in several battles against the imperial government troops as the captain of one of the rebel ships. When the Enomoto forces were finally vanquished, he was apprehended together with other leaders. Incarcerated in Tokyo, he became sick and died in 1871, just before an imperial pardon was proclaimed.[45] Another victim, Yoshioka Ryōdayū Yūhei (the author of *A-kō nikki*) was in the honor guard as the last Shogun retired to Mito in accordance with the agreement with the imperial forces. Upon his return to Edo, many Tokugawa faithfuls zealously flocked around Yoshioka in an attempt to resist the government troops to the bitter end. Yoshioka was not keen on the futile battle, and tried to avoid a leadership role. Having been captured, he managed to escape, but did not remain on the loose for long. He was again apprehended in 1870, and this time successfully beheaded after a short imprisonment in Tokyo's Kodenmachō Prison.[46]

Sincere and dutiful in their own fashion, perhaps these men all deserved better ends, and one idly dreams what might have awaited them had the samurai code been otherwise. Still, one does note that there is something peculiarly public and personally passive in their final decisions. Suzufuji took his life because his samurai honor unambiguously dictated this resolution; Matsuoka decided to go with the rebel force because his position called on him to do so; Yoshioka did struggle against the role imposed on him, but the harsh legal system was simply blind to any evidence of such inner conflicts. These men, in short, were all victims, not so much active executors of their own will and plan as accidental participants in the unalterable affairs of state. This impression is even stronger with the similar death of Tamamushi Sadayū Yasushige, the most lucid-minded of all the 1860 diarists.

After his return Tamamushi was formally readmitted into the

Sendai fief in 1861.[47] Though he bore the title of page *(koshō)*, his actual duties consisted of intelligence assignments. In those pre-journalism days, every clan administration was compelled to employ at least some intelligence agents to keep abreast of what went on in other parts of Japan. Tamamushi, the author of reports on northern Japan and the United States, was a natural choice. Accordingly, he was sent as a spy *(saisaku)* to various areas all over the country from Edo to Kyoto, from Satsuma to Chōshū. His numerous and voluminous accounts have survived as a useful source of information for present-day historians. An examination of one of these, *Kanbu tsūki* (Survey of the political situations), that covers the period between 1862 and 1864 in a modern, finely printed 1,100-page text, reveals how scrupulous his observations were and how tireless his endeavors on topics such as the attack on Andō Tsushima-no-Kami, the second assault on the British Legation at the Tōzenji Temple, or the affairs of the Chōshū and Satsuma fiefs. Tamamushi collected astonishingly minute facts, all the while displaying his familiarity with a vast range of political circumstances throughout Japan.[48] As a reward for his efforts, he was promoted to the directorship of the fief's official school, Yōkendō, under the noted Confucian scholar Ōtsuki Bankei.

After the Restoration proclamation, it so happened that the imperial forces, largely made up of the Chōshū and Satsuma samurai, were set to subjugate by force the northeastern clans that had been sympathetic with the Tokugawa government. An imperial order was handed down to Tamamushi's master, Lord Date of Sendai, to send an expeditionary force to the neighboring Aizu clan whose lord had attacked the Chōshū-Satsuma allies in Kyoto in support of the retired Shogun. The Sendai administration was divided on whether or not they should comply with the order. Many men felt too committed to the Tokugawas, and thus to the Aizu clan, to carry out the open fire command, while others thought it more advantageous to side with the imperial forces (that is, the Chōshū-Satsuma southwestern alliance) and battle with the "traitorous" Aizu. Tamamushi was one of the leaders of the first group. In the earlier stages he tried on the one hand to persuade the Aizu men to surrender, and on the other to plead with the imperial forces to refrain from an all-out confrontation. As Aizu refused to surrender, the imperial forces in turn hardened their policy toward the indecisive Sendai fief as well as the Aizu. In the final rounds, Tamamushi was no longer a pacifist mediating between the conflicting powers but an active organizer of the Northern Alliance *(Ōu Dōmei)*, calling on the twenty-five domains in the region to bear arms against the southwestern invaders who, as they saw them, illegitimately presented themselves as "imperial" forces. An open conflict, known as the War of 1868 *(Boshin sensō)*, ensued. As the major expeditionary troops arrived from the western parts of Japan under the banners of the imperial emblem, the Northern Alliance crumbled at once. Within months the entire oppositions were crushed, and peace was restored in the region.

As one of the rebel commanders, Tamamushi found himself in serious trouble by the time Lord Date of Sendai decided to yield. Tamamushi planned to escape by joining the Enomoto loyalist fleet that happened to be at anchor outside of Sendai. But the seven-ship fleet abruptly sailed away, leaving just one last Tokugawa ship that would arrive two days later in order to pick up Tamamushi and other faithfuls. Tamamushi was captured on the day between. After a six-week imprisonment he was ordered, as a traitor to the emperor, to commit *seppuku*, and in accordance with the rules of the rite his head was severed as he disemboweled himself. He was forty-six years old.

For the reader of Tamamushi's various reports as well as the 1860 diary, the circumstances of his death are not at all easy to accept. His doubt and criticism of the feudal structure were movingly personal, and theoretically radical, and yet he was willing to defend the old regime to his end. He knew much about the political situations of the whole of Japan, yet apparently believed the Northern Alliance could brake the gathering momentum of the Chōshū-Satsuma coalition. The alliance even contemplated the possibility of a new Shogunate, under a new northern emperor, to rival the Kyoto version.[49] He understood the international power games thoroughly, but tried, together with other leaders, to draw various Western nations to the northeastern-Tokugawa side against the Kyoto-southwestern forces, thus risking, as did Oguri, the integrity and independence of Japan. Somehow one cannot help feeling that thrown into the political vortex of a relatively unimportant feudality, Tamamushi misspent his intelligence and energy. Perhaps so much of what decided his life—and death—was accidental. Had he been a direct vassal *(hatamoto)* of the Tokugawa regime, as were Katsu and Oguri, or a member of Chōshū and Satsuma, as were the leaders of the next age, what might his course of action have been? Like Katsu's, in trying to bring about the death of the old world while not quite ready to help with the birth of the new? Or like Oguri's, in stubbornly trying to stay the now vanishing world? Or like Ōkubo Toshimichi's, in guiding his clan to vanquish the Tokugawa world? One does regret, in this extraordinary scholar-activist's case, that the accidents of history played a foul game on his remarkable vision and imagination.

From Shimmi to Tamamushi, these men were primarily known for their action rather than their thought. Although Tamamushi and Katsu came close to being writers and ideologues, they nonetheless considered themselves, and were considered by others, men of action, samurai, that is, administrators and officers of essentially military governments. Unlike them all, there was one man who was from his earliest days to his last known for his ideas, as a philosophe, an intellectual: Fukuzawa Yukichi (1834–1901), the attendant for Commodore Kimura of the *Kanrin Maru*. His books, enormously popular when published a century ago, are still read not only by the students and faculty of Keio University, who worship him as their founding father, but by the general reading public as well as critics and historians.[50] Fukuzawa is, for many, the first introducer of the West and its civilization to the Japanese.

To sketch his life briefly, Fukuzawa was hired out of the Nakatsu clan into the Office of Foreign Affairs of the Tokugawa government soon after his return, translating diplomatic documents and foreign books. Because of his expertise in Western matters, he was recruited by another embassy in 1862, visiting France, England, Holland, Prussia, Russia, and Portugal. During this travel he was one of the specialists who together did more or less systematic research on the social and political institutions of European countries. By this time, Fukuzawa was an established teacher of "Western learning" and began gathering students around him, although these were indeed dangerous years for all pro-Western men. In 1867 he was ordered again to accompany a delegation to the United States headed by Ono Tomogorō, also a former member of the *Kanrin Maru* crew. The mission was to bring home a warship purchased from the United States. On the voyage back, Fukuzawa's autobiography claims, he uttered some anti-Tokugawa remarks, which were duly reported by Ono to the higher authorities. The account seems to have belied the fact: he merely quarreled with Ono.[51] At any rate, Fukuzawa was placed under house arrest *(kinshin)* while the Tokugawa government was suffering through its final death throes. The confinement worked in his favor, for during this time of inaction he was able to intensify his writing efforts. A number of books and pamphlets on the subject of Western matters, all commercially very successful, were published in

Fukuzawa Yukichi abroad as a young samurai.

rapid sequence in the midst of the turbulent Restoration. *Seiyō jijō* (The conditions of the West), *Seiyō tabi annai* (A tourist's guide to the West), *Seiyō ishokujū* (Western clothing, food, and houses), *Sekai kuni zukushi* (All the nations of the world)—such primers were devoured by all literate people starved for information concerning the newly opened outside world.

Fukuzawa insists in his autobiography *(Fukuō jiden)* and elsewhere that he was never tempted by a career either in the Tokugawa or the new Meiji government. But he is most probably interpreting his past with considerable liberty here. It is more likely that he was—at least initially—unable, rather than unwilling, to obtain a satisfactory position on the administrative ladder.[52] Anyway, he remained an outsider, establishing in 1868 a school called Keio Gijuku, which has since become one of the more influential institutions in Japan. The ten years following 1867 proved to be Fukuzawa's most fertile and intellectual decade. He authored during this period books like *Gakumon no susume* (An encouragement of learning, 1872–1876) and *Bunmei ron no gairyaku* (An outline of a theory of civilization, 1875) both masterpieces in explaining and interpreting Western civilization in terms that are plain and comprehensible to the utterly bewildered Japanese readers.[53] One needs to recall once more how insular Japanese culture was at the time in order to appreciate Fukuzawa's achievement properly. The centuries-long seclusion naturally affected the very language, conspicuously devoid of terms that corresponded to many Western ideas and objects. Which meant that Fukuzawa not only had to invent words and phrases, or borrow them from Chinese and other languages, but to make sure as well that the reader understood them. It may be easy enough to coin words for "postage stamps" and "trousers" and "ice cream," but it is no laughing matter to create expressions equivalent to "liberty," "right," or "equality" in a language long soaked in the hierarchic, authoritarian, feudal ethos in which no such concepts existed. Fukuzawa's contribution to modern Japanese is, more than anything else, quite irrefutable.

Fukuzawa became in 1873 a member of a political research-action group called Meirokusha (Meiji Six Club) together with Nishi Amane, Mori Arinori, Katō Hiroyuki, Nishimura Shigeki, and others. Most of these scholars had been associated with the Institute for the Study of Barbarian Books and were known advocates of the cause of modernizing Japan, via the promotion of "civilization" *(bunmei)* and "enlightenment" *(kaika)*. Heavily biased though it was toward the defense of the newly organized power structure of Japan, the Meirokusha was undeniably a leading intellectual circle in those early Meiji years, selling the new culture and spreading the modern gospels of utilitarianism, egalitarianism, civil libertarianism, freedom of speech, pragmatism, feminism, and so forth. While most Meirokusha members were important officials within the Meiji government, Fukuzawa, it is true, remained outside. At the same time, his relationship to the Meiji government was never that of a forthright critic. In the complex history of the national Diet (parliament), for instance, Fukuzawa was a warm defender in its infancy, but once the populist movement became a real political program he turned aloof, if not outright negative, to the lower populace. Requested in 1880 to edit a government-sponsored newspaper, he declined the offer once, but then just as arbitrarily changed his mind. When the whole plan miscarried, he moved ahead to establish his own paper, *Jiji shimpō*, in 1882, which played a significant role in molding public opinion. From this time on, Fukuzawa used editorials and articles as his principal weapon in an engagement with the political problems of his time, both domestic and international. He was not always supportive of the administration lines, and yet to think of Fukuzawa as a bourgeois conscience of a bourgeois society, a sort of Japanese equivalent of John Stuart Mill, would be a grievous error. On so many fundamental issues, his ideology radically approached—especially in his later years—that of an absolutist-imperialist, the representative Meiji founding-father type of an Ōkubo Toshimichi or an Itō Hirobumi.

In his earliest days (say, up to 1875), Fukuzawa was indeed an innovative writer. In the *Encouragement of Learning*, he adopted pivotal ideas of bourgeois democracy via a minor American writer, Francis Wayland (*The Elements of Moral Science*, 1835), as he did later on more directly from Mill, Spencer, Tocqueville, Buckle, and others. But for Fukuzawa, all civil libertarian issues were strictly subordinated to what always remained the foremost goal in his mind, namely, the realization in Japan of *bunmei kaika*, "civilization" and "enlightenment." Obviously, Fukuzawa was beyond a mere infatuation with what struck him as the glossy life of Americans and Europeans which he had closely witnessed while still impressionably young. At the same time, much of what he seems to have meant by these terms comes dangerously close to the image of the West as it presented itself as Japan's model in the 1850s and 1860s. Of course, the "West," too, is a vague notion just like "civilization," but for

Fukuzawa—as for many other Meiji leaders—the West embodied everything that Japan was not and should be. The West was wealthy and powerful; Japan should be wealthy and powerful. As soon as possible. But how?

When Fukuzawa maintained in the 1860s and early 1870s that the Japanese should be free and independent so that Japan as a nation could be free and independent in the world, he assumed that the civilized countries of the world should, and in fact *did*, abide by the "law of nations" *(bankoku no kōhō)*. As Albert Craig convincingly argues, Fukuzawa readily embraced the notion of the "law of nations" because it was based on a concept of "natural laws," which bore some resemblance to the *ri* of Neo-Confucianism.[54] As he gradually realized that the Western nations did not live up to the so-called "law of nations," Fukuzawa began to adjust to the changed understanding of the West all his socio-political ideas from civil rights to international justice. The West was wealthy and powerful; Japan too should be wealthy and powerful. How? Militarily and economically. During his entire career as the head of the *Jiji shimpō* after 1882, he supported every single administration program for military expansion, strengthening of capitalism, and territorial invasion of Korea and China. In fact, Fukuzawa personally involved himself at least twice in active patriotic schemes: during the Korean incident of 1884 *(Kōshin Jihen)*, he sent his disciples to Korea to take a part in a coup d'état attempt; and in the Sino-Japanese Wars of 1894–1895, he was frantically absorbed in a campaign to raise funds and himself donated a large sum.[55] His attitude toward the rest of the Asian nations was a brutally simple one: Japan must be "civilized"; China and Korea are uncivilized and uncivilizable; in the sacred name of civilization, therefore, Japan must arm itself and conquer the two countries. If the rhetoric is similar to that of the contemporary European and American imperialists used in confronting Japan as well as China and Korea, it also anticipates the propaganda of the Japanese militarists several decades later. The Japanese, as I noted earlier were diligent students of the West in those days, and Fukuzawa, as the most influential educator of Meiji Japan, was an avid pupil in this aspect of "Western learning" as in others.

It may be a little distortive to look at Fukuzawa Yukichi from so narrow an angle. After all, as a feminist, he went as far as anybody had ever dared, and he remained the most vocal advocate for the empire's fair sex even long after his time. True, his is a far cry from present-day feminism; he never considered women men's professional equals, in separation from and independent of men. He was, however, the first to challenge and ridicule the teaching of the seventeenth-century *Onna daigaku*, in a series of newspaper articles and pamphlets such as "Nihon fujin ron" (A theory of Japanese women), "Danjo kōsai ron" (A theory of relationships between sexes), "Nihon danshi ron" (A theory of Japanese men), *Onna daigaku hyōron; Shin onna daigaku* (A critique of Onna daigaku; The new Onna daigaku). Similarly, however tenuous his political independence, as a political analyst he belongs to the very few who at least tried to maintain some semblance of distance from the government in power—no small task in those days barely out of the feudal authoritarianism of Tokugawa Japan. Earlier, especially, he was more effective than anybody else in soothing people's fear of the strange customs and ideas of the barbaric Westerners. No matter how rudimentary and opportunistic, his discussion of civil rights and national autonomy was essential to the further development of such ideas in the hands of his successors. Finally, Maruyama Masao's subtle defense of Fukuzawa's speculative method as modern, a sort of philosophical pragmatism which saved itself from opportunism by sustaining the tension between the dictates of an ideology and the acute perception of reality, may indeed deserve serious consideration.

And yet, after all, Fukuzawa Yukichi is likely to elude one's unconditional respect. He did write, one cannot forget, those numerous essays like "Datsu-A ron" (A theory for moving out of Asia) and "Ni-Shin no sensō wa bunya no sensō nari" (The war between Japan and China is a war between the civilized and the barbarians).[56] In these articles and many others, he repeatedly insists that Japan should distance itself from Asia, since Japan is the only civilized country in the area—a notion that is even now tacitly held, if not openly proclaimed, after so many wars and devastations, by many Japanese, businessmen, students, housewives, even scholars. His support of the imperial system, too, became, as time went on, nearly unqualified and absolute. Too bad, that Fukuzawa's attitude after his first contact with the West in 1860 seemed to have steadily progressed toward this position, psychologically pervert, historically absurd, and politically both destructive and self-destructive. And in the searing light of this racist-imperialist posture, his other contributions to the growth of a bourgeois capitalist Japan would have to pale considerably, be they his efforts for industrialization or his agitation for feminism, Tory republicanism, or Machiavellian patriotism. When Fukuzawa died in 1901, 150,000 people reportedly attended his funeral.

It may be in order here to round up—somewhat in the manner of the last chapter of a Dickensian novel—the later careers of some of the men who played roles in the dispatch of the Embassy. I begin with minor characters like Joseph Heco, the shipwrecked sailor who worked for a while as Captain Brooke's secretary and returned to the United States in 1861 to escape from the threats of assassination. He met his old friends and added another President, Abraham Lincoln, to the previous two, Pierce and Buchanan, who shook his hand. After his return to Japan in 1862, he became involved in the munitions trade, and through it in various political intrigues. Having sided with the right Chōshū men, he was treated well by the new government, preserving friendly relationships with the new leaders, whom he might never have had a chance to know had his fishing boat not been wrecked many years back.[57] As for Captain John M. Brooke, who navigated the *Kanrin Maru*, he was soon drawn into the Civil War, serving the Confederate States Navy. As Chief of the Bureau of Ordnance and Hydrography, he designed the Brooke Gun, the most powerful cannon produced by the Confederacy. After the war, he taught at the Virginia Military Institute for two decades; he died in 1906.[58]

Iwase Tadanari, the negotiator with Townsend Harris and most likely the initial planner of the Embassy to Washington, was, as I have mentioned earlier, demoted by Regent Ii in 1859. And even after Ii's assassination he was not reinstated to his diplomatic position. Still under house arrest, he died in 1861 without the chance to attempt a comeback to the Tokugawa political scene.[59] As for Townsend Harris himself, he returned to his native New York City in September 1862. He never married, living a quiet bachelor's life in a modest apartment. His remaining years were lonely and frugal ones, as if his isolated ascetic life in the Shimoda village had forever molded the opener of Japan into a hermit. The quiet was broken only by a few events: he became a member in 1862 of the exclusive Union Club, where he was known as the "old Tycoon"; he traveled to Europe in 1867, and on his return was awarded a modest stipend by Congress in recognition of his great service; he was visited by a member of the 1871 Iwakura Mission, Kikuchi Gen'ichirō (Ōchi), and happily reminisced about his encounters with able Tokugawa men like Iwase and Inoue;[60] in 1862 he was honored with a citation by the faculty of the Free Academy of the City of New York, which he had helped to establish before his assignment to Japan. He died alone in his New York apartment in February 1878.[61] The Free Academy was later expanded to become the City College of New York, where Harris's diary and documents, together with the American flag he hoisted in Shimoda and in Zempukuji Temple, are still housed in a now sadly dilapidated Rare Books Room. Though largely forgotten in the United States, his is indeed very much a household name in Japan, even in this last quarter of the twentieth century.

Thus the men traveled and returned home. Their mission accomplished and the treaty duly ratified, people resumed their lives and died. Once begun, Japan's intercourse with the West—the enraged samurai patriots' menacing protests and bloody assassinations notwithstanding—flourished. The Tokugawa government dispatched a few more embassies before its fall. The second one went in 1862 to England, France, Holland, Prussia, Russia, and Portugal. This delegation was sponsored by Rutherford Alcock, Great Britain's Minister, and Duchesne de Bellecourt, French Minister, who were no doubt challenged if not piqued by the New World's victory in the race. The purpose of this Embassy, however, was to slow down the calendar for the opening of ports and cities as stipulated by the treaties and negotiate compensatory terms for the delay. Essentially negative though the errand was, the members of the Embassy continued to be profoundly impressed by what they saw and heard in Europe.[62] The group included six men who had already toured on the 1860 Mission—Hidaka Keizaburō, Masuzu Shunjirō, Dr. Kawasaki Dōmin, Sano Kanae, Satō Tsunezō, and Fukuzawa Yukichi. Moriyama Takichirō, Japan's best Dutch interpreter of the time, joined the Embassy at a later stage, accompanying Minister Alcock, who happened to be returning home. This time around, the government was careful to include several young men known for their expertise in Western lore. Their intelligence reports, called *tansaku*, were centralized and systematic, and better informed than the documents left by the individual members of the previous Embassy.[63] Their mission was partly successful in the sense that the port openings were delayed, though not as long as the Tokugawa government would have liked. The information gathered and brought back was, in the intensely anti-Western atmosphere of the first half of the sixties, more or less ignored, and the records were presumably shelved among all the other musty unopened documents.[64]

The third Embassy, of 1864, was sent to talk about the possibility of resuming seclusion, which even the Tokugawa government knew full well to be an utter impossibility. Ikeda Chikugo-no-Kami, the Chief Ambassador, and his two Vice-Ambassadors were all so persuaded of the absolute necessity of foreign trade that they defied the Council order and concluded an agreement on their own, filing a strongly worded recommendation on their return for expanded diplomatic programs. They paid dearly for their initiative, as they were swiftly arrested and condemned to house confinement for a whole year. Rumors flew that the Council's dispatch of the Embassy was merely a show to appease the imperial court and other anti-Western agitators, and that Ikeda and his retinue were merely a decoy.[65]

A delegation was sent to France in 1865, another to Russia in 1866, and still another—the last Tokugawa Embassy, in 1867, headed by the fourteen-year-old Tokugawa Mimbu-dayū Akitake—to Europe. The purpose of this Embassy was to represent the Shogunate in the World Fair in Paris. In the light of the Tokugawa-Roches intrigue, this delegation was clearly a strategic one, and the Tokugawas emphasized its importance by sending, for the first time, a real prince, a brother of the Shogun himself. By this time, however, all was too late. While the young boy was beginning to behave like a Japanese version of the Prince of Wales at the courts of Napoleon III, Queen Victoria, and other European monarchs, the foundation of the Tokugawa House was rapidly caving in back in Japan. And by the time he hurried home, his brother no longer ruled over Japan.

Alongside the embassies, various groups of people were increasingly venturing out to the West. First, the Tokugawa government itself was pressured by the ever solicitous Western ministers to send students to their countries. There was also mounting domestic lobbying for acquiring Western technology from America and Europe. The Tokugawa government yielded in 1862 and dispatched nine officers (including Akamatsu Daisaburō) and six artisans to Holland to study mainly navigation, ship building, and medicine. This group included Nishi Amane and Tsuda Shin'ichiro, who were directed to study more broadly "the way of governing and enriching the country," meaning disciplines in law and the social sciences. While in Holland, they were individually and informally tutored, but because of their deficiencies in the language (they could somehow read, but barely spoke, Dutch), even Nishi and Tsuda had to start from the basics—a primary school teacher instructed the two in Dutch.[66] After 1865, the Tokugawa government added more students to go to Russia, England, and France. But the men on Tokugawa's exchange program were generally passive and conservative, since the assignments were

Students from Chōshū in London, 1863. Four out of these five men (including Itō Hirobumi, rear right) were given peerage by the Meiji government.

usually awarded to the sons of high-ranking vassals rather than to those eager and talented. Also, they were too committed to the political status quo of Japan to stake out and experiment with the new.

The second group of students were those sent secretly—in violation of the Tokugawa rules—by the southwestern fiefs. Chōshū again took the initiative. Determined to remain isolationist, several officers of the domain were paradoxically eager to acquire Western sciences which they felt were nonetheless necessary to expel the hairy invaders. Some of the fief leaders moved ahead with a plan of sending out five of their best "Western experts," among them Itō Shunsuke (Hirobumi), later one of the most powerful men in the Meiji government. As they resided in London taking private tutorials, their view of the international situation, quite understandably, changed rapidly. Itō and another man hurried home as soon as they learned about the imminent conflict between their fief and the Western powers, which was to lead into the 1864 allied action in the Shimonoseki Straits. Although they failed to turn the tide of xenophobia at this time, they were set to persuade Chōshū into a friendly relationship with the Westerners after the battle.

The process was more or less the same in Satsuma. Soon after the British bombardment of Kagoshima, the best Dutch scholars advised the domainal administration to initiate a systematic study abroad program, and in 1865 a fifteen-man delegation was ordered to England and France. Many were selected from the Kaiseisho School of the clan, having already spent years studying Western languages. The actual travel arrangements, all under cover, were made with the cooperation of Thomas B. Glover, one of the most important behind-the-scenes munitions traders of the time. A majority of the Satsuma men studied at the University of London, Oxford and Cambridge being too classics-oriented and, besides, closed to non-conformists, among whom were included presumably those heathens from the Far East. The Tokugawa government soon found out about the contraband students, but preferred to look the other way.[67]

There were other clans active in the illegitimate student exchange, although the prohibitive costs of maintaining students in Europe confined the list mainly to the great and wealthy fiefs. But more intriguing were the separate individuals who disobeyed the ban of the Tokugawas even without the backing of their fiefs. The most memorable of these, Niijima Jō, smuggled himself out in 1864 and studied at Amherst College, returning in 1874 to establish Dōshisha University in Kyoto.[68] Such defiances combined to influence the

Shogunate finally to repeal in 1866 the centuries-long ban against traveling abroad. Although the voyage out was still carefully supervised and selective, the last vestige of the seclusion policy was finally discarded.

During the last years of the Tokugawa reign about 150 students traveled Westward, roughly half from the Tokugawa House, and the others from various feudalities.[69] Most of these men were not adequately prepared either psychologically or linguistically, and their specific academic achievements were rather dubious. Some, like those sent to Russia by the Shogunate in 1865, are reported to have been illiterate even in their own language.[70] And yet, even these dullards did see and experience the outside world. And they inevitably brought back, however undefined, a different view of their country and the world. Their "country" was no longer a Chōshū, or a Satsuma, or a Tosa, but Japan, the whole state that superseded the separate authorities of fiefs. And even among the Tokugawa students, there were some—like Nishi and Tsuda—who began to feel the need to transcend the interests of the Tokugawa House itself and to see a unified Japan under a different arrangement of government if necessary.

When the Shogunate collapsed in 1867, most students still abroad were summoned home, but the policy of swift importation of Western technology was only reaffirmed and reemphasized. During the very first years of the new regime, the program of sending students abroad was already regarded as an essential part of the elite career. Among the earliest students sponsored by the Meiji government were many who were born to the highest social ranks, regardless of their individual talents.[71] The notion of elitism, however, had to be quickly readjusted to the altered social conditions. The need for modern technology in all branches—from military management to educational administration—was so acute that the Meiji bureaucracy could no longer afford to be selective except on the basis of personal merit. By 1874 nearly six hundred people were allowed to study abroad.[72] And as the cant of "civilization" and "enlightenment" swept through the islands, Japan invited many Western teachers and advisors, while at the same time sending out students who would on their return replace the costly foreign employees.[73] By the mid-seventies, the system of government-sponsored students was so smoothly streamlined that it could choose mainly from among the finest graduates of Kaisei College (formerly the Institute for the Studies of Barbarian Books; it would soon become Tokyo Imperial University).[74] Since those admitted to Kaisei College were already the cream, the students chosen for studies abroad were indeed the very best, that is, the fittest for the management of the empire.

The country favored by the largest number of students was the United States, followed by Great Britain, Germany, and France. Very few opted for Holland or Russia, now realizing that these countries did not figure among the leading nations of the West. The reasons for the overwhelming partiality to the United States were several: Japan's traditional sense of America as the friendliest occidental country; the widespread myth of the United States as a new nation unencumbered by social, moral, and humanistic values and resolutely devoted to the pursuit of money and might; and accidental incentives such as America's physical proximity and her evangelical zeal that packed off more missionaries to Japan than all the Old World put together. That accidents and tradition played an important role is evident also in the distribution of these students in America: the majority elected to live around New Brunswick, New Jersey. The reasons for this rather unexpected preference of Rutgers and its surrounding communities are: (1) the very first Japanese students—Mori Arinori, for instance—who transferred to the United States after an initial stay in England settled in New Brunswick on account of their American sponsors; (2) since then, there happened to have been many influential American residents in Japan who were graduates of Rutgers, like R. H. Pruyn, James H. Ballagh, William E. Griffis, Edward W. Clark, and David Murray (a professor at Rutgers). During the two decades after 1866, as many as three hundred Japanese went to study around New Brunswick, although only a handful actually enrolled at the college.[75]

Japan's carefully screened elites began to leave respectable academic records by 1880 on various campuses of the West. At Yale, the Sorbonne, or the University of London, they no longer passively looked on, and especially in natural sciences some of these students were fully competing with their native friends.[76]

Of course, the Meiji administration was continually sending its own investigators and observers to the Western countries from various departments and ministries. Of all such official missions, the most important was the 1871 Iwakura Embassy, which set in many ways the future course of the newly reborn empire. The primary aim of the Embassy was to observe the West and negotiate with the treaty nations about what they had begun to realize as inequities, that is, extraterritoriality and surrendered tariff autonomy.[77] The constitution of the Embassy was quite unlike the 1860 version: the retinue of the former virtually consisted of more than half the leaders of the

Emperor Meiji (Mutsuhito).

Meiji government. Beginning with Iwakura Tomomi, "the Minister of the Right" (or the "Junior Prime Minister," as he was called by Westerners) as the Envoy Extraordinary Ambassador Plenipotentiary, the Mission included Kido Kōin, Ōkubo Toshimichi, Itō Hirobumi, and Yamaguchi Naoyoshi as Vice-Ambassadors. They were real decision makers fully empowered to coordinate their findings abroad with the future policy of the empire.[78] The Mission, fifty-one members altogether, traveled from the United States to Europe between November 1871 and September 1873. Everywhere they went, their resolution to Westernize Japan was warmly cheered. And yet their proposals for treaty revision were peremptorily dismissed as out of the question.

While they were stunned by the vast economical difference between the Western countries and their own, they were also shrewd enough to notice that Japan trailed not far behind: even Europe had been materially undeveloped but half a century earlier. At the same time, their discovery that international relations were not governed by the "law of nations," but by sheer brute power, had a profoundly chilling effect on their initial naive optimism. Bismarck's lecture during a state dinner on the predatory reality of world politics lingered in the memories of several men, Ōkubo Toshimichi and Itō Hirobumi especially, who were later to cast themselves as "Bismarcks of Japan."[79] It is interesting to note that Ōkubo boasted in one of his letters from England that they had studied "courts, prisons, schools, trading firms, factories and shipyards, iron foundries, sugar refineries, paper plants, wool and cotton spinning and weaving, silver, cutlery, and glass plants, coal and salt mines, not to speak of old castles and temples—there is nowhere we haven't gone."[80] The one institution this list does not include is Congress or Parliament, the branch of government that represents citizens' rights.[81]

Now convinced of the clear priority of industrialization and military buildup before cultural and institutional Westernization, the Ambassadors were resolved, upon their return, to initiate those measures required for survival in the brutal nineteenth-century world. As a group they fought against Saigō Takamori and others who in their absence had lobbied for war with Korea. Their pacifism had nothing whatsoever to do with international justice, but rather with the simple conviction that Japan desperately needed immediate domestic reforms before launching out on an aggressive Asian policy. In fact, the anti-Korean-war group did not at all hesitate in 1874, the following year, to invade Formosa when the expedition appeared to serve the purpose of unifying the divided populace and diverting the clamor of the people's rights movement.

The West "taught" Japan. Japan in time was to "teach" the rest of Asia. Toward this goal, the Japanese worked to become rich and powerful *(fukoku, kyōhei)*. In the process the imperial system was made absolute, and subjects' rights severely inhibited. At the same time, the West stood for some modern Japanese as a pastoral dreamland, a Shangri-la, where individual rights were guaranteed and free criticism encouraged, and people lived happily with all kinds of cultural and material amenities. Those aspirants visited there at least once so they could cherish for the rest of their lives the memory of the fairyland of America or Europe. For others, the West was a hell inhabited by sensualists and materialists, from which the messengers of death and destruction were continually sent out threatening the very existence of the empire. They would do anything to fight back so that the holy ambition of the empire could be fulfilled. There were others, of course, who tried to see the West for what it was, but their number was frightfully small. Either way, the Japanese no longer thought of themselves in isolation. The land of the rising sun was now a full-fledged member of the world, even if the West was not always mindful of its existence.[82]

Epilogue

A century later. Wars have been fought, empires lost; and as the world economy inflates, jets fly faster and the globe has steadily shrunk its dimensions. Traveling is no longer the adventure it once was. It is recreation, a mere vacation activity—unless of course one is on business. As a recent theorist of traveling puts it, "we are all tourists."[1]

And Japan sends out a fair share. In Paris and Rome, London and Copenhagen, these pilgrims from the East are to be found everywhere. American airports lately receive so many planefuls of visitors from Japan that many have added Japanese words to the signs and instructions at their facilities. On the West coast especially, group tours (called *pakku*, "package") are numerous and varied: several weeks of English instruction for the summer, a whirlwind seven-day sight-seeing of California and Hawaii, a leisurely stay in San Francisco for four whole days—all programmed to satisfy the increasingly matter-of-fact need to get away. The word *yōkō* (traveling abroad), once an awe-inspiring word which signified the indispensable notch in very elite careers—be they in civil service, business, academia, or even in literature and the arts—was irrevocably overthrown for the new vulgarism "tsuā" (tour). The West obviously has altered its meaning for the Japanese.

Or has it? Are today's Japanese travelers in America—about a million a year, as against around one-third of that figure of Americans visiting Japan[2] —essentially changed from those of the 1860s? The answer must clearly be yes. They know a lot about America through books and magazines, movies and television; many have been abroad before; they—the young in particular—dress like Americans; life in

183

Japan is not that different from life in America; technology dominates in both countries. But then, one wonders. In their behavior and movements, there persists something distinctly and undeniably Japanese. They almost always travel in groups; the cliché image of the camera-happy Japanese tourist—often drawn in disdain if not outright hostility—is surprisingly close to the mark. At any famous scenic or historic site, one sights Japanese tourists snapping pictures of each other, often taking pictures of their friends taking pictures. They bring charming enigmatic gifts, as has been mentioned earlier. They are also reluctant to talk to Americans, understandably perhaps in view of their acute sensitivity to their imperfect English. But even when fairly fluent in English they seem to prefer smiling silence to brash experiment. They are introverts; even now "Tommies" are the exception.

Admittedly, these are no more than impressions I have gathered as I have watched Japanese visitors in New York and Berkeley, at San Francisco and O'Hare airports, or spoken with a good number of them in both English and Japanese. And yet the group movement, the photographic addiction at any memorable place or time, and the self-defensive posture and observation are features I see time and time again in those numerous travelers who come from widely different backgrounds. Whether they are high school students or farm cooperative members, business people or university professors, they seem to share these familiar traits.

I am not interested in discussing in detail the implications of such characteristics. But one does recall that traveling in a group has a history in Japan much older than the recent Western invention of jamming people into economy buses and jumbo jets. Group tourism is an ancient custom that dates back to the Heian period around the ninth to the twelfth century. Called *kō* (association), it first began as aristocratic seminars in Buddhist teaching held at various temples. Later on, the pilgrimage to Buddhist temples and Shinto shrines grew both in variety and social range. After the thirteenth century *kō* was participated in by people of all classes; and since around 1600 it has gradually turned into mutuals and credit unions that help finance their members' excursions. There were many kinds of *kō* by this time, some even functioning as appraisers of inns and guarantors of the travelers' character and credit. Beyond the 1860 version of group supervision, the *pakku* tour claims a long lineage.

Photographing famous places, say, the Empire State Building, the Golden Gate Bridge, or Walden Pond (or what's left of it) seems not unrelated to the conventions of *uta makura* (poetic pillow: literary antecedents and associations) and *meisho* (famous places), which have been touched on in Chapter III. The tourist's being at a well-known or significant site is an imaginative act in itself. As the old traveler who stood, say, at Suma Beach related to the spirit of the place by recalling the layers and layers of poetic and historical associations such as the *Tale of Genji*, the *Tale of Heike*, *Tadanori* (a Noh play by Zeami), and Bashō, so do today's Japanese travelers try to relate to the famous American sites *(Amerika no meisho)*. Since poetic and historical associations are relatively unavailable to them around these foreign *meisho*, they evoke instead the pictures of the towering Empire State Building, now passed by for the World Trade Center, or the Golden Gate in the translucent fog which they have seen many times before. Photography is the means to cope with the alien American space: while they are unable to put themselves verbally and intellectually in America, within the pictures they take they do stand *in* the place. One might say the photograph itself creates the relationship, and this extension of the *uta makura* convention consecrates the profane space.

Thousands of travelogues and travelogue fictions have been composed since the mid-nineteenth century by novelists and others who visited America and Europe.[3] In the course of writing this book, I have read scores of those memoirs—for example, by Narushima Ryūhoku, Mori Ōgai, Natsume Sōseki, Nagai Kafū, Arishima Takeo, Shimazaki Tōson, and Tokutomi Roka, as well as more recent ones by Ōoka Shōhei, Yasuoka Shōtarō, Takeyama Michio, Etō Jun, Oda Makoto, and Mori Arimasa. What I have remarked in connection with the 1860 Embassy records stands to be adjusted, of course. And yet here again familiar features are discernible. Few of them make universalist speculative comments about the West. They tend to assemble day-to-day impressions without structuring them into a personal interpretation. Instead of individuals experiencing a place in all its stark immediacy, they refer themselves back to the Japanese idea of it. They are seldom free from the consciousness of being from Japan, their home country unceasingly hovering over them wherever they go. Individuals confronting a foreign culture in their separate ways and finding their own terms for entering into it are not commonplace even among these documents. It is Japan that they inevitably face as they tour in the West. Yokomitsu Riichi's shapeless and sprawling novel *Ryoshū* (Homesickness, 1937) may still be a good specimen of these unresolved cogitations that seem to preoccupy Japanese intellectuals, nearly always torn between the will to discover and reassert the uniquely Japanese and the sighting of the disturbingly, overwhelmingly attractive and/or repulsive West. Agonized people's agonized documents, many are not unlike Tamamushi's *Kō-Bei nichiroku*, book eight.

So seen, today's travelers may yet be found to share much with the 1860 Embassy members. In history's longer terms, a century of contact may still prove to be a very limited one. An intense relationship that culminated in a total war, occupation, and so-called economic cooperation thereafter gives the impression of the two countries mingling and constantly merging in so many aspects. But America and Japan, one might stop to reflect, lie as far apart now as they did a century ago. Before all cultures are made undistinguishable by the ingratiating blight of technology and consumer culture, one might even now recognize and cherish the tenacious difference between the two cultures.[4] It is in this context that the records of the 1860 Embassy seem still fresh and cogent after all that has happened in the intervening century and more.

Notes

Prologue

1. *The Complete Journal of Townsend Harris* (hereafter referred to as *CJH*), p. 531. According to Iwase Higo-no-Kami, this was the only time Harris expressed surprise throughout the entire negotiation. See Nakane Yukie, *Sakumu kiji*, 2:319.

2. See *Dai Nihon komonjo, bakumatsu gaikoku kankei monjo* (hereafter referred to as *BGKM*), 15:85. Nishimura Shigeki, for instance, applied in 1853 for permission to go abroad. Several proposals were made for the dispatch of students to the West by Sakuma Shōzan, Nagai Gemba-no-Kami Naomune, Sugi Kyōji, and others in subsequent years. One of the most remarkable suggestions made to the Council of State was Tokugawa Nariaki's. This powerful and eccentric lord proposed that the Shogunate should send him to America, together with "three or four hundred" *rōnin* (samurai out of service), younger sons of farmers and townspeople, "instead of granting the Americans permission to establish consulates in Japan" (*BGKM*, 18:360–368). The recommendation is translated by W. G. Beasley in his *Select Documents on Japanese Foreign Policy*, pp. 168–169.

3. *Despatches from the United States Ministers to Japan*, roll 1, no. 20, November 25, 1856.

4. *Japan Journal* (by Henry Heusken), trans. and ed. Jeannette C. van der Corput and Robert A. Wilson, p. 158. Hereafter referred to as *JJ*.

5. *JJ*, p. 179.

Chapter One

1. For the general background of the seclusion period, the best book in English remains G. B. Sansom's *The Western World and Japan*. His two other books, *Japan: A Short Cultural History* and *A History of Japan*, are both authoritative. In the vast literature on Tokugawa Japan, some of the more conspicuous books on the subject of seclusion are: Iwao Shigeichi's *Shuinsen bōeki-shi no kenkyū*, and the same author's more popularized study, *Sakoku. Nihon no rekishi*; and Numata Jirō, *Nihon to seiyō. Tōzai bunmei no kōryū*, 6.

A convenient book on the subject of "Dutch learning" is Donald Keene's *The Japanese Discovery of Europe*. Among good reference books in Japanese on

Tokugawa studies of the West are: Hani Gorō, *Hakuseki; Yukichi;* Takahashi Shin'ichi, *Yōgaku ron;* Ienaga Saburō, *Gairai bunka sesshū-shi ron;* Numata Jirō, *Bakumatsu yōgaku-shi;* Ayuzawa Shintarō and Ōkubo Toshikane, eds., *Sakoku jidai no Nihonjin no kaigai chishiki;* Kure Shūzō, *Shīboruto* [Siebold] *sensei* and *Mizukuri Gempo,* Koga Jūjirō, *Nagasaki yōgaku-shi;* Arisaka Takamichi, *Nihon yōgaku-shi no kenkyū;* Satō Naosuke, *Seiyō bunka juyō no shiteki kenkyū;* Ogata Tomio, ed., *Rangaku to Nihon bunka;* Araki Ihei, *Nihon Eigo-gaku shoshi;* Sugimoto Tsutomu, *Edo jidai Ran-gaku-go no seiritsu to sono tenkai.* The best theoretical treatment is Satō Shōsuke's *Yōgaku-shi kenkyū josetsu.* See also Chapter II, below.

2. Iwao, *Sakoku,* pp. 205–223, 322–341; Numata, *Nihon to seiyō,* pp. 147–172.

3. A brief account of Kōdayū's adventure, *Hokusa bunryaku* (1794), written by Katsuragawa Hoshū, was widely read at the time. There are two biographies of the sailor by Kamei Takayoshi, *Daikokuya Kōdayū* and *Kōdayū no hiren.*

4. The best account in English of the rescued sailors of the time is Sakamaki Shunzō's *Japan and the United States.* In Japanese there are several collections of the shipwreck narratives: Ishii Kendō, ed., *Hyōryū kidan zenshū* and *Ikoku hyōryū kitan shū;* Arakawa Hidetoshi, ed., *Kinsei hyōryūki shū.* See also Ayuzawa Shintarō's survey, *Hyōryū.*

5. *Manjirō hyōryūki* and *Hikozō hyōryūki* are two of the five stories of rescued sailors allowed publication during the Tokugawa period (Arakawa Hidetoshi, p. 188), and they are both collected in Arakawa's edition. As for Manjirō's modern biographies, *Nakahama Manjirō den,* by his son Nakahama Tōichirō, is the most authoritative. There is a fictionalized life of Manjirō by Ibuse Masuji, *Jon Manjirō hyōryū-ki,* but it offers nothing interesting either literarily or biographically. There is a more recent biography in English by Kaneko Hisakazu, *Manjirō: The Man Who Discovered America.* As for Hikozō's life, see his autobiography: Joseph Heco, *The Narrative of a Japanese.* Also, there is a recent biography in Japanese, *Joseph Heco,* by Chikamori Haruyoshi.

6. Koga, *Nagasaki yōgaku-shi,* 1:41–73; Takahashi, *Yōgaku ron,* pp. 52–57; Numata, *Nihon to seiyō,* pp. 185–192.

7. Koga, *Nagasaki yōgaku-shi,* 1:73–93.

8. Samuel Wells Williams, *A Journal of the Perry Expedition to Japan,* p. 150.

9. *CJH,* p. 550. For Heusken's entry, see *JJ,* pp. 192–193.

10. The following is the Dutch version of the first letter Shogun Tokugawa Iesada sent to the U.S. President in May 1858 (the English version of it is reproduced in the text of this chapter:

"Aan zyne Majesteit, Franklin Pierce, President der Vereenigde Staten van Amerika, enz. enz. enz.

"Ik Minamoto Ië Sada, Taikoen van het Japansche Ryk, antwoord aan Uwe Majesteit met genoegen, dat Gy, sedert onlangs meenigmaal over de vrede en vriendschap tusschen beide Ryken geschreven hebt, en tevens bewys U myne opregte erkentelykheid van de zending van zyne Excellentie Townsend Harris, Consul Generaal der Vereenigde Staten van Amerika, met Uwen vriendschappelyken Brief, welke omtrent het openen van den handel en de voortdurende vrede tusschen beide Natien is voorgesteld; dan, de onmogelykheid om het tydelyke Tractaat spoedig uit te wisselen, komt daar op aan dat er eene Zamenkomst en beraadslaging van myn geheele Ryk vereischt worden, neemt dit in eene gunstige aanmerking. En, Ik wensch aan Uwe Majesteit het geluk en den voorspoed van Uw Ryk.

"dem Zesden dag der vyfde maand van het vyfde jaar van Ansei Tsutsinoye Mma"

Not being a native Dutch speaker, I consulted with two Dutch scholars about the linguistic competence of this letter. Their opinion is that, while it is quite clear in meaning, the syntactic structure and idiomatic usage are both less than adequate. Also, they pointed out that the formal style of a diplomatic document was perhaps beyond the ability of the Tokugawa Dutch scholar. All in all, the letter seems to display a degree of mastery more or less similar to that of its English version. I found this letter in the Townsend Harris Collection housed in the Rare Books Collection of the City College of New York, City University of New York.

11. For the general history of studies of English in Japan, see Sakamaki, *Japan and the United States*, pp. 87–111; Koga, *Nagasaki yōgakū-shi*, 2:121–161; also Tokyo-to Tosei Shiryōkan, comp., *Tokyo no Eigaku*. The most recent and ambitious study on the subject is the four-volume work *Nihon no Ei-gaku hyaku-nen*, eds. Doi Kōchi et al., published by Kenkyūsha. Its first volume is devoted to the Japanese studies of English before 1916.

12. See William S. Lewis and Murakami Naojirō, *Ranald MacDonald*.

13. Quoted by Sakamaki, *Japan and the United States*, p. 103.

14. Quoted by Nakahama Tōichirō, *Nakahama Manjirō den*, p. 303. There are several other letters quoted in Kaneko's *Manjirō*, all at the same level in the mastery of English. This letter varies in insignificant details in Kaneko's text.

15. Quoted by Chikamori Haruyoshi, *Joseph Heco*, p. 221. Of course, the text of this fragment may have been corrupted in the process of transcription by Chikamori. But Tominaga Makita's careful examination of the three manuscripts of *The Narrative of a Japanese*, housed in the Tenri Library in Nara, argues that in the earlier two versions Heco's English is quite unidiomatic. Mr. Tominaga's conjecture is that the first two versions are Heco's own work, while the third version is thoroughly edited by James Murdoch; see Tominaga's "Amerika Hikozō 'narrativu' shohon o megutte." I did obtain a microfilm copy of one of the three versions—which happens to be in much more idiomatic English than, say, Nakahama Manjirō's letters. The only trouble is that the film nowhere identifies whether it is the first, second, or third version!—and my attempt to determine that has so far been unsuccessful.

16. *Notes from the Japanese Legation in the United States to the Department of State*, roll 1.

17. Toyoda Minoru, *Nihon Ei-gaku-shi no kenkyū*, pp. 53–57; Koga, *Nagasaki yōgaku-shi*, 1:139–142; Doi Kōchi et al., eds., *Nihon no Ei-gaku hyaku-nen*, 1.

18. Hawks, *Narrative of the Expedition*, 1:485–486.

19. According to Mrs. Williams, "Wells went with Commodore Perry rather against his own (and much against *my*) will, in consequence of leaving his office of Chinese printers in inexperienced hands, and feeling his own want of preparation for such a position. His reputation as a Japanese scholar is based upon the slight ground of his having studied that language ten years ago, under a sailor teacher!—nor has he since that time had the opportunity to practice a word of it." Quoted by Frederick Williams, *The Life and Letters of Samuel Wells Williams*, p. 185.

20. Alcock's 70-page pamphlet, *Elements of Japanese Grammar for the Use of Beginners*, was published in 1861 in Shanghai. Almost completely forgotten now, it is nonetheless an attempt to explain the Japanese language employing English grammatic concepts. Of course, they do not work in Japanese, and the reader of the primer must have become more confused than before opening it. Still it is a brave try—especially in view of the fact that Alcock had little help other than a native interpreter, the Abbé Girard, and the famous seventeenth-century Japanese grammar book by Rodriguez. For the story of Dankichi, see

Alcock's *The Capital of the Tycoon*, 1:292–297; also, Payson J. Treat, *Diplomatic Relations between the United States and Japan*, 1:94.

21. *Narrative of the Earl of Elgin's Mission*, 2:177.

22. Fukuchi Gen'ichirō, *Bakufu suibō ron*, chaps. 3 and 4, pp. 19–39.

23. Harris tended to exaggerate the importance of his office. While he was still in Paris, he was "distributing cards of an Envoy Extraordinary and Minister Plenipotentiary," according to reports that reached Secretary of State William L. Marcy. Marcy's angry letters to General Prosper M. Wetmore, Harris's chief advocate, fols. 47754-5 and 47764-5, are quoted by Oliver Statler, *Shimoda Story*, pp. 31–32.

24. The Tokugawa records of the diplomatic sessions published in the *Dai Nihon komonjo, bakumatsu gaikoku kankei monjo* (hereafter referred to as *BGKM*) reveal the insight and shrewdness of the Tokugawa negotiators. They knew, for instance, that Harris was using the British navy as a rhetorical weapon. They also realized, however, that they could indeed use Harris's help. The correctness of this judgment is proven in the difference between the British-Chinese Treaty and the British-Japanese Agreement, both signed by Lord Elgin. Because of the precedent of the Harris Treaty, Lord Elgin was bound to be more favorable to Japan than to China. See Fukuchi Gen'ichirō, *Bakufu suibō ron*, p. 60.

25. See Tōyama Shigeki, *Meiji ishin*, pp. 45–64. Tōyama's view of Britain's interest in Japan as chiefly economical was questioned by Inoue Kiyoshi and Ishii Takashi. See the latter's *Meiji ishin no kokusai-teki kankyō*, 1:12–33.

26. Fukuchi Gen'ichirō, *Kaiō jidan; Bakumatsu seijika*, pp. 284–302. See also his *Bakufu suibō ron*, pp. 72–85. There is an interesting study of Kawaji Toshiakira by Satō Seizaburō, "Seiō no shōgeki e no taiō," pp. 3–67.

27. Harris's own account was not available, and this is my translation of the record on the Japanese side. *BGKM*, 30:84–86, and Ishin-shi gakkai, *Bakumatsu ishin gaikō shiryō shūsei* (hereafter referred to as *BIGS*), 3:658–659. See also Tanabe Taichi, *Bakumatsu gaikō dan*, 1:144–145, and Fukuchi Gen'ichirō, *Kaiō jidan*, pp. 31–32.

28. *Memories*, 1:384.

29. *The Capital of the Tycoon*, 1:210 and 162.

30. *JJ*, p. 96. Also see *JJ*, p. 155; *CJH*, pp. 299, 337; Goncharov, *The Voyage of the Frigate Pallada*, p. 143; Hawks, 1:328, 359; Ernest Satow, *A Diplomat in Japan*, p. 69.

31. Referring to the Metsuke system, Norman describes it as "astonishingly similar to modern secret police," *Origins of the Modern Japanese State*, p. 121.

32. See W. G. Beasley's introduction to his *Select Documents on Japanese Foreign Policy*, pp. 18–35. For the complicated office hierarchy and job categories of the Tokugawa government, see Shinji Yoshimoto, ed., *Edo jidai bushi no seikatsu* and his *Edo jidai buke no seikatsu*; Matsudaira Tarō, *Edo jidai seido no kenkyū*.

33. *BGKM*, 33:84–85, 151–153.

34. See, for instance, Fukuzawa Yukichi's explanation of his recruitment in his *Fukuō jiden*, p. 106.

35. For the list of the members of the Embassy, see chap. 3 of the general introduction in the *Man'en gannen ken-Bei shisetsu shiryō shūsei*, comp. Nichi-Bei Shūkō Tsūshō Hyakunen Kinen Gyōji Uneikai (hereafter referred to as *SS*), 7:63–75. As for the fief background, see a list compiled by Katō Somō in his memoir, *Futayo gatari*, collected in *SS*, 3:6–13.

36. Dated September 6, 1858. *Despatches from the United States Ministers to Japan*, roll 2.

37. Dated November 15, 1859. In ibid.

38. The first proposal was made to the Council of State by Mizuno Chikugo-no-Kami Tadanori, Nagai Gemba-no-Kami Naomune, Tsuda Hanzaburō Masa-michi, and Katō Shōzaburō Norikaki on October 6, 1858. The proposal is reprinted in *BGKM*,, 21:211–214.

39. This is Fukuzawa Yukichi's version as he recalled the event in his *Fukuō jiden*, p. 110. Kimura Yoshitake, however, disagrees, arguing that Katsu was disgruntled by his position as Kimura's inferior and was sulking in his cabin. See "*Kanrin Maru* senchū no Katsu," in Katsu's *Kaishū zadan*, pp. 144–195. Whatever the reason, Katsu remained in his cabin throughout, and this is confirmed by Lt. John M. Brooke's numerous references to Katsu in his *Kanrin Maru Journal, SS*, 5:67–96, and his letter to the Secretary of Navy, dated March 25, 1860, *SS*, 5:109.

40. Many Japanese historians seem to believe that the Japanese crew were quite competent during the voyage. This view, perhaps based on Fukuzawa's memory (*Fukuō jiden*, p. 110), is, however, contradicted by some of the diarists as well as Lieutenant Brooke. See, for instance, Saitō Tomezō's *A-kō shinsho, SS*, 4:366–367. Interesting in this connection is Brooke's recording in the *Kanrin Maru Journal* of a conversation between him and the captain of a passing ship: "He wished us a pleasant passage. I remarked that we had a high old crew on board. He said he should think so from their looks. Said this vessel sailed very well for a steamer and a Japanese. I told him he must not let a Japanese vessel beat him. He replied . . ." (*SS*, 5:84). This exchange, quite clearly ironic on the part of both Brooke and the captain, is always translated by the Japanese historians as a straightforward compliment by Brooke for the experienced crew!

41. *CJH*, p. 412.

42. These English translations are in the *Notes from the Japanese Legation in the United States to the Department of State*, roll 1 (May 22, 1858 to April 5, 1875). The Japanese drafts of these letters appear in *BGKM*, 30:133–138; 33:35–41; and 34:181–187. Several more drafts—proposed by the offices of *metsuke*, foreign affairs, and treasury—are to be found in *BIGS*, 4:121–126.

43. The treaty is reproduced in Beasley's *Select Documents*, pp. 183–189. For an incisive discussion of its inequities, see Tōyama Shigeki, "Kaikoku, taisei hōkan," 3:14–16. See also Marlene Mayo, "Rationality in the Meiji Restoration," for a discussion of the earliest realization of the treaty inequities by the Japanese.

44. Commodore Kimura wanted to go on to Washington, D.C., but Captain Katsu was reluctant, according to Kimura's reminiscence. See *Kaishū zadan*, p. 195. Actually, Kimura was given another assignment of taking the place of the Ambassadors in case anything should happen to them before reaching the capital (*BGKM*, 34:98–99). He fulfilled the assignment by waiting in San Francisco until the news of the Embassy's imminent arrival at Washington reached him.

45. To take just one example, Hirose Hōan is deeply impressed by the American crew's hospitality, although he explains it as a manifestation of Japan's "importance." *Kankai kōro nikki*, 1:16th leaf.

46. *China and Japan*, pp. 304–305.

47. *The Capital of the Tycoon*, 1:253–254.

48. Dated February 14, 1860. *Despatches from the United States Ministers to Japan*, roll 3.

49. *BGKM*, 34:23–33; *BIGS*, 4:343–357.

50. *Fukuō jiden*, pp. 107–108. For details of the shipped coins, see *SS*, 7:29–31.

51. *The Diary of George Templeton Strong*, 3 (*The Civil War*):32–33.

52. Quoted from the *New York Times* for June 27, 1860. When this poem was collected in the 1865 *Drum-Taps,* the title was changed to "A Broadway Pageant (Reception Japanese Embassy, June 16, 1860)."

53. Congress voted to appropriate $50,000 for the reception of the Embassy. U.S. Congress, Senate, *Bills and Joint Resolutions of the Senate of the United States for the Thirty-Sixth Congress,* April 3, 1860. Various municipal governments, however, seem to have spent far more. According to the San Francisco *Daily Evening Bulletin,* the New York Common Council was presented with bills amounting to $125,000, including the hotel bill for $91,000 (which meant "$137 per day for each guest") that itemized, for instance, 10,000 bottles of champagne. August 2, 1860.

54. These letters are in the *Notes from the Japanese Legation in the United States to the Department of State,* roll 1. The note of urgency is unmistakable in their painfully composed English letters. By the time they wrote the third letter (dated the 9th day of the fourth month of the seventh year of Ansei, i.e., May 28, 1860), they had been advised that the return trip would have to be via the Cape of Good Hope. Their response was: "So we think that as many days will now be lost by the going of the *Niagara* to Panama, we have determined to make the voyage by the Cape of Good Hope, as Dupont mentioned, and to set forth directly from Washington without visiting part of the United States, because we would necessarily give many days to that, and the views of our Government would not be followed out. Therefore we request the Niagara may come to Hampton Roads about the 1st of June, if that be not troublesome to you." In the last letter they wrote on the subject (dated the 16th day of the fourth month of the seventh year of Ansei, i.e., June 4, 1860), they reluctantly accept the invitations to Baltimore, Philadelphia, and New York, but even then they plead, "[the *Niagara* should stop] at such ports only as necessary for providing such articles, as most urgently requested, and in such cases to remain not longer than absolutely necessary for such purposes. They request this for the reason, that their departure has been delayed beyond their calculation and they are much pressed for time; they also think, as the 'Niagara' is a large and strong ship, that sufficient coal, wood, water, and provisions may be put on board of here." See also Muragaki, *Ken-Bei-shi nikki,* contained in (Ōtsuka Takematsu, ed.) *Kengai shisetsu nikki sanshū* (hereafter referred to as *KSNS*), 1:116–118, 138.

55. A letter from the offices of *ōmetsuke* and *metsuke,* dated the 11th month of the sixth year of Ansei, *BGKM,* 31:35–39.

56. *BIGS,* 5:1–2. The Embassy's first official report to the Council of State, sent from San Francisco, interestingly enough says nothing about this Hawaiian diplomatic approach. The Ambassadors are indeed very timid in the letter, even in mentioning that they had contact with the kingdom, a non-treaty country; they emphasize the absolute need to replenish the ship's supply and apologetically point out that the ship's movement was not up to them, but to its captain. *BGKM,* 37:124–130. It was not until two days after their return to Edo that the Ambassadors reported about the Hawaiian government's approach. They were obviously afraid of a possible censure for even having had a talk with a foreign government outside of the agreed plan. *BIGS,* 5:2–3.

57. For a dietary crisis, see Morita Kiyoyuki, *A-kō nikki, SS,* 1:114. Tamamushi Sadayū is highly critical of his colleagues' complaints about American food. But even he admits his dislike of the taste of the foreign food. *Kō-Bei nichiroku,* p. 51.

58. The vast quantity of food carried by the *Kanrin Maru* is itemized in Katsu Rintarō's *Kanrin kan Beikoku tokō, Zenshū,* 12:226–227. For the detail of the

remodeling of a special kitchen at Willard's in Washington, D.C., see *Harper's Weekly*, May 26, 1860.

59. Kimura Tetsuta, *Kō-Bei-ki*, p. 333.

60. Yanagawa Kenzaburō Masakiyo, *Kōkai nikki*, *KSNS*, 1:240. The Continental Hotel in Philadelphia provided them with specially made pillows. See *The Philadelphia Press*, June 11, 1860.

61. *Fukuō jiden*, pp. 112-113.

62. *Kanrin-kan Beikoku tokō, Zenshū*, 12:239-309.

63. Namura Gohachirō and Tateishi Tokujūrō, the Embassy's interpreters, had borrowed from the Institute Bomhoff's *English-Dutch, Dutch-English Dictionary*, *BGKM*, 33:58-61.

64. See Chapter IV, pp. 174 and 181, below.

65. *Kaki kōkai nisshi, SS*, 3:326.

66. *Kōkai nichiroku, SS*, 3:209.

67. *BGKM*, 37:69-71. When the Ambassadors were invited to an evening party by the Hawaiian court, for example, they declined the invitation on the ground that going out at night was against the Japanese customs *(kokufū)*. The same expression was used even in Washington to avoid unnecessary exposure to the Americans. See Muragaki's *Ken-Bei-shi nikki, KSNS*, 1:32, 91, 106.

68. *Kaki kōkai nisshi, SS*, 3:325. Sano Kanae, too, describes the ban in his *Man'en gannen hō-Bei nikki*, p. 52.

69. *Kō-Bei nichiroku*, pp. 98, 111. The accuracy of Tamamushi's observation is confirmed by Morita Kiyoyuki's *Personal Account-Book*. See *SS*, 1:327-340.

70. *Kō-Bei nichiroku*, pp. 241-242.

71. This point is also made by Matsuzawa Hiroaki in his excellent analysis of the pre-Meiji foreign travel diaries, "Samazama na seiyō kenbun," pp. 621-679.

72. The two lexiconophiles are Fukuzawa Yukichi and Nakahama Manjirō (see Chapter IV, below). Their purchase of the *Webster's*, however, was in fact neither Japan's first importation of a Western dictionary nor the Embassy's only purchase of the *Webster's*. As early as 1844, Sakuma Shōzan, one of the most accomplished students of "Dutch learning," was avidly reading a sixteen-volume Dutch encyclopedia (one of the world's earliest and largest "do-it-yourself" handbooks, by Noel Chomel), applying whatever he found there to technical inventions and innovations. See Ōhira Kimata, *Sakuma Shōzan*, pp. 80-82. Also, the item identified as "Worushisutoru chojutsu, *Eigo jibiki*" in the list of books and presents brought back by the Ambassadors is no other than Webster's *Dictionary of the English Language* abridged by J. E. Worcestor, first published in 1829 and revised in 1841, and often reissued thereafter. See Emily Ellsworth Skeel and Edwin H. Carpenter, eds., *A Bibliography of the Writings of Noah Webster*, pp. 249-255. For the list of books and presents brought back by the Ambassadors, see Muragaki, *Man'en gannen dai ichi ken-Bei shisetsu nikki*, ed. Shibama Chikakichi, pp. 334-371, and *BIGS*, 4:258-281.

73. The brawl is reported in Tamamushi's *Kō-Bei nichiroku*, p. 63, Fukushima's *Kaki kōkai nisshi, SS*, 3:306, and in *America tokai nikki*, by an anonymous writer, pp. 37-38.

74. See Chapter II.

75. *Bei-kō nikki, KSNS*, 1:411-412.

76. *Kaki kōkai nisshi, SS*, 3:336-337.

77. *Kankai kōro nikki*, 1:28th leaf.

78. *Ikoku no koto no ha, SS*, 4:340.

79. *Hōshi Meriken kikō, SS*, 4:32.

80. See, for example, Kimura Tetsuta, *Kō-Bei-ki*, p. 193; Kahachi, *Ikoku no*

koto no ha, SS, 4:338; Muragaki, *Ken-Bei-shi nikki, KSNS,* 1:59, 196; Tamamushi, *Kō-Bei nichiroku,* p. 74; Sano Kanae, *Man'en gannen hō-Bei nikki,* p. 32.

81. See Maruyama Masao, *Nihon seiji shisō-shi kenkyū,* pp. 6–19; Tōyama Shigeki, *Meiji ishin,* pp. 66–74.

82. Nagao Kōsaku's *A-kō nikki* mentions a discussion he had on board the *Kanrin Maru* with Nakahama Manjirō, Makiyama Shūkyō, and Hideshima Tōnosuke about the relationship between Japan and the United States. He records that Nakahama Manjirō's idea was received with enthusiasm, but refuses to specify it on the ground that it contains "some confidential matters." *SS,* 4:223. This kind of reference to any political discussion among themselves or with the Americans is extremely rare in any of the diary-travelogues.

83. Ambassador Shimmi condemned Tamamushi for his use of the word *i* (barbarian) for "American" and "English" in the conversation, fearing that the Americans might discover the written document and become angered. Tamamushi criticizes Shimmi in his confidential book eight of *Kō-bei nichiroku* and insists that the Americans are "broad-minded." The Tamamushi-Chinese emigré conversation is reproduced in book eight, pp. 229–236.

84. Letter dated 2nd day of the second month of the first year of Ansei (1854), quoted by Nakahama Tōichirō, *Nakahama Mankirō den,* p. 231.

85. John Mercer Brooke, *Kanrin Maru Journal, SS,* 5:77.

86. Nakahama Tōichirō, *Nakahama Manjirō den,* pp. 313–315.

87. *BGKM,* 34:22–23.

88. *Philadelphia Inquirer,* June 15, 1860, and *New York Herald,* June 17, 1860.

89. *The Diary of George Templeton Strong,* 3:45.

90. August 20, 1860.

91. The American reporters sensed that "Tommy" was under continual surveillance by the *metsuke* officers. See, for instance, the *New York Herald,* June 20, 1860: "His every movement is jealously watched by the Censors . . ." A brief and flattering bit of news about "Tommy" did reach the Commissioners for Foreign Affairs in Edo via the newspaper clippings Townsend Harris transmitted to them. In the course of translation and transcription, however, the report was so garbled that no one could have known who "Tomushi" was. *BIGS,* 4:84.

92. The Ambassadors' letter, dated "9th day of the fourth month of the seventh year of Ansei" (May 26, 1860). *Notes from the Japanese Legation in the United States to the Department of State,* roll 1.

93. June 15, 1860.

94. The only business they conducted while in the United States was some talks about the exchange rate of the Japanese and American currencies. In this connection, they visited the mint in Philadelphia for the purpose of having the Japanese coins assayed so that Japan could establish a more favorable exchange rate with the Western countries. Ironically, by the time they returned to Japan the rate had already been improved, thus making vain the Embassy's efforts.

95. There are numerous documents that record the endless discussions about gifts to be taken by the Ambassadors. See *BGKM,* passim, and *SS,* 7:143–149.

96. Hawks, 1:356–357; *CJH,* p. 260. The Japanese side, characteristically, left far more complete lists, *BGKM,* 5:208–232. A similarly complete list of the Japanese gifts is contained in *BGKM,* 5:304–316.

97. Take, for example, the word *hassaku* (literally, the first day of the eight month). In order to commemorate the occupation of Edo, on the first day of the eighth month, 1600, by Ieyasu, the founder of the Tokugawa dynasty, all the *daimyō* were expected to give gifts to the Shogunate on that day every year. Hence, the word came to signify "present." There is, of course, a heavy political meaning loaded in the gift-offering ceremony. For a study of the Japanese

custom of gift-giving, see Harumi Befu, "Gift-Giving in a Modernizing Japan."

98. January 30, 1861. The Japanese records more or less confirm this report. If anything, the initial report prepared by the dock official and transmitted to the Commissioners for Foreign Affairs lists the gifts of that day as only "10 ducks, fresh fish, and 1 containerful of fruit and cakes." Later on, however, the Tokugawa officers seem to have relaxed their purse strings considerably: they gave, among other things, "5 cows, 500 carrots, 25 sacks of sweet potatoes, 500 horse radishes, 200 bunches of scallion, 15 sacks of wheat flour, 20 pigs, 300 chickens and ducks, 50 sacks of rice, and 5000 eggs" (*BIGS,* 4:216–226).

Chapter Two

1. *Ken-Bei-shi nikki, KSNS,* 1:51; see also his *Kōkai nikki,* trans. Uno, p. 43.
2. *Ken-Bei-shi nikki, KSNS,* 1:30–31; also, his *Kōkai nikki,* p. 26.
3. *Kōkai nichiroku, SS,* 3:214.
4. *Kaki kōkai nisshi, SS,* 3:333–334.
5. *A-kō nikki, SS,* 4:208–209.
6. See "The Attack on the British Legation in Japan in 1861," in Oliphant's *Episodes in a Life of Adventure,* pp. 152–173.
7. *Ken-Bei-shi nikki, KSNS,* 1:81; also, his *Kōkai nikki,* p. 68.
8. *Kō-Bei-ki,* p. 42; Tamamushi, *Kō-Bei nichiroku,* book eight, reproduces the dialogue between Tamamushi and the Chinese emigré in Honolulu (pp. 228–236).
9. *Kaki kōkai nisshi, SS,* 3:333.
10. G. B. Sansom, *Japan: A Short Cultural History,* p. 84.
11. Tōyama Shigeki, *Meiji ishin,* pp. 72–74.
12. *Kōkai nikki, KSNS,* 1:221.
13. *A-kō nikki, SS,* 1:10.
14. *Ikoku no koto no ha, SS,* 4:347–348.
15. Morita, *A-kō nikki, SS,* 1:221.
16. *Kō-Bei nichiroku,* pp. 172–176.
17. *A-kō kōkai nikki, SS,* 2:134.
18. *A-kō nikki, SS,* 2:253.
19. *Kōkai nikki, KSNS,* 1:288.
20. *Kō-Bei-ki,* p. 157.
21. *Man'en gannen hō-Bei nikki,* p. 128.
22. *Bei-kō nikki, KSNS,* 1:435, 444–445.
23. *Kō-Bei nichiroku,* pp. 156–157.
24. *A-kō nikki, SS,* 1:118.
25. Ibid., 1:156.
26. *Kankai kōro nikki,* 1:21st leaf.
27. *Futayo gatari, SS,* 3:100–101.
28. There is an interesting comparative discussion of the Japanese attitudes toward China and the West in Satō Seizaburō's "Bakumatsu Meiji shoki ni okeru taigai ishiki no shoruikei."
29. Katō Shūichi makes a similar observation of Japanese racism manifest in the official reports of the Iwakura Embassy *(Tokumei zenken taïshi Bei-Ō kairan jikki)* in his "Nihon-jin no sekaizō."
30. For instance: "They readily admit our superiority, and seem to be strongly impressed with the power of our country. The frequent presence of this power is therefore imperative, with this people, to the establishment of trade and the introduction of Christianity. The missionary and the commercial interests are equally benefited by naval protection. For, as Christianity and

commerce are carried into heathen and uncivilized lands, their supervision and defense necessarily follow." Andrew H. Foote, "A Visit to Simoda and Hakodadi in Japan."

31. *New York Illustrated News,* May 26, 1860.

32. Originally this appeared in the *Tribune;* it was later quoted in *New York Life Illustrated,* June 23, 1860. The Japanese side is, of course, completely silent about the incident.

33. *Harper's Weekly,* June 23, 1860.

34. June 2, 1860.

35. *Frank Leslie's Illustrated Newspaper,* June 2, 1860.

36. June 9, 1860.

37. May 26, 1860.

38. May 26, 1860.

39. May 14, 1860.

40. June 11, 1860.

41. March 18, 1860.

42. March 19, 1860.

43. March 23, 1860.

44. April 4, 1860.

45. May 26, 1860.

46. J. F. Steiner, *The Japanese Invasion.*

47. See Bernard Semmel, *Jamaican Blood and Victorian Conscience.*

48. For the history of Japanese women, see Inoue Kiyoshi, *Nihon josei-shi;* Mary R. Beard, *The Force of Women in Japanese History;* Takamure Itsue, *Josei no rekishi;* Morosawa Yōko, *Onna no rekishi.*

49. *Kaibara Ekken,* ed. Matsuda Michio, p. 234. For a slightly different version of *Onna daigaku,* see Morosawa, *Onna no rekishi,* pp. 215–216. There were more than thirty guidebooks for women during the Tokugawa period, but none deviated from the official line set by Kaibara—with the sole exceptions of Kumazawa Banzan's *Joshi-kun* and Andō Shōeki's *Tōdō shinden.* See Inoue Kiyoshi, *Nihon josei-shi,* pp. 144, 196. Banzan emphasizes the need of women to acquire learning and independent judgment. The *Joshi-kun* appears in Banzan's selected works, 2:371–418. As for Andō Shōeki's text, Noguchi Takehiko's edition is convenient. See also E. H. Norman, *Andō Shōeki and the Anatomy of Japanese Feudalism.*

50. Kaibara Ekken, p. 211. Age seven in Japanese means "the seventh year," thus corresponding to the Western age six.

51. Commodore Perry was requested to agree that no American women would be brought to Japan. See Hawks, 1:385. There had been very few female Western visitors to Japan before the formal opening: a few in Nagasaki in the earlier nineteenth century; three American women in Shimoda in 1855; the wife of an English consul at Hakodate (C. Pemberton Hodgson, who was in Japan between 1859 and 1860). Yoshida Tsunekichi, *Tōjin Okichi,* pp. 46–53, and Hodgson, *A Residence at Nagasaki and Hakodate;* Kawaji Toshiakira, *Nagasaki nikki, Shimoda nikki,* pp. 209–210.

52. *Ken-Bei-shi nikki, KSNS,* 1:84; *Kōkai nikki,* p. 71.

53. *Ken-Bei-shi nikki, KSNS,* 1:91–93; *Kōkai nikki,* pp. 78–80.

54. The Westerners' eyes were often compared to those of dogs. See, for instance, Amano Shinkei, *Shiojiri zuihitsu* (1782), quoted in Osatake Takeshi, *Meiji ishin,* 1:112.

55. *A-kō nikki, SS,* 1:129.

56. *Kanrin Maru kō-Bei nisshi,* pp. 607, 611.

57. *Bei-kō nisshi, SS,* 2:16.

58. *Kaki kōkai nisshi, SS,* 3:297.

59. *Kōkai nichiroku, SS,* 3:202.

60. *Ken-Bei-shi nikki, KSNS,* 1:111–112; *Kōkai nikki,* pp. 96–97.

61. *Kaki kōkai nisshi, SS,* 3:326.

62. *Fukuō jiden,* p. 114.

63. *Kōkai nikki, KSNS,* 1:288.

64. *A-kō kōkai nikki, SS,* 2:99.

65. *A-kō nikki,* p. 47.

66. *Futayo gatari, SS,* 3:49, 79.

67. This quotation appears in the second part of *Futayo gatari, SS,* 3:79–80. According to Mizuno Masanobu, who wrote down and edited Katō Somō's talk, the second part is actually his, Mizuno's, work, based on Katō's talk plus another work which he identifies as *Gasshūkoku schichōroku.* The latter work has never been discovered, but the second part of *Futayo gatari* is largely identical with the anonymous *America tokai nikki,* published in the *Yashidai ishin shiryō sōsho,* 8:27–70. *Gyokuseki shirin,* by Mizukuri Gempo, is reproduced in toto in the *Gaikoku bunka hen,* vol. 16 of the *Meiji bunka zenshū.* Katō's (or Mizuno's) passage is a quite random and careless extraction from a few pages (pp. 81–83) of the work where the American "manners and customs" are described.

68. *CJH,* p. 308.

69. Yoshida Tsunekichi, *Tōjin Okichi;* Sakata Seiichi, *Harris;* and Oliver Statler, *Shimoda Story.*

70. *Journal,* pp. 183–184. But Perry's own Dutch interpreter, Portman, wrote Moriyama Einosuke, during his stay in 1854, that he wanted to "become friends" with one of these lewd girls of Japan. The Japanese translation of the letter is in *BIGS,* 3:102. Portman, incidentally, later officiated as the interpreter for the 1860 Embassy, and then as Acting Minister for the United States.

71. Morita Kiyoyuki, *A-kō nikki, SS,* 1:71–72.

72. San Francisco *Daily Evening Bulletin,* March 21, 1860.

73. *Frank Leslie's Illustrated Newspaper,* June 9, 1860.

74. *New York Illustrated News,* May 26, 1860.

75. Ibid.

76. *Fukuō jiden,* pp. 115–116.

77. Ibid., pp. 125, 129.

78. *Konyo zushiki* is in five books *(kan),* printed in three separate volumes; *Konyo zushiki ho* is in four books and printed in four separate volumes. They were published in 1845 and 1846 in Edo.

79. Satō Seizaburō, "Seiō no shōgeki e no taiō," p. 29.

80. *Kō-Bei nichiroku,* p. 109.

81. There are numerous editions of *Kaikoku zushi.* I have used the sixty-volume edition published in Yōshū, China, that was used by the Japanese translators.

82. Written by Tsurumine Boshin in 1853, *Meriken shinshi* tried to cash in on the curiosity aroused by Perry's visit. Aimed at a wide audience, it offered no new information.

83. Robert N. Bellah, *Tokugawa Religion,* pp. 42–43.

84. *A-kō nikki, SS,* 1:49.

85. *Kanrin-kan Beikoku tokō, Zenshū,* 12:285.

86. "The Japanese could hardly believe that such a modest, unassuming, quiet little man could be a governor. If he had been attended by an army of office-seekers in cocked hats, they might have appreciated more easily his dignity." San Francisco *Daily Evening Bulletin,* March 19, 1860.

87. Many of these terms were found in the Chinese geography books such as *Kaikoku zushi*. Some — like *kuni* — are of course Japanese.

88. *Kōkai nichiroku, SS,* 3:201, 213; Yanagawa, *Kōkai nikki, KSNS,* 1:278. Both Nonomura and Yanagawa, at the same time, also use terms like *daitōryō*. See also Osatake Takeshi, *Ishin zengo ni okeru rikken shisō,* chaps. 1-3.

89. Nonomura, *Kōkai nichiroku, SS,* 3:201.

90. Kimura Tetsuta, *Kō-Bei-ki,* p. 188; Satō Hidenaga, *Bei-kō nikki, KSNS,* 1:456-457.

91. *Kōkai nikki, KSNS,* 1:277-278.

92. Fukushima, *Kaki kōkai nisshi, SS,* 3:325; Nonomura, *Kōkai nichiroku, SS,* 3:213.

93. Yanagawa, *Kōkai nikki, KSNS,* 1:335; Fukushima, *Kaki kōkai nisshi, SS,* 3:359.

94. *Ken-Bei-shi nikki, KSNS,* 1:69; *Kōkai nikki,* p. 59.

95. *Ken-Bei-shi nikki, KSNS,* 1:79; *Kōkai nikki,* p. 66.

96. *Ken-Bei-shi nikki, KSNS,* 1:84; *Kōkai nikki,* p. 71.

97. *Ken-Bei-shi nikki, KSNS,* 1:88-89; *Kōkai nikki,* pp. 76-77.

98. Wei-Ming Tu, "*Li* as Process of Humanization," pp. 194, 187.

99. Tsuda Sōkichi, *Jukyō no jissen dōtoku,* pp. 56-57, 127, 209-227.

100. I have discussed this system of honorifics elsewhere. See *Accomplices of Silence,* passim.

101. Tokugawa Nariaki's vision of the feudal order is firmly based on the theory of hierarchic distinctions. And as such it has a kind of holism involving the entire nation. See Tōyama Shigeki, *Meiji ishin,* pp. 76-78. The best document to illustrate the relationship between *rei* and the hierarchic distinction is Fujita Yūkoku's *Seimei ron* (1791), reproduced in *Mito gaku,* eds. Imai Usaburō et al.

102. *Ken-Bei-shi nikki, KSNS,* 1:104-105; *Kōkai nikki,* pp. 90-91.

103. *The Voyage of the Frigate Pallada,* pp. 150-151.

104. Ibid., p. 152.

105. *Mudai tehikae, SS,* 1:281-282.

106. *Kō-Bei nichiroku,* pp. 63-64. A variant of this entry appears in book eight, pp. 236-237.

107. *Kō-Bei nichiroku,* pp. 94-96.

108. Ibid., pp. 107-108.

109. Sano Kanae, a member of an "outside" fief, who volunteered to serve as a manservant for Masuzu, a Tokugawa vassal, during the voyage, was very much like Tamamushi in his position in the Embassy. He, too, describes the visit to the Capitol, but expresses total bewilderment as to the nature of Congress. *Man'en gannen hō-Bei nikki,* pp. 64-65.

110. See Bellah, *Tokugawa Religion,* p. 25.

111. Tōyama, *Meiji ishin,* pp. 66-74; Norman, *Origins of the Modern Japanese State.*

112. The Ambassadors and the Council of State repeatedly discussed whether or not they should request a presidential interview. See *BGKM,* 30:138-142, and *BIGS,* 4:30-32. Thus, the proposal for the interview was made — matter of factly — by Secretary Cass, not by the Japanese, according to the Japanese record. *BIGS,* 4:65.

113. See the Ambassadors' letter to Cass dated "the 25th day of the second-third month of the seventh year of Ansei" (May 4, 1860). *Notes from the Japanese Legation in the United States to the Department of State,* roll 1.

114. The meeting reproduced here is nearly a verbatim translation of Morita Kiyoyuki's record in his *A-kō nikki, SS,* 1:119-122. A reference is made by

Muragaki to the same preparatory talk, *Ken-Bei-shi nikki, KSNS,* 1:84–85; *Kōkai nikki,* pp. 71–72.

115. Buchanan, following Secretary Marcy's instructions, chose to appear in the court in the simple dress befitting an American citizen. Carl Russel Fish, "James Buchanan," *DAB.*

116. See above, pp. 86–87.

117. See, for instance, the Washington *Evening Star,* May 17, 1860.

118. On August 16, 1860, before the Embassy's return to Japan, Townsend Harris transmitted a selection of Washington newspaper clippings to the Commissioners for Foreign Affairs. But the Japanese translation (based on Heusken's Dutch translation) is so garbled that it does not reveal anything about this ceremonial bungle (which wasn't even recognized as such by the Americans). *BIGS,* 4:82–85. Maruyama Kunio, who edited the *BIGS,* notes that the translation was probably made by Moriyama Takichirō. If it is indeed his work, this is additional evidence of his linguistic limitations: the translator clearly does not know what is meant by the "Secretary of State," or the "cabinet," nor does he understand the American newspaper account of the ceremony.

Chapter Three

1. Fukuzawa Yukichi describes the fanatic xenophobic atmosphere after his return to Japan in his *Fukuō jiden,* p. 120. As for the circumstance of the withdrawn application, see Mori Mutsuhiko's "Tokugawa bakufu no yōgakusho no honyaku shuppan kisei," in *Rangaku to Nihon bunka,* ed. Ogata Tomio, pp. 113–120. Mori is, of course, wrong in attributing the withdrawn manuscript to a member of the 1860 Embassy.

2. The massive bibliography contained in the last volume of *SS* is indispensable to anyone interested in this event. The techniques employed in this descriptive bibliography, however, are far from ideal. Aside from several typographical errors, there are a few confusions, ambiguities, omissions, and contradictions. As far as I can determine, I have read every standard version of the records listed in the bibliography, except the very insignificant ones identified in it as 123, 180, and 183. There are a few publications since the *SS* bibliography; see my bibliography to this volume.

The *SS* bibliography indicates that there was *Seishi suiroki* (no. 181), published in 1860 (p. 217). But the item is merely a seven-sheet leaflet briefly describing most places visited by the Embassy, plus a few simplified maps. I am grateful to Professor Kawakita Nobuo of Keio University for providing me with a photocopy of this work. Copies of Hirose's work have survived (one of which is in the Diet Library [Kokkai Toshokan]), although a modern version is not yet published.

3. The *SS* bibliography lists only fourteen copies, but Numata Jirō's essay "Tamamushi Sadayū to *Kō-Bei nichiroku,*" pp. 551–564, gives the higher figure.

4. Of course, the existence of the original diary copy (entered day by day during the voyage itself) neither confirms the author's lack of interest in talking about his experience to others nor proves that no other versions remained. Katō Somō, for instance, left a day-by-day diary (item 159 in the *SS* bibliography), but he also revised it in several other copies (items 160 through 168) as well as told the whole story to Mizuno Masanobu, who in turn wrote it down as *Futayo gatari* (collected in *SS,* 3:1–130). In short, most diarists were eager storytellers about the most important experience in their lives. According to the descriptions in the *SS* bibliography, the works by Masuzu Hisatoshi (item 124) and Ishikawa Masatarō (item 251) are definitely in the initial diary form, while the

records by Namura Motonori (item 139) and Nagao Kōsaku (item 221) seem to be in the raw form though not explicitly so stated.

5. Kimura Tetsuta's "Atsumegusa" and Katō Somō's *Futayo gatari* are both oral reports recorded by others.

6. The official memoranda of the Embassy, called "Shimmi Buzen-no-Kami, Muragaki Awaji-no-Kami, Oguri Bungo-no-Kami, A-kō goyōdome," in six manuscript volumes, are in the Shiryō Hensanjo of the University of Tokyo. Several documents in the record have already been published in *BIGS*. There are in the same library memorandum books by Muragaki and Oguri. I have checked the former by Muragaki, a copy of the original on Gaimushō (Ministry for Foreign Affairs) stationery, which does not seem to contain any significant new material. I was told about Oguri's *Goyōdome* by Professor Ishii Takashi, but I have not had a chance to examine the document itself.

7. *SS*, 7:223 (under item 198).

8. See footnote to p. 82, Chapter II.

9. See Edwin Reischauer, *Ennin's Travels in T'ang China* and *Ennin's Diary*. Largely factual, this immense medieval record of a pilgrimage, written in Chinese, is yet fully informed with the sense of intimate knowledge of the country. Ennin's diary is also quite dramatic, i.e., organized with an interpretation.

10. *SS*, 3:236–237.

11. Engelbert Kämpfer, who traveled between Nagasaki and Edo several times during his stay in Japan toward the end of the seventeenth century, calls Tōkaidō, the main trunk road, "more crowded, than the publick streets in any [of] the most populous town[s] in Europe." *The History of Japan*, 2:330. The Tokugawa government maintained an overall control of the nation's main highways. Their checkpoints (*sekisho*), principally established to guard the hostage system and security measures, numbered over fifty altogether throughout Japan, and survived until 1869. All travelers were required to submit for inspection their passports (*tegata*), issued by registered officials. In the case of samurai, their masters or the deputies of their masters (and in the case of commoners, village masters [*nanushi*], landlords, parish priests, etc.) were authorized to grant passports. The fiefs had their own checkpoints (*kuchidome bansho*) along the borders. Although the strictness of control over travelers and merchandise shipments varied from fief to fief, some domains were quite reluctant to permit strangers to enter their territories. Kämpfer describes the Hakone checkpoint in *The History of Japan*, 2:59–61. See Toyoda Takeshi and Kodama Kōta, eds., *Kōtsū-shi*, pp. 105–233; Ōshima Nobujirō, *Nihon kōtsū-shi gairon* and *Nihon kōtsū-shi ronsō*; and Hibata Setsuko, *Edo jidai no kōtsū bunka* and *Nihon kōtsū-shi wa*.

12. See Tōyama Shigeki, *Meiji ishin*, pp. 73–74. This is, of course, the basis of the Meiji ideology of "family state" *(kazoku kokka)*.

13. Mircea Eliade, *Patterns in Comparative Religion*, esp. chap. 10.

14. "Danpen," dated October 1900.

15. *Hokuyūki* is by Akiba Tomoemon and Okutani Shingorō, collected in Suzuki Tōzō, *Kinsei Kikō bungei nōto*.

16. See footnote to p. 82, Chapter II.

17. *Ken-Bei-shi nikki*, *KSNS*, 1:40; Kokai nikki, p. 35.

18. *Akō nikki*, *SS*, 1:45.

19. *JJ*, pp. 124–125.

20. For studies of the literary diary tradition as a whole, see Tamai Kōsuke's *Nikki bungaku no kenkyū* and Ikeda Kikan's *Nikki waka bungaku*. Also see Earl Miner's *Japanese Poetic Diaries*. For the contemporary Tokugawa travelogues, see Suzuki Tōzō's *Kinsei kikō bungei nōto*, which, however, makes no mention of the 1860 Embassy records. Numerous studies of Bashō, the traveling

poet, are quite helpful for reflection about the travelogue form. *Hyōhaku no tamashii,* ed. Imoto Nōichi, for instance, is a convenient collection of essays on Bashō and the *tabi-nikki* conventions. Although I disagree with practically everything said by Mr. Herbert Plutschow, his unpublished talk entitled "Some Characteristics of Medieval Japanese Travel Diaries," given at Berkeley on December 5, 1975, was suggestive in several ways, and I thank him for the help I found in opposing his ideas. *Kokubungaku: kaishaku to kyōzai no kenkyū* 20, a special issue on the diary and travelogue, is also useful.

21. *Notes from the Japanese Legation in the United States to the Department of State,* roll 1.

22. *SS,* 2:290–291.

23. *Kōkai nichiroku, SS,* 3:160.

24. Respectively, *Futayo gatari, SS,* 3:23; *Man'en gannen hō-Bei nikki,* p. 19; *Kō-Bei-ki,* pp. 74–75; *Kankai kōro nikki,* 2:7th leaf; *Kō-Bei nichiroku,* p. 47. Tamamushi's entry reads as follows: "We did not know what it was, and — as is always the case with our countrymen — [we were] frightened; but the Americans were not; seeing us [*yora*] baffled, [they said] there was nothing like this in Japan; apparently there is no phenomenon of this kind in Japan; the American name for it is 'north light.' "

25. *A-kō-ei, SS,* 2:356.

26. The poem is reproduced in Yamamoto Akira, ed., *Kō-Bei nichiroku* (Sendai, 1930).

27. Fukuchi Gen'ichirō (Ōchi), for instance, reminisces how severely he was criticized by Hayashi for preferring Dutch learning to Confucianism, in *Kaiō jidan,* pp. 37–39. As for the history of the Shōheikō Institute, see Wajima Yoshio, *Shōheikō to hangaku.*

28. For Tamamushi's life, see pp. 164–167, Chapter IV.

29. *Kō-Bei nichiroku,* pp. 229–231.

30. *Ken-Bei-shi nikki, KSNS,* 1:200–206; *Kōkai nikki,* pp. 177–180.

31. *The Voyage of the Frigate Pallada,* pp. 156, 160.

32. *CJH,* pp. 362–363.

33. See, for instance, Thomas C. Smith's "Ōkura Nagatsune and the Technologists," pp. 127–154.

34. Arai Hakuseki, *Seiyō kibun,* ed. Miyazaki, pp. 16–17. Miyazaki's comments in the edition are quite helpful. Also, see Satō Shōsuke, *Yōgaku-shi kenkyū josetsu,* and Miyazaki Michio, *Arai Hakuseki no yōgaku to kaigai chishiki.*

35. The text of *Taga Bokkyō kun ni kotaeru sho* is in the Iwanami Bunko edition of *Miura Baien shū,* ed. Saegusa Hiroto. For Miura's philosophy, see Saegusa's *Miura Baien no tetsugaku* and Taguchi Masaharu's *Miura Baien.*

36. For the understanding of Nakae Tōju and Kumazawa Banzan, I found the collections of their works in the *Nihon shisō taikei,* 29 and 30, which include several concise discussions, most helpful. There is also an edition in the *Nihon no meicho* series. See also Bitō Masahide, *Nihon hōken shiso-shi kenkyū,* pp. 136–276.

37. In addition to the studies mentioned earlier in connection with "Dutch learning," see Numata Jirō et al., eds., *Yōgaku,* 1; *Nihon shisō taikei,* 64 (which includes important selections from Sugita Genpaku and Shiba Kōkan); Haga Tōru's selection of works by Sugita Genpaku, Hiraga Gennai, and Shiba Kōkan in the *Nihon no meicho* series, 22; Tsukatani Akihiro et al., eds., *Honda Toshiaki; Kaiho Seiryō, Nihon shisō taikei,* 44; Satō Shōsuke et al., eds., *Watanabe Kazan, Takano Chōei, Sakuma Shōzan, Yokoi Shōnan, Hashimoto Sanai, Nihon shisō taikei,* 55. As for monographs on individual writers, I read

Katagiri Kazuo, *Sugita Genpaku;* Tatsuno Sakito, *Sakuma Shōzan;* Ōhira Kimata, *Sakuma Shōzan;* Matsuura Rei, *Yokoi Shōnan;* Tamamuro Taijō, *Yokoi Shōnan;* Yamaguchi Muneyuki, *Hashimoto Sanai;* Kumura Toshio, *Yoshida Shōin no shisō to kyōiku;* Kawakami Tetsutarō, *Yoshida Shōin.* In "Science and Confucianism in Tokugawa Japan," Albert Craig characterizes these Dutch scholars by their "eclectic syncretism" (p. 156). As for the later development of the "Japanese soul and Western technology" attitude, see Hirakawa Sukehiro's *Wakon yōsai no keifu,* which discusses it in relation to Mori Ōgai.

38. The text of *Gekibun* is in *Ōshio Heihachirō shū; Satō Issai shū, Dai-Nihon shisō zenshū,* 16:470–475.

39. Various papers by Miura Meisuke are reproduced in *Minshū undō no shisō,* eds. Shōji Kichinosuke et al., *Nihon shisō taikei,* 58.

40. Maruyama Masao, *Nihon no shisō,* esp. pp. 1–66.

41. See p. 174 in Chapter IV.

42. "The Legacy of Tokugawa Education," pp. 109–110. This is a revised version of the last chapter of *Education in Tokugawa Japan.*

43. *CJH,* pp. 468–480.

44. *Ken-Bei-shi nikki, KSNS,* 1:85–90; *Kōkai nikki,* pp. 72–77. A reminder is in order at this point to stress that we are comparing Harris's English with a translation of Muragaki's Japanese, undoubtedly a risky undertaking. Yet I feel less apprehensive about such a comparison here than I might elsewhere, for a few reasons: (1) many of the questions raised go beyond the particular language involved; (2) whenever individual words or phrases are in question, they can be adequately explained—perhaps not as accurately as one wishes, but still adequately; (3) there is no other option, insofar as we are interested in formal comparison of works in different languages. It appears that the advantages seem to more than compensate for the risks.

45. What dress uniforms the Ambassadors should wear was the topic of a serious discussion in the Tokugawa government. The triumvirate proposed a detailed list, which was commented on by the Commissioners of the Treasury, the Chancellery *(Hyōjōsho),* protocol experts, etc. The discussion ranged from the choice of summer fabric as against winter fabric, and the antecedent cases, to the propriety of a given style to a given rank, etc. *BIGS,* 4:126–139.

46. For a suggestion of particularity in the narrative texture, see Carol T. Christ's *The Finer Optic: The Aesthetic of Particularity in Victorian Poetry.* Harris refers to the novels by these writers in his *Journal.*

Chapter Four

1. Akamatsu Daisaburō, *Amerika yuki kōkai nikki, SS,* 4:183–184; Anon., *Amerika kihan nikki, SS,* 4:305–306.

2. *Fukuō jiden,* pp. 119–120.

3. Muragaki, *Ken-Bei-shi nikki, KSNS,* 1:196; *Kōkai nikki,* p. 174. According to another report, twenty-one guns (Namura Motonari, *A-kō nikki, SS,* 2:276). Actually, the custom of firing guns as a salute was not established in Japan till 1862. For the solemn diplomatic negotiations on whether Japan should adopt this foreign ritual, see *BIGS,* 1:490–542, and Tanabe Taichi, *Bakumatsu gaikō dan* (1898), 1:151–154.

4. *Kō-Bei nichiroku,* p. 221. Among the welcoming crowd was Joseph Heco, who describes the Embassy's return in *The Narrative of a Japanese,* 1:261.

5. Muragaki, *Ken-Bei-shi nikki, KSNS,* 1:196–207; *Kōkai nikki,* pp. 174–180. Also, the "Embassy Chronology," *SS,* 7:78–105.

6. February 5, 1861.

7. The *Daily Evening Bulletin,* February 5, 1861.

8. Muragaki, *Ken-Bei-shi nikki, KSNS,* 1:196–207; *Kōkai nikki,* pp. 174–180. Also, Katsu Kaishū, *Zenshū,* 12:305–309.

9. *JJ,* pp. 223–226.

10. *JJ,* pp. 223–226; also, *Ishin-shi,* 2:965–974.

11. Oliphant's own account appears in chap. 10 ("The Attack on the British Legation in Japan") of his *Episodes in a Life of Adventure,* pp. 152–173.

12. The literature dealing with the Bakumatsu-Meiji Ishin period is vast, and threatens to expand day by day as Japan's nostalgia for these "simple, exciting days" intensifies. I have read many standard Japanese books, but would like to limit myself here to referring to the bibliography volume of the *Meiji ishin-shi kenkyū kōza,* compiled by Rekishigaku Kenkyūkai. As for works specifically treating the diplomatic history of this time, see Ishii Takashi, *Meiji ishin no kokusai-teki kankyō; Nihon kaikoku-shi; Gakusetsu hihan, Meiji ishin ron; Meiji ishin no butai ura;* and *Bakumatsu ishin no gaikō.* Also *Iwanami kōza,* [1st and 2nd ser.], *Nihon rekishi 14 (Kindai, 1);* vol. 3 of Rekishigaku Kenkyūkai, comp., *Meiji ishin-shi kenkyū kōza;* Ōtsuka Takematsu, *Bakumatsu gaikō-shi no kenkyū;* Numata Jirō, *Nihon to seiyō;* Tōyama Shigeki, *Meiji ishin;* Oka Yoshitake, *Kindai Nihon no keisei* and *Sōmeiki no Meiji Nihon;* Osatake Takeshi, *Meiji ishin, Bakumatsu gaikō hishi-kō,* and *Kokusai-hō yori mitaru bakumatsu gaikō monogatari;* Kamikawa Hikomatsu, ed., *Nichi-Bei bunka kōshō-shi,* 1. For books in English, see Robert Schwantes's "Japan Cultural Foreign Policy, 1868–1941," in James W. Morley's *Japan's Foreign Policy,* pp. 153–183.

13. According to Ishii Takashi, there was one shrewd observer at the time who noted that the anti-Tokugawa fiefs were opposed to the Tokugawa policy of foreign trade so that they (the opposition fiefs) could trade directly with foreigners for profits as well as challenge the Shogunate authority. The observer, unidentified by Ishii, is no other than Tamamushi Sadayū, *Kanbu tsūki,* 1:122 (quoted by Ishii, *Meiji ishin no kokusai-teki kankyō,* 2:456).

14. Ishii Takashi's chap. 4 in vol. 2 of the rev. ed. of *Meiji ishin no kokusai-teki kankyō* contains the most authoritative discussion of the time of this Japanese-English relationship. See also Ōtsuka Takematsu, *Bakumatsu gaikō-shi no kenkyū.*

15. The biographical materials of Shimmi Buzen-no-Kami are to be found in the "Shimmi-ke keifu shōroku," in Muragaki, *Man'en gannen daiichi ken-Bei shisetsu nikki,* ed. Shibama Chikakichi, pp. 1–10; and Yoshida Tsunekichi, "Shimmi Masaoki no A-kō ei ni tsuite," *SS,* 2:395–399.

16. The information about Muragaki's life was gathered from "Muragaki-ke keifu shōroku," in *Man'en gannen daiichi ken-Bei shisetsu nikki,* ed. Shibama, pp. 11–32. His Hakodate diary, *Kōmu nikki,* is collected in *BGKM.*

17. Kurata Kurakichi, "Hōshi Meriken kikō." *SS,* 4:401–409. A dull conventional chronicle, *Sanjū-nen-shi* does not reveal Kimura as much of a historical writer. See also Fumikura Heijirō, *Bakumatsu gunkan Kanrin Maru,* pp. 679–686.

18. For the circumstance of Oguri's confrontation with the Russians, see George Alexander Lensen, *The Russian Push toward Japan,* pp. 448–451.

19. Ninagawa Shin, *Ishin zengo no seisō to Oguri Kōzuke no shi,* p. 150. This book and its second volume, *Zoku ishin zengo no seisō to Oguri Kōzuke,* are, together with another full-volume biography by Abe Dōzan, *Kaigun no senkusha, Oguri Kōzukenosuke seiden,* quite incoherent as well as inaccurate and irresponsible. As of now, the biographical materials concerning this interesting Tokugawa man must be culled from various sources such as Ishii Taka-

shi's numerous diplomatic historical books. There are several contemporary references to Oguri: Fukuchi Gen'ichirō, *Bakumatsu seijika* (1896–1897), Tanabe Taichi, *Bakumatsu gaikō dan* (1898), Kurimoto Joun, *Hōan jusshu (1892).* Ishii Takashi is presently working on a biography.

20. Ishii Takashi, *Meiji ishin no kokusaite ki kankyō,* 2, chap. 6, esp. pp. 622, 673–674.

21. Hirao Michio, *Boshin sensō-shi,* p. 85; Fumikura Heijirō, *Bakumatsu gunkan Kanrin Maru,* p. 407.

22. Unlike all others so far mentioned in this connection, Katsu has no shortage of biographers. I have consulted: Tanaka Sōgorō, *Katsu Kaishū;* Yamaji Aizan, *Katsu Kaishū;* Matsuura Rei, *Katsu Kaishū;* Etō Jun, *Kaishū yoha: Waga dokusho yoteki;* Ishii Takashi, *Katsu Kaishū;* Tamura Eitarō, and Tanaka Eitarō, *Shiryō kara mitaru Katsu Kaishū;* Ozaki Hideki and Ozawa Kenshi, *Shashin hiroku: Katsu Kaishū.* Ishii's work, though dry, is the best. Etō Jun fails to deliver the goods promised by his overly dramatic, and pedantic, narrative structure, a watered-down imitation of *Lord Jim.*

23. For Sakamoto Ryōma, see Marius Jansen's *Sakamoto Ryōma and the Meiji Restoration.*

24. Ishii Takashi, *Katsu Kaishū,* pp. 177–182.

25. Katsu's chats with these worshippers are recorded in two collections, both included in *Katsu Kaishū zenshū:* Iwamoto Yoshiharu's *Kaishū zadan* and Yoshimoto Jō's *Hikawa seiwa.*

26. Matsuura Rei, *Katsu Kaishū,* p. 187. Ishii Takashi, *Katsu Kaishū,* pp. 231–232.

27. Ishii Takashi, *Katsu Kaishū,* p. 237.

28. Katsu Kaishū's father, Katsu Kokichi, was a fascinatingly free-spirited man. His autobiography, *Musui dokugen* (A monologue in drunken dreams), is a very revealing record of the freedom enjoyed by the lowest-rank samurai in the tight Tokugawa society. It is hard not to see traits of Kokichi in Katsu Kaishū.

29. Fumikura Heijirō, *Bakumatsu gunkan Kanrin Maru,* chap. 4, "A-kō *Kanrin Maru* norikumiin ryakureki," pp. 679–749.

30. Fumikura Heijirō, *Bakumatsu gunkan Kanrin Maru,* pp. 737–738.

31. Ibid., p. 738.

32. Kawakita Nobuo, "Kaidai," *SS,* 1:419–433.

33. Konishi Shirō, "Hidaka Tameyoshi no *Bei-kō nisshi* ni tsuite," *SS,* 2:379–381.

34. I owe much of this information about "Tommy" Tateishi Onojirō's later life to Professor Kanai Madoka of Tokyo University. See also Professor Kanai's "Tommy to yū na no Nihon-jin," in *Kokusai bunka,* nos. 100, 101. As for the record referred to, see Sasaki Takayuki's diary, *Hogo-hiroi,* 5:244. Although there are two Naganos in the Iwakura Mission, this roué is unquestionably our man. The other Nagano was Sasaki's secretary, and is mentioned often throughout the diary without any special qualification as is "Tommy" Nagano.

35. Fumikura Heijirō, *Bakumatsu gunkan Kanrin Maru,* pp. 689–729.

36. Shimizu Masashi, "Amerika-yuki kōkai nikki," *SS,* 4:409–412; Fumikura Heijirō, *Bakamatsu gunkan Kanrin Maru,* pp. 708–713.

37. Yoshida Tsunekichi, "Masuzu Shunjirō no *A-kō kōkai nikki* ni tsuite," *SS,* 2:382–386.

38. Konishi Shirō, "Namura Motonari no *A-kō nikki* ni tsuite," *SS,* 2:387–392.

39. Yoshida Tsunekichi, "Murayama Hakugen no *Hōshi nichiroku* ni tsuite," *SS,* 2:393–394.

40. Muramatsu Shikō, "Hirose Hōan no to-Bei monogatari," *Kōshū sōwa*, pp. 233–260. I am grateful to Professor Muramatsu Sadataka of Sophia University for telling me about this book by his father and giving me a copy.

41. Yoshida Tsunekichi, "Nonomura Tadazane no *Kōkai nichiroku* ni tsuite," *SS*, 3:413–415.

42. Nakahama Tōichirō, *Nakahama Manjirō den;* Kaneko Hisakazu, *Manjirō: The Man Who Discovered America.*

43. Fumikura Heijirō, *Bakumatsu gunkan Kanrin Maru*, pp. 727–729.

44. Ibid., pp. 694–695.

45. Ibid., pp. 701–702.

46. Ibid., pp. 717–720. See also Kojima Chōzō, ed. *Yoshida Ryōdayū shōden*, App., pp. 14–19.

47. There is no full-length treatment of Tamamushi's life. The main source of information is still Tamamushi Bun'ichi and Yamamoto Akira, *Tamamushi Sadayū ryakuden*, which consists of a chronology, a brief outline of Tamamushi's life, a lecture by Shimizu Tōshirō on his life, selected passages related to Tamamushi that appeared in Fujiwara Ainosuke's *Sendai boshin-shi*, and a few *kanbun* poems and letters by Tamamushi, published together with an edition of *Kō-Bei nichiroku*, by Yamamoto Akira, in 1930 in Sendai. Recently, however, there have been a number of entries on this hitherto little-known man in various books discussing the late Tokugawa years. See, for instance: Hanzawa Hiroshi, "Hi-baku, hi-Satchō no mezashita mono: Tamamushi Sadayū," in *Meiji no gunzō*, 1; Tsurumi Shunsuke, ed., *Goisshin no arashi. Nihon no hyakunen*, 10:74–84; Numata Jirō, "Tamamushi Sadayū to *Kō-Bei nichiroku*," in *Seiyō kenbun shū*, pp. 551–564. As for the role of Tamamushi in the general context of the War of 1868 (Boshin sensō), see Fujiwara Ainosuke, *Sendai boshin-shi;* and Haraguchi Kiyoshi, *Boshin sensō.*

48. *Kanbu tsūki* appeared in two volumes in 1913. *Hazankiji*, a copiously detailed report of the March 1864 Tsukubasan anti-Western, anti-Tokugawa insurrection in the Mito fief, was published in 1918. This account alone amounts to 928 modern pages. Another two-volume report, *Ihi nyūkō roku*, this time on the movements of Westerners in Japan, is a collection of translations of diplomatic correspondence, public records, and Yokohama newspapers, between 1862 and 1864, plus several comments *(Muryo zasshū)* by Tamamushi himself. Most documents contained in the work must have been classified and certainly hard to obtain and translate. Tamamushi surely cannot have read them in the original languages. That means that he had fairly free access to the Office of Foreign Affairs—an efficient intelligence agent, indeed. As for sophistication of his observations, see n. 13, above.

49. If this plan, sketched in a document discovered in 1952, had anything to do with Tamamushi, some of its features may have come from what he saw in Washington: the Shogunate envisioned for the north was something along the line of a "republican" government ruled by a council of lords *(kōgisho)*, with an emperor presiding above. See Mushakōji Minoru, "Boshin-eki no ichi-shiryō." See also Tsurumi Shunsuke, *Goisshin no arashi*, pp. 82–84.

50. There are a number of books on Fukuzawa written by Keio-associated historians. The Keio University Press, for instance, has published important books, from the authoritative *Fukuzawa Yukichi, zenshū*, 21 vols., to Aida Kurakichi's bibliography in the *Juku-shi*, March 1955 to September 1962. But it is also undeniable that many of the Keio works are characterized by pietism, contributing zero critically. Among the works on Fukuzawa that are intellectually serious are: Hani Gorō, *Hakuseki; Yukichi;* Hattori Shisō, "Fukuzawa Yukichi," "Bunmei kaika," and "Zettaishugi to Fukuzawa Yukichi"; Maruyama

Masao, "Fukuzawa ni okeru jitsugaku no tenka," "Fukuzawa Yudichi no te-tsugaku — toku ni sono jiji hihan tono kanren," and "Kaidai" (contained in the 6-vol. Iwanami ed. of the *Senshū*); Ienaga Saburō, "Fukuzawa Yukichi no kaikyū ishiki"; Tōyama Shigeki, *Fukuzawa Yukichi;* Shikano Masanao, *Nihon kindai shisō no keisei,* pp. 165–269; Albert M. Craig, "Fukuzawa Yukichi." There is also a general introduction in English by Carmen Blacker, *The Japanese Enlightenment: A Study of the Writings of Fukuzawa Yukichi.*

51. The records of the whole affair, Ono's complaint and Fukuzawa's apology, are both in Fukuzawa's *Zenshū,* 20 and 21. Also see Tōyama, *Fukuzawa Yukichi,* p. 32.

52. Craig calls Fukuzawa's self-characterization (as "a strict neutralist during the disturbances of the bakumatsu period") "an old man's imagining," having no resemblance to the real Fukuzawa ("Fukuzawa Yukichi," p. 103). See also Tōyama, *Fukuzawa Yukichi,* pp. 18–44.

53. There are English translations available: *An Encouragement of Learning,* trans. David A. Dilworth and Umeyo Hirano; *An Outline of a Theory of Civilization,* trans. David A. Dilworth and G. Cameron Hurst. His *Autobiography (Fukuō jiden)* is also made available by Eiichi Kiyooka. Also, there is *The Speeches of Fukuzawa,* trans. Wayne H. Oxford.

54. "The *ri* of Chu Hsi that had been stretched to encompass natural science was now further stretched and distorted to cope with the 'natural laws' of society. As a consequence the metaphysical status that earlier had been ascribed to scientific laws was now assumed to inhere in the Enlightenment natural rights as well. An early form of the juncture of ideas from the two traditions can be seen in the phrase 'universal ethical principles' [*sekai fūtsū no dōri*] used by Fukuzawa in an 1866 letter to a friend. Or, in his earliest translations, Fukuzawa frequently takes statements that stress the empirical discovery of the God-given, natural laws of society and transforms them into statements about the metaphysical nature of man. He translates from a deistic framework into one that is tinged with Confucianism." ("Fukuzawa Yukichi," p. 114.) "Where did Fukuzawa's early universalism come from? I am inclined to answer that the source was Chu Hsi Confucianism, or better, the late Tokugawa blend of Neo-Confucianism and Dutch learning. Fukuzawa appears to have moved from a relatively open position within the Tokugawa tradition to that of nineteenth century British liberalism." (Ibid., p. 145.) As for the coinage of the term *bankoku kōhō,* see Osatake Takeshi's fascinating tracing of its importation from the Chinese in *Kinsei Nihon no kokusai kannen no hattatsu,* chap. 3, pp. 26–50.

55. Tōyama, *Fukuzawa Yukichi,* pp. 183–197, 225–240.

56. A great number of his newspaper articles repeat this theme. To take two more, "Chōsen no dokuritsu" (The independence of Korea) and "Tadachini Pekin o tsukubeshi" (Attack Peking at once). As for Fukuzawa's stand on the Sino-Japanese War, see Tōyama, Hattori Shisō, Ienaga, and Shikano.

57. Joseph Heco, *The Narrative of a Japanese.* See also Chikamori Haruyoshi, *Joseph Heco.*

58. George M. Brooke, Jr., "John Mercer Brooke: A Biographical Sketch," *SS,* 5:133–137.

59. Fukuchi Gen'ichirō, "Iwase Higo-no-Kami," in *Bakumatsu seijika,* pp. 374–381; Kurimoto Joun, *Hōan jusshu,* pp. 313–317; Shimane Kiyoshi, "Bakumatsu gaikō no suishinsha Iwase Tadanari o chūshin to shite," *Meiji no gunzō,* 1:69–102.

60. Fukuchi Gen'ichirō, *Bakufu suibō ron,* p. 60.

61. W. E. Griffis, *Townsend Harris,* and Sakata Seiichi, *Harris.* Carl Crow's *He*

Opened the Door of Japan is thoroughly undocumented and offers nothing new.

62. A popular account of the 1862 Embassy is given in Haga Tōru's *Taikun no shisetsu*. Some of the travelogues by the members of this mission are in *KSNS*, 2, 3. See also Fukuchi Gen'ichirō, *Kaiō jidan;* Tanabe Taichi, *Bakumatsu gaikō dan;* and Fukuzawa Yukichi, *Fukuō jiden.*

63. *Eikoku tansaku (The report on England),* transcribed by Fukuda Sakutarō, written by Fukuzawa and other Western experts, is collected in *Seiyō kenbun shū,* pp. 477–544. Matsuzawa Hiroaki's comments on this report (pp. 579–598) are very helpful.

64. See Matsuzawa's comments in *Seiyō kenbun shū,* pp. 579–598.

65. For the accounts of the later Tokugawa embassies, see Numata Jirō, "Bakumatsu no kengai shisetsu ni tsuite," *Seiyō kenbun shū,* pp. 601–620: also, numerous and often redundant studies of the Tokugawa embassies by Osatake Takeshi (*Iteki no kuni e,* e.g., is identical with *Bakumatsu kengai shisetsu monogatari*). See also Ōtsuka Takematsu, *Bakumatsu gaikō-shi no kenkyū,* and Ishii Takashi, *Meiji ishin no kokusai-teki kankyō.* There is a pamphlet devoted to this mission: Kishi Kashirō, *Ikeda Chikugo-no-Kami Nagaoki to Pari.*

66. Ishizuki Minoru, *Kindai Nihon no kaigai ryūgaku-shi,* pp. 12–25. My debt to this detailed study of the Japanese students abroad around this time is quite obvious. I also consulted Ogata Hiroyasu's *Seiyō kyōiku inyū no hōto.*

67. Ishizuki Minoru, *Kindai Nihon no kaigai ryūgaku-shi,* chap. 2, pp. 28–59.

68. For a study of Niijima Jō, see Irwin Scheiner, *Christian Converts and Social Protest in Meiji Japan,* pp. 127–155.

69. Ishizuki, *Kindai Nihon no kaigai ryūgaku-shi,* pp. 103–106.

70. Ibid., pp. 62–66.

71. Ibid., pp. 148–153. Special encouragement was given, for instance, to the peers to go abroad in 1870 in the name of the Prime Minister *(Dajōkan).* Ogata Hiroyasu, *Seiyō kyōiku inyū no hōto,* pp. 38–39.

72. Ishizuki, *Kindai Nihon no kaigai ryūgaku-shi,* p. 154.

73. Shigehisa Tokutarō, *Kyōiku, shūkyō. Oyatoi gaikokujin,* gives a convenient survey of the foreign teachers and advisors.

74. Ishizuki, *Kindai Nihon no kaigai ryūgaku-shi,* pp. 195–196.

75. Ibid., pp. 155–158.

76. Ibid., pp. 198–202.

77. The official record of the Iwakura Embassy was published in 1878 under the title *Tokumei zenken taishi Bei-Ō kairan jikki,* ed. Kume Kunitake. The document is a compilation of various individual records, thus more impersonal and public than those left by the members of the 1860 Embassy. Their comments on the United States, at the same time, are not unlike those in most 1860 Embassy records: they are as racist and anti-feminist, e.g. Kume Kunitake's own reminiscences of the travel are contained in vol. 2 of *Kume Hakase kyūjūnen kaikoroku.* There is a recent book-length study of this Embassy: Ōkubo Toshikane, ed., *Iwakura shisetsu no kenkyū.* Concise accounts are to be found in Tanaka Akira, *Meiji ishin. Nihon no rekishi,* 24:194–231; Nagai Hideo, "Tōitsu kokka no seiritsu," *Iwanami kōza: Nihon rekishi,* [2nd ser.], 14:121–133; Katō Shūichi, "Nihon-jin no sekaizō," *Sekai no naka no Nihon,* pp. 225–282; Marlene Mayo, "The Iwakura Mission to the United States and Europe" and "Rationality in the Meiji Restoration"; Eugene Soviak, "On the Nature of Western Progress."

78. At the same time, the Embassy was not authorized to conclude anything. Mayo, "Rationality in the Meiji Restoration," p. 358.

79. Inoue Kiyoshi, *Meiji ishin. Nihon no rekishi,* p. 290.

80. Quoted by Marius Jansen, "Modernization and Foreign Policy in Meiji Japan," p. 153.

81. Inoue Kiyoshi asserts that the Iwakura Embassy did not visit any of the Western parliamentary organizations such as the U.S. Congress (*Meiji ishin,* p. 289), but that is, of course, untrue. At the same time, the Embassy was, as Inoue maintains, more and more impressed by the great power invested in the government in every country they visited. The Meiji leaders began during the trip to become firmly convinced of the need to consolidate, rather than disperse, power of the central government.

82. The best collection of the travel reports published in the early Meiji years (before 1890) is vol. 16 (*Gaikoku bunka hen*) of the *Meiji bunka zenshū,* ed. Yoshino Sakuzō.

Epilogue

1. Dean MacCannell, *The Tourist,* p. 9.

2. These figures were made available by the Japan National Tourist Organization in San Francisco.

3. "Japanese mass tourism has continued the travelogue tradition and has produced a vast quantity of travel literature. There always seems to be a market for travelogues, even those with an amateurish style. According to the *Japanese Publishers Yearbook,* 2,300 travelogues were published in Japan between 1950 and 1970. Most dealt with trips to Europe; only 250 concerned the United States. Thus, even though nearly a third of the passports issued in Japan have been for travel to the United States, the proportion of travelogues about that country has been relatively low." Katō Hidetoshi, "America as Seen by Japanese Travelers," p. 196.

4. The most incisive treatment of change and tradition in modern Japan is Robert N. Bellah's "Continuity and Change in Japanese Society."

Bibliography

I. Works by the Members of the Embassy
(Including the Kanrin Maru Escort Group)

1. Collections

Nichi-Bei Shūkō Tsūshō Hyakunen Kinen Gyōji Uneikai, comp. *Man'en gannen ken-Bei shisetsu shiryō shūsei.* 7 vols. Tokyo: Kazama Shobō, 1961. Referred to throughout as *SS.*

Ōtsuka Takematsu, ed. *Kengai shisetsu nikki sanshū.* 3 vols. Tokyo: Nihon Shiseki Kyōkai, 1928. Referred to throughout as *KSNS.*

2. Individual Works

Akamatsu Daisaburō. *Amerika yuki kōkai nikki.* 3 vols. In *SS,* 4.

Anon. *Amerika tokai nikki.* Ed. Yoshida Tsunekichi. In *Yashidai ishin shiryō sōsho,* 8. Tokyo: Tokyo Daigaku Shuppankai, 1972.

Anon. *Seishi suiro-ki.* 8 sheets. Maps and brief comment. Published in 1860. The Keio Gijuku Daigaku Bungakubu Shigakka.

Fukushima Keisaburō Yoshikoto. *Kaki kōkai nisshi.* 3 vols. In *SS,* 3.

Fukuzawa Yukichi. *Fukuō jiden.* Tokyo: Iwanami Shoten, 1954.

———. *Fukuzawa Yukichi zenshū.* 21 vols. Tokyo: Iwanami Shoten, 1958–1964.

———. *Autobiography.* Trans. Eiichi Kiyooka. New York: Columbia University Press, 1966.

———. *An Encouragement of Learning.* Trans. David A. Dilworth and Umeyo Hirano. Tokyo: Sophia University Press, 1969.

———. *An Outline of a Theory of Civilization.* Trans. David A. Dilworth and G. Cameron Hurst. Tokyo: Sophia University Press, 1973.

———. *The Speeches of Fukuzawa.* Trans. Wayne H. Oxford. Tokyo: Hokuseidō, 1973.

Hidaka Keisaburō Tameyoshi. *Bei-kō nisshi.* In *SS,* 2.

Hirose Kakuzō Hōan Kaneaki. *Kankai kōro nikki.* 2 vols. Ed. Hirose Ikkō and Aishin. Edo: Suharaya Mohei, 1862.

Ishikawa Masatarō. *Amerika kihan nikki.* In *SS,* 4.

———. *Nikki.* In *SS,* 4.

Kahachi. *Ikoku no koto no ha.* In *SS,* 4.

Katō Somō. *Futayo gatari.* Ed. Mizuno Masanobu in 1861. 2 vols. In *SS,* 3.

Katsu Awa-no-Kami Rintarō (Kaishū). *Hikawa seiwa.* in *Katsu Kaishū zenshū,* 14, ed. Etō Jun et al. Tokyo: Keisō Shobō, 1970.

———. *Kanrin-kan Beikoku tokō.* 3 vols. In *Katsu Kaishū zenshū,* 12, ed. Etō Jun et al. Tokyo: Keisō Shobō, 1971.

———. *Kaishū zadan.* Ed. Iwamoto Yoshiharu. In *Katsu Kaishū zenshū,* 11, ed. Katsube Mitake et al. Tokyo: Keisō Shobō, 1975.

Kimura Settsu-no-Kami Kaishū Yoshitake. *Hōshi Meriken kikō.* In *SS,* 4.

———. *Sanjū-nen-shi.* Introduction by Fukuzawa Yukichi. Tokyo: Kimura Shunkichi, 1892.

———. *Nikki.* Ed. Nakai Nobuhiko and Kawakita Nobuo. Tokyo: Hanawa Shobō, 1977.

Kimura Tetsuta. *Kō-Bei-ki.* 6 vols. Ed. Matsumoto Masaaki. (Includes "Atsumegusa" and "A-Boku Kimura Tetsuta kikitorisho.") Kumamoto: Seichōsha, 1974.

Kosugi Masanoshin. "Akoku jōge sonohoka nikki narabini sōmoku shashin." 2 vols. Manuscript. Kokkai Toshokan.

KSNS. see Ōtsuka Takematsu, ed. *Kengai shisetsu nikki sanshū.*

Masuzu Shunjirō Hisatoshi. *A-kō kōkai nikki.* 3 vols. In *SS,* 2.

———. *Ō-kō-ki.* 5 vols. In *KSNS,* 3.

Morita Kiyoyuki. *A-kō nikki.* 6 vols. In *SS,* 1.

———. *Mudai tehikae.* In *SS,* 1.

———. *Shutsu-nyū bo.* In *SS,* 1.

Morita Kiyoyuki, ed. Various documents related to the 1860 Embassy. In *SS,* 1.

Muragaki Awaji-no-Kami Norimasa. *Kōmu nikki.* 5 vols. *Bakumatsu gaikō kankei monjo (BGKM),* supp., 2–6. Tokyo: Tokyo Daigaku Shiryō Hensanjo, 1917–1967.

———. *Ken-Bei-shi nikki.* In *KSNS,* 1. Available also as: (1) *Kōkai nikki.* Ed. Yoshida Tsunekichi. In *Nichi-Bei ryōkoku kankeishi,* II. Tokyo: Jijitsūshinsha, 1959. (2) *Man'en gannen daiichi ken-Bei shisetsu nikki.* Ed. Shibama Chikakichi. Tokyo: Nichibei Kyōkai, 1918.

———. *The First Japanese Embassy to the United States of America.* Ed. Shibama Chikakichi; trans. Miyoshi Shigehiko. Tokyo: Nichibei Kyōkai, 1920.

———. *Kōkai nikki: The Diary of the First Japanese Embassy to the United States of America.* Trans. Helen M. Uno. Tokyo: Foreign Affairs Association of Japan, 1958.

Murayama Hakugen. *Hōshi nichiroku.* In *SS,* 2.

Nagao Kōsaku. *A-kō kiroku.* In *SS,* 4.

———. *A-kō nikki, kō-moku kai-ji.* In *SS,* 4.

Namura Motonori. *A-kō nikki.* In *SS,* 2.

Naruse Zenshirō Masanori (or Osakabe Tetsutarō Masayoshi). "Akoku kōkai nikki." Manuscript, transcr. Fukuda Sakutarō. Tokyo Daigaku Shiryō Hensanjo.

Nonomura Tadazane. *Kōkai nichiroku.* 3 vols. In *SS,* 3.

Ono Tomogorō. *Kanrin Maru kō-Bei nisshi.* In Fumikura Heijirō, *Bakumatsu gunkan Kanrin Maru.* Reprinted. Tokyo: Meicho Kankōkai, 1969.

Saitō Tomezō. *A-kō shinsho.* In *SS,* 4.

Sano Kanae. *Man'en gannen hō-Bei nikki.* Kanazawa: Kanazawa Bunka Kyōkai, 1946.

Satō Hidenaga. *Bei-kō nikki.* In *KSNS,* 1.

Shimanouchi Einosuke Kanetaka. *Man'en gannen ken-Bei shisetsu Bei-kō nichiroku.* Kumamoto: Seichōsha, forthcoming.

Shimmi Buzen-no-Kami Masaoki. *A-kō-ei.* In *SS,* 2.

"Shimmi Buzen-no-Kami, Muragaki Awaji-no-Kami, Oguri Bungo-no-Kami, A-kō goyōdome." 6 vols. Huge unpublished memoranda. Tokyo Daigaku Shiryō Hensanjo.

SS. See Nichi-Bei Shūkō, *Man'en gannen* . . .

Suzufuji Yūjirō. "Kō-A nikki." Manuscript. Tokyo Daigaku Shiryō Hensanjo.

Tamamushi Sadayū Yasushige. *Kanbu tsūki.* 2 vols. Tokyo: Kokusho Kankōkai, 1913.

———. *Hazankiji.* Tokyo: Nihon Shiseki Kyōkai, 1918.

[———.] *Ihi nyūkō roku.* Ed. Ōtsuka Takematsu. 2 vols. Tokyo: Nihon Shiseki Kyōkai, 1930.

———. *Kō-Bei nichiroku.* 8 vols. Ed. Numata Jirō. In *Seiyō kenbun shū. Nihon shisō taikei,* 66, ed. Numata Jirō and Matsuzawa Hiroaki. Tokyo: Iwanami Shoten, 1974. Also available in: *Kō-Bei nichiroku,* with *Tamamushi Sadayū ryakuden.* Ed. Yamamoto Akira. Sendai, 1930.

Tateishi Tokujūrō. "Kyūbaku shisetsu Bei-kō kikō." Manuscript. Tokyo Daigaku Shiryō Hensanjo.

Yanagawa Kenzaburō Masakiyo. *The First Japanese Mission to America (1860): Being a Diary Kept by a Member of the Embassy.* Trans. Jun'ichi Fukuyama and Roderick H. Jackson, ed. M. G. Mori. New York: Frederick A. Stokes, 1938.

———. *Kōkai nikki.* In *KSNS,* 1.

Yoshioka Ryōdayū Yūhei. *A-kō nikki.* In *Yoshioka Ryōdayū shōden,* ed. Kojima Chōzō. Tokyo: Shūeisha, 1919.

II. Selected References

Abe Dōzan. *Kaigun no senkusha, Oguri Kōzukenosuke seiden.* Tokyo: Kaigun Yūshūkai, 1941.

Adams, Francis Ottiwell. *The History of Japan.* 2 vols. London: Henry S. King, 1874–1875.

Adams, Henry. *Letters of Henry Adams.* Ed. Worthington Chauncey Ford. 2 vols. Boston: Houghton Mifflin, 1930–1938.

Aida Kurakichi. "Fukuzawa sensei kankei bunken mokuroku kō." *Juku-shi,* March 1955–September 1962.

Aizu Wakamatsu-shi Shuppan Iinkai. *Gekidō suru Aizu.* In *Aizu Wakamatsu-shi,* 5. Aizu Wakamatsu, 1966.

Akiba Tomoemon and Okutani Shingorō. *Hokuyūki.* In Suzuki Tōzō, *Kinsei kikō bungei nōto.* Tokyo: Tokyodō Shuppan, 1974.

Alcock, Rutherford. *Elements of Japanese Grammar for the Use of Beginners.* Shanghai, 1861.

———. *The Capital of the Tycoon: A Narrative of a Three Years' Residence in Japan.* 2 vols. New York: Harper & Brothers, 1863.

Allen, J. F. "First Voyage to Japan." *Historical Collections of the Essex Institute* 2 (1860):166–169.

Andō Shōeki. [*Selected Works.*] Ed. Noguchi Takehiko. *Nihon no meicho,* 19. Tokyo: Chūōkōronsha, 1971.

Arai Hakuseki. *Nikki* (1693–1705). 2 vols. Dai Nihon Kokiroku. Comp. Tokyo Daigaku Shiryō Hensanjo. Tokyo: Iwanami Shoten, 1952–1953.

———. *Seiyō kibun* (1715–1725). Ed. Miyazaki Michio. Tokyo: Heibonsha, 1968.

Arakawa Hidetoshi, ed. *Kinsei hyōryūki shū.* Tokyo: Hōsei Daigaku Shuppankyoku, 1969.

Araki Ihei. *Nihon Eigo-gaku shoshi.* Tokyo: Sōgensha, 1931.

Arisaka Takamichi. *Nihon yōgaku-shi no kenkyū.* Osaka: Sōgensha, 1968.

Asao Naohiro. *Sakoku. Nihon no rekishi,* 17. Tokyo: Shōgakkan, 1975.

Ayuzawa Shintarō. *Hyōryū: sakoku jidai no kaigai hatten.* Tokyo: Shibundō, 1956.

Ayuzawa Shintarō and Ōkubo Toshikane, eds. *Sakoku jidai no Nihonjin no kaigai chishiki.* Tokyo: Kangensha, 1953.

Bakumatsu ishin gaikō shiryō shūsei. Ed. Ishin-shi Gakkai. 6 vols. Tokyo: Zaisei Keizai Gakkai, 1942–1944.

Barr, Patricia. *The Coming of the Barbarians: A Story of Western Settlement in Japan.* London and Melbourne: Macmillan, 1967.

Beard, Mary R. *The Force of Women in Japanese History.* Washington: Public Affairs Press, 1953. Trans. into the Japanese as *Nihon josei-shi* by Katō Shizue. Tokyo: Kawade Shobō, 1953.

Beasley, W. G. *Great Britain and the Opening of Japan.* London: Luzac, 1951.

———. *Select Documents on Japanese Foreign Policy: 1853–1868.* London, New York, Toronto: Oxford University Press, 1955.

———. *The Meiji Restoration.* Stanford: Stanford University Press, 1972.

———. *The Modern History of Japan,* 2nd ed. London: Weidenfeld & Nicolson, 1973.

Befu, Harumi. "Gift-Giving in a Modernizing Japan." In *Japanese Culture and Behavior: Selected Readings.* ed. Takie Sugiyama Lebra and William P. Lebra, pp. 208–221. Honolulu: University Press of Hawaii, 1974.

Bellah, Robert N. *Tokugawa Religion: The Values of Pre-Industrial Japan.* Glencoe: Free Press, 1957.

———. "Continuity and Change in Japanese Society." In *Stability and Social Change,* ed. Bernard Barber and Alex Inkeles, pp. 377–404. Boston: Little, Brown, 1971.

BGKM. See *Dai Nihon komonjo, bakumatsu gaikoku kankei monjo.*

BIGS. See Ishin-shi Gakkai. *Bakumatsu ishin gaikō shiryō shūsei.*

Bird, Isabella L. *Unbeaten Tracks in Japan.* 2 vols., 1880. Reprinted. Rutland and Tokyo: Charles E. Tuttle, 1973.

Bitō Masahide. *Nihon hōken shisō-shi kenkyū.* Tokyo: Aoki Shoten, 1961.

Black, John R. *Young Japan: Yokohama and Yedo.* 2 vols. London: Trubner, 1880.

Blacker, Carmen. *The Japanese Enlightenment: A Study of the Writings of Fukuzawa Yukichi.* Cambridge: Cambridge University Press, 1964.

Borton, Hugh. *Japan's Modern Century: From Perry to 1970,* 2nd ed. New York: Ronald Press, 1970.

Bridgman, Elijah Coleman. *Mirika gassei-koku shiryaku.* Singapore: Kenka Shoin, 1838.

Brooke, John Mercer. *Yokohama Journal* [and] *Kanrin Maru Journal.* Introduction by George M. Brooke. In *SS,* 5.

Brower, Robert H., and Earl Miner. *Japanese Court Poetry.* Stanford: Stanford University Press, 1961.

Brzezinski, Zbigniew. *The Fragile Blossom: Crisis and Change in Japan.* New York: Harper & Row, 1972.

Bush, Lewis. *77 Samurai: Japan's First Embassy to America, Based on the Book by Itsurō Hattori.* Tokyo: Kōdansha International, 1968.

[Busk, Mary Margaret.] *Manners and Customs of the Japanese in the Nineteenth Century: From the Accounts of Recent Dutch Residents in Japan, and from the German Work of Dr. PH. Fr. Von Siebold.* London: John Murray, 1841.

Chang, Richard T. *From Prejudice to Tolerance: A Study of the Japanese Image of the West, 1826–1864.* Tokyo: Sophia University Press, 1970.

Chikamori Haruyoshi. *Joseph Heco.* Tokyo: Yoshikawa Kōbunkan, 1963. *CJH.* See Townsend Harris. *The Complete Journal . . .*

Chomel, Noël. *Algemeen Huishoudelijk-, Natuur-, Zedekundig- en Konst-Woordenboek.* Revised and enlarged by J. A. de Chalmot et al. 16 vols. Leyden: J. le Mair, 1778–1793.

Chomsky, Noam. *American Power and the New Mandarins: Historical and Political Essays.* New York: Pantheon, 1967.

Christ, Carol T. *The Finer Optic: The Aesthetic of Particularity in Victorian Poetry.* New Haven: Yale University Press, 1975.

Clyde, Paul H., and Burton F. Beers. *The Far East: A History of the Western Impact and the Eastern Response, 1830–1965,* 4th ed. Englewood Cliffs, N.J.: Prentice-Hall, 1966.

Craig, Albert M. *Chōshū in the Meiji Restoration.* Cambridge: Harvard University Press, 1961.

———. "Science and Confucianism in Tokugawa Japan." In *Changing Japanese Attitudes toward Modernization,* ed. Marius B. Jansen, pp. 133–160. Princeton: Princeton University Press, 1965.

———. "Fukuzawa Yukichi: The Philosophical Foundations of Meiji Nationalism." In *Political Development in Modern Japan,* ed. Robert E. Ward, pp. 99–148. Princeton: Princeton University Press, 1968.

Crow, Carl. *He Opened the Door of Japan: Townsend Harris and the Story of His Amazing Adventures . . .* New York and London: Harper & Brothers, 1939.

Dai Nihon komonjo, bakumatsu gaikoku kankei monjo, 12–37. Tokyo: comp. and pub. Tokyo Daigaku Shiryō Hensanjo, 1920–1974. Referred to as *BGKM.*

Daily National Intelligencer. Washington, D.C.

Delano, Amasa. *A Narrative of Voyages and Travels . . .* Boston: E. G. House, 1817.

Despatches from the United States Ministers to Japan. File microcopies of records in the National Archives, no. 133. 3 rolls.

Dickins, F. V., and Stanley Lane-Poole. *The Life of Sir Harry Parkes.* 2 vols. London: Macmillan, 1894.

Doi Kōchi et al., eds. *Nihon no Ei-gaku hyaku-nen.* 4 vols. Tokyo: Kenkyūsha, 1968–1969.

Dōmon Tōji. *Shiden: Katsu Kaishū.* Tokyo: Tairiku Shobō, 1973.

Dore, Ronald P. *Education in Tokugawa Japan.* Berkeley and Los Angeles: University of California Press, 1965.

———. "The Legacy of Tokugawa Education." In *Changing Japanese Attitudes toward Modernization,* ed. Marius B. Jansen, pp. 99–132. Princeton: Princeton University Press, 1965.

Dulles, Foster Rhea. *America in the Pacific: A Century of Expansion,* 2nd ed. Boston and New York: Houghton Mifflin, 1938.

———. *Yankees and Samurai: America's Role in the Emergence of Modern Japan, 1791–1900.* New York: Harper & Row, 1965.

Earl, David Magarey. *Emperor and Nation in Japan.* Seattle: University of Washington Press, 1964.

Eliade, Mircea. *Patterns in Comparative Religion.* Trans. Rosemary Sheed. Cleveland and New York: World, 1963.

Etō Jun. *Kaishū yoha: Waga dokusho yoteki.* Tokyo: Bungei Shunjūsha, 1974.

Fish, Carl Russell. "James Buchanan," in *Dictionary of American Biography.*

Fonblanque, Edward Barrington de. *Niphon and Pe-che-li: Or, Two Years in Japan and Northern China,* 2nd ed. London: Saunders, Otley, 1863.

Foote, Andrew H. "A Visit to Simoda and Hakodadi in Japan." *Journal of the Shanghai Literary and Scientific Society* 1 (June 1858).

Fortune, Robert. *Yedo and Peking: A Narrative of a Journey to the Capitals of Japan and China*. London: John Murray, 1963.

Frank Leslie's Illustrated Newspaper. New York.

Fujiwara Ainosuke. *Sendai Boshin-shi*. Sendai, 1911.

Fukuchi Gen'ichirō (Ōchi). *Fukuchi Ōchi shū*. Ed. Yanagida Izumi. *Meiji bungaku zenshū*, 11. Tokyo: Chikuma Shobō, 1966.

———. *Bakufu suibō ron* (1891–1892). Ed. Ishizuka Hiromichi. Tokyo: Heibonsha, 1967.

———. *Kaiō jidan* (1892) [and] *Bakumatsu seijika* (1896–1897). *Bakumatsu ishin shiryō sōsho*, 8. Tokyo: Jinbutsu Ōraisha, 1968.

Fukuda Kiyohito, ed. *Meiji kikō bungaku shū*. *Meiji bungaku zenshū*, 94. Tokyo: Chikuma Shobō, 1974.

Fukuda Sakutarō, comp. *Eikoku tansaku*. Ed. Matsuzawa Hiroaki. In *Seiyō kenbun shū*. *Nihon shisō taikei*, 66, ed. Numata Jirō and Matsuzawa Hiroaki. Tokyo: Iwanami Shoten, 1974.

Fumikura Heijirō. *Bakumatsu gunkan Kanrin Maru*. Reprinted. Tokyo: Meicho Kankōkai, 1969.

Gi Gen (Wei Yüan). *Kaikoku zushi [Hai-kuo t'uchi]*. 60 vols. Yōshū: Kokidō, 1847.

Golownin, Captain Wassly Michaelovitsch. *Memoirs of a Captivity in Japan, during the Years 1811, 1812, and 1813: With Observations on the Country and the People*. 3 vols. London: Henry Colburn, 1824.

Goncharov, Ivan. *The Voyage of the Frigate Pallada*. Ed. and trans. N. W. Wilson. London: Folio Society, 1965.

Gragg, William F. *A Cruise in the U.S. Steam Frigate Mississippi . . . to China and Japan from July 1857 to February 1860*. Boston: Damrell & Moore, 1960.

Griffis, William Elliot. *The Mikado's Empire*, 2nd ed. New York: Harper & Brothers, 1895.

———. *Townsend Harris: First American Envoy in Japan*. Boston and New York: Houghton Mifflin, 1895.

Gubbins, J. H. *The Progress of Japan, 1853–1871*. Oxford: Clarendon, 1911.

Haga Tōru. *Taikun no shisetsu*. Tokyo: Chūōkōronsha, 1968.

Hall, John W., and Marius B. Jansen, eds. *Studies in the Institutional History of Early Modern Japan*. Princeton: Princeton University Press, 1968.

Hani Gorō. *Hakuseki; Yukichi*. Tokyo: Iwanami Shoten, 1937.

Hanzawa Hiroshi. "Hi-baku hi-Satchō no mezashita mono: Tamamushi Sadayū." In *Kaikoku no kurushimi*, ed. Ichii Saburō, pp. 153–179. *Meiji no gunzō*, 1. Tokyo: San'ichi Shobō, 1969.

Haraguchi Kiyoshi. *Boshin sensō*. Tokyo: Hanawa Shobō, 1963.

Harootunian, H. D. *Toward Restoration: The Growth of Political Consciousness in Tokugawa Japan*. Berkeley and Los Angeles: University of California Press, 1970.

Harper's Weekly. New York.

Harris, Townsend. *The Complete Journal of Townsend Harris*. Ed. Mario Emilio Cosenza. New York: Doubleday, Doran, 1930. Referred to as *CJH*.

———. *Some Unpublished Letters of Townsend Harris*. Ed. Shio Sakanishi. New York: Japan Reference Library, 1941.

———. Commonplace book. 1 ms. file. Rare Books Room, City College, City University of New York.

———. Letters and Papers. 2 ms. vols. Rare Books Room, City College, City University of New York.

———. Private letter books. 5 ms. vols. Rare Books Room, City College, City University of New York.

Hashikawa Bunzō and Matsumoto Sannosuke, eds. *Kindai Nihon seiji shisō-shi*, 1. *Kindai Nihon shisō-shi taikei*, 3. Tokyo: Yūhikaku, 1971.

Hattori Itsurō. *77-nin no samurai Amerika ni yuku: Man'en gannen ken-Bei shisetsu no kiroku*. Tokyo: Kōdansha, 1974.

Hattori Shisō. "Bunmei kaika." In *Meiji no shisō*, pp. 165–185. *Hattori Shisō chosaku shū*, 6. Tokyo: Rironsha, 1955.

———. "Fukuzawa Yukichi." In *Meiji no shisō*, pp. 187–205. *Hattori Shisō chosaku shū*, 6. Tokyo: Rironsha, 1955.

———. "Zettai shugi to Fukuzawa Yukichi." *Hattori Shisō zenshū*, 10:309–326. Tokyo: Fukumura Shuppan, 1974.

Hawks, Francis L. *Narrative of the Expedition of an American Squadron to the China Seas and Japan: Performed in the Years 1852, 1853, and 1854, under the Command of Commodore M. C. Perry, United States Navy*. 3 vols. Washington, D.C.: A. O. P. Nicholson, 1856.

Hawthorne, Nathaniel. *Notes of Travel*, 1. *The Complete Writings of Nathaniel Hawthorne*, 19. Boston: Houghton Mifflin, 1900.

Hayashi Daigaku-no-Kami Fukusai. "Dairy of an Official of the Bakufu." *Transactions of the Asiatic Society of Japan*, 2nd ser., 7 (1930):98–119.

Heco, Joseph. *The Narrative of a Japanese*. 2 vols. Ed. James Murdoch. San Francisco: Japanese Publishing Association, 1950.

———. Draft of *The Narrative of a Japanese*. Tenri University Library.

———. *Hikozō hyōryū-ki*. In *Kinsei hyōryū-ki shū*, ed. Arakawa Hidetoshi, pp. 233–283. Tokyo: Hōsei Daigaku Shuppankyoku, 1969.

———. *Kaigai shinbun*. Comp. Joseph Heco Kinenkai, Waseda University. Tokyo: Waseda Daigaku Shuppanbu, 1977.

Henderson, Philip. *The Life of Laurence Oliphant, Traveller, Diplomat, and Mystic*. London: Robert Hale, 1956.

Heusken, Henry. *Japan Journal, 1855–1861*. Trans. and ed. Jeanette C. Van der Corput and Robert A. Wilson. New Brunswick: Rutgers University Press, 1964. Referred to as *JJ*.

Hibata Setsuko. *Kōtsū fūzoku. Nihon fūzoku-shi kōza*, 11. Tokyo: Yūzankaku, 1929.

———. *Edo jidai no kōtsū bunka*. Tokyo: Tōkō Shōin, 1931.

———. *Nihon kōtsū-shi wa*. Tokyo: Yūzankaku, 1937.

Hildreth, Richard. *Japan and the Japanese*. Boston: Bradley, Dayton, 1860. (Originally published as *Japan as It Was and Is*.)

Hirakawa Sukehiro. *Wakon yōsai no keifu: Uchi to soto kara no Meiji Nihon*. Tokyo: Kawade Shobō Shinsha, 1971.

Hirao Michio. *Boshin sensō-shi*. Tokyo: Misaki Shobō, 1971.

Hisamatsu Sen'ichi et al., eds. *Nihon no tabibito, hyaku-ichi-nin. Kokubungaku: Kaishaku to kyōzai no kenkyū* 20 (November supp. 1975). Tokyo: Gakutōsha.

Hodgson, C. Pemberton. *A Residence at Nagasaki and Hakodate in 1859–60*. London: Richard Bentley, 1861.

Honda Toshiaki and Kaiho Seiryō. [*Selected Works.*] Ed. Tsukatani Akihiro et al. *Nihon shisō taikei*, 44. Tokyo: Iwanami Shoten, 1970.

Ibuse Masuji. *Jon Manjirō hyōryū-ki. Zenshū*, 2. Tokyo: Chikuma Shobō, 1974.

Ichii Saburō, ed. *Kaikoku no kurushimi. Meiji no gunzō*, 1. Tokyo: San'ichi Shobō, 1969.

Ienaga Saburō. *Gairai bunka sesshu-shi ron*. Tokyo: Iwasaki Shoten, 1948.

———. "Fukuzawa Yukichi no kaikyū ishiki." In *Kindai seishin to sono genkai*. Tokyo: Kadokawa Shoten, 1952.

———. "Fukuzawa seishin no rekishi-teki hatten: Fukuzawa to Min'yūsha tono shisō-teki renkan." In *Nihon kindai shisō-shi kenkyū*. Tokyo: Tokyo Daigaku Shuppankai, 1953.

———. " 'Fuku-ō hyakuwa'. . . kō." In *Nihon kindai shisō-shi kenkyū*. Tokyo: Tokyo Daigaku Shuppankai, 1953.

Ikeda Kikan. *Nikki waka bungaku*. Tokyo: Shibundō, 1968.

Illustrated London News.

Imai Hiromichi et al. *Takahashi Ryūzō sensei kiju kinen ron shū: Kokiroku no kenkyū*. Tokyo: Zoku Gunsho Ruijū Kanzenkai, 1970.

Imai Usaburō et al., eds. *Mito gaku. Nihon shisō taikei*, 53. Tokyo: Iwanami Shoten, 1973.

Imoto Nōichi, ed. *Hyōhaku no tamashii. Bashō no hon*, 6. Tokyo: Kadokawa Shoten, 1970.

Inoue Kiyoshi. *Nihon josei-shi*. Tokyo: San'ichi Shobō, 1949.

———. *Meiji ishin. Nihon no rekishi*, 20. Tokyo: Chūōkōronsha, 1966.

Inoue Tadashi. *Kaibara Ekken*. Tokyo: Yoshikawa Kōbunkan, 1963.

Iriye, Akira. *Across the Pacific: An Inner History of American-East Asian Relations*. New York: Harcourt, Brace & World, 1967.

Iriye, Akira, ed. *Mutual Images*. Cambridge: Harvard University Press, 1975.

Ishii Kendō, ed. *Hyōryū kidan zenshū*. Tokyo: Hakubunkan, 1900.

———. *Ikoku hyōryū kitan shū*. Tokyo: Fukunaga Shoten, 1927.

Ishii Takashi. *Bakumatsu ishin no gaikō. Shinkō dai-Nihon-shi*, 9. Tokyo: Yūzankaku, 1941.

———. *Meiji ishin no butai ura*. Tokyo: Iwanami Shoten, 1960.

———. *Gakusetsu hihan, Meiji ishin ron*. Tokyo: Yoshikawa Kōbunkan, 1961.

———. *Nihon kaikoku-shi*. Tokyo: Yoshikawa Kōbunkan, 1972.

———. *Meiji ishin no kokusai-teki kankyō*, 3rd rev. ed. 3 vols. Tokyo: Yoshikawa Kōbunkan, 1973.

———. *Katsu Kaishū*. Tokyo: Yoshikawa Kōbunkan, 1974.

Ishikawa Mikiaki. *Fukuzawa Yukichi den*. 4 vols. Tokyo: Iwanami Shoten, 1932.

Ishin-shi. Comp. Ishin Shiryō Hensan Jimukyoku, Mombushō. 6 vols. Tokyo: Meiji Shoin, 1939–1941.

Ishin-shi Gakkai. *Bakumatsu ishin gaikō shiryō shūsei*. Ed. Maruyama Kunio. 6 vols. Tokyo: Zaisei Keizai Gakkai, 1942–1944. (Referred to as *BIGS*.)

Ishizuki Minoru. *Kindai Nihon no kaigai ryūgaku-shi*. Tokyo: Mineruba Shobō, 1972.

Itō Masao. *Fukuzawa Yukichi ronkō*. Tokyo: Yoshikawa Kōbunkan, 1969.

Iwanami kōza: Nihon rekishi. [1st ser.] 13. *Kinsei*, 5. Edited by Yagi Haruo et al. Tokyo: Iwanami Shoten, 1964.

Iwanami kōza: Nihon rekishi. [1st ser.] 14. *Kindai*, 1. Edited by Tōyama Shigeki et al. Tokyo: Iwanami Shoten, 1962.

Iwanami kōza: Nihon rekishi. [2nd ser.] 14. *Kindai*, 1. Edited by Ōishi Kaichirō et al. Tokyo: Iwanami Shoten, 1975.

Iwao Shigeichi. *Shuinsen bōeki-shi no kenkyū*. Tokyo: Kōbunkan, 1958.

———. *Sakoku. Nihon no rekishi*, 14. Tokyo: Chūōkōronsha, 1966.

Jansen, Marius B. *Sakamoto Ryōma and the Meiji Restoration*. Princeton: Princeton University Press, 1961.

———. "Modernization and Foreign Policy in Meiji Japan." In *Political Development in Modern Japan*, ed. Robert E. Ward. Princeton: Princeton University Press, 1968.

Jephson, R., and E. Elmhirst. *Our Life in Japan*. London, 1869.

JJ. See Henry Heusken. *Japan Journal*.

Jo Kei-ban. *Ei kan shiryaku*. 5 vols. Ed. Inoue Shun'yō et al. Edo, 1861.

Johnston, James D. *China and Japan: Being a Narrative of the Cruise . . . in the*

Years 1857, '58, '59, and '60. Philadelphia: Charles Desilver; Baltimore: Cushings & Bailey, 1860.

Kaibara Ekken. *Zenshū.* Ed. Ekken-kai. Vol. 7. Tokyo: Ekken Zenshū Kankōbu, 1911.

Kaikoku Hyakunen Kinen Bunka Jigyō-kai, *Sakoku jidai Nihonjin no kaigai chishiki.* Ed. Ayuzawa Shintarō and Ōkubo Toshikane. Tokyo: Kangensha, 1953.

Kamei Shunsuke, ed. *Nihon to Amerika: hikaku bunka ron,* 1. Tokyo: Nan'undō, 1973.

Kamei Takayoshi. *Daikokuya Kōdayū.* Tokyo: Yoshikawa Kōbunkan, 1964.

———. *Kōdayū no hiren.* Tokyo: Yoshikawa Kōbunkan, 1967.

Kamikawa Hikomatsu, ed. *Nichi-Bei bunka kōshō-shi,* 1. *Sōsetsu, gaikō.* Tokyo: Yōyōsha, 1956.

Kämpfer, Engelbert. *The History of Japan.* Trans. J. G. Scheuchzer. 3 vols., repr. New York: AMS Press, 1971.

Kanai Madoka. "Tommy to yū na no Nihon-jin." *Kokusai bunka,* no. 100 (October 1962), pp. 9–11, and no. 101 (November 1962), pp. 16–19.

———. "Suzufuji Chikō to Kanrin Maru nankō-zu." *Kokusai bunka,* no. 102 (December 1962), pp. 6–8.

———. "Shoki ni okeru Amerika bunka no shōgeki." In *Nihon to Amerika: hikaku bunka ron,* 1. Ed. Kamei Shunsuke. Tokyo: Nan'undō, 1973.

Kaneko Hisakazu. *Manjirō: The Man Who Discovered America.* Boston: Houghton Mifflin, 1956.

Katagiri Kazuo. *Sugita Genpaku.* Tokyo: Yoshikawa Kōbunkan, 1971.

Kato Hidetoshi. "America as Seen by Japanese Travelers." In *Mutual Images,* ed. Akira Iriye. Cambridge: Harvard University Press, 1975.

Katō Shūichi. "Nihon-jin no sekaizō." In *Sekai no naka no Nihon. Kindai Nihon shisō-shi kōza,* 8. Ed. Takeuchi Yoshi and Karaki Junzō. Tokyo: Chikuma Shobō, 1961.

Katsu Kokichi. *Musui dokugen.* Ed. Katsube Mitake. Tokyo: Kadokawa Shoten, 1974.

Kawai Koume. *Nikki [1849–1861].* 3 vols. Ed. Shiga Yasuharu and Murata Shizuko. Tokyo: Heibonsha, 1974.

Kawaji Toshiakira. *Nagasaki nikki, Shimoda nikki.* Ed. Fujii Sadabumi and Kawada Sadao. Tokyo: Heibonsha, 1968.

Kawakami Tetsutarō. *Yoshida Shōin: Bu to ju ni yoru ningenzō.* Tokyo: Bungei-Shunjūsha, 1969.

Kawakita Nobuo. "Kaidai." In *SS,* 1.

Keene, Donald. *The Japanese Discovery of Europe: 1720–1830,* rev. ed. Stanford: Stanford University Press, 1969.

Kikuchi Katsunosuke. *Sendai boshin monogatari.* Sendai: Miyagi-ken Jinja-chō, 1968.

Kimura Motoi. *Kakyū bushi ron.* Tokyo: Hanawa Shobō, 1967.

Kimura Tsuyoshi, ed. *Nichi-Bei bunka kōshō-shi,* 4. *Gakugei, fūzoku.* Tokyo: Yōyōsha, 1955.

Kipling, Rudyard. *From Sea to Sea: Letters of Travel,* pt. 1. *The Writings in Prose and Verse of Rudyard Kipling,* 15. New York: Charles Scribner's Sons, 1909.

Kishi Kashirō. *Ikeda Chikugo-no-Kami Nagaoki to Pari.* Okayama: Okayama UNESCO Kyōkai, 1975.

Kiyokawa Hachirō. *Saiyūsō* (1855). Ed. Koyamamatsu Katsuichirō. Tokyo: Heibonsha, 1969.

Koga Jūjirō. *Nagasaki yōgaku-shi.* 2 vols. Nagasaki: Hakueisha, 1966.

Kojima Chōzō. *Yoshida Ryōdayū shōden.* Tokyo: Shūeisha, 1919.

Konishi Shirō. "Hidaka Tameyoshi no *Bei-kō nisshi* ni tsuite." In *SS,* 2.
——. *Kaikoku to jōi. Nihon no rekishi,* 19. Tokyo: Chūōkōronsha, 1966.
——. "Namura Motonori no *A-kō nikki* ni tsuite." In *SS,* 2.
Konishi Shirō, ed. *Meiji ishin. Shin-Nihon shi taikei,* 5. Tokyo: Asakura Shoten, 1952.
KSNS. See Ōtsuka Takematsu, ed. *Kengai shisetsu nikki sanshū.*
Kumazawa Banzan. *Joshi-kun.* In *Zenshū,* 2. Ed. Masamune Atsuo. Tokyo: Ogawa Tetsunosuke, 1941.
——. [*Selected Works.*] Ed. Gotō Yōichi et al. *Nihon shisō taikei,* 30. Tokyo: Iwanami Shoten, 1971.
Kumazawa Banzan [and Nakae Tōju]. [*Selected Works.*] Ed. Itō Tasaburō. *Nihon no meicho,* 11. Tokyo: Chūōkōronsha, 1976.
Kume Kunitake. *Tokumei zenken taishi Bei-Ō kairan jikki.* 5 vols. Tokyo: Hakubunsha, 1878.
——. *Kume Hakase kyūjūnen kaikoroku.* 2 vols. Tokyo: Waseda Daigaku Shuppanbu, 1934.
Kumura Toshio. *Yoshida Shōin no shisō to kyōiku.* Tokyo: Iwanami Shoten, 1942.
Kurata Kurakichi. "Hōshi Meriken kikō." In *SS,* 4.
Kure Shūzō. *Shīboruto [Siebold] sensei: sono shōgai oyobi kōgyō.* 3 vols. Ed. Iwao Seiichi. Tokyo: Heibonsha, 1967–1968.
——. *Mizukuri Gempo.* 1914. Reprinted, Kyoto: Onbunkaku, 1971.
Kurimoto, Joun. *Hōan jusshu* (1892). In *Narushima Ryūhoku, Hattori Nadematsu, Kurimoto Joun. Meiji bungaku zenshū,* 4. Tokyo: Chikuma Shobō, 1969.
Kuroda, S.-Y. "Where Epistemology, Style, and Grammar Meet: A Case Study from Japanese." In *A Festschrift for Morris Halle,* Ed. Stephen R. Anderson and Paul Kiparsky. New York: Holt, Rinehart & Winston, 1973.
——. "Reflections on the Foundations of Narrative Theory." In *Pragmatics of Language and Literature,* ed. Teun A. van Dijk. North Holland Publishing, 1976.
LaFarge, John. *An Artist's Letters from Japan.* New York: Century, 1903.
Lanman, Charles. *The Japanese in America* (1872). Reprinted in *Leaders of the Meiji Restoration in America,* ed. Y. Okamura. Tokyo: Hokuseidō Press, 1931.
Lensen, George Alexander. *The Russian Push Toward Japan: Russo-Japanese Relations, 1697–1875.* Princeton: Princeton University Press, 1959.
Levine, L. E. *Behind the Silken Curtain.* New York: Julian Massner, 1961.
Lewis, Charles Lee. *Admiral Franklin Buchanan: Fearless Man of Action.* Baltimore: Norman Remington, 1929.
Lewis, William S., and Murakami Naojirō. *Ranald MacDonald.* Spokane: Eastern Washington State Historical Society, 1923.
MacCannell, Dean. *The Tourist: A New Theory of the Leisure Class.* New York: Schocken, 1976.
MacFarlane, Charles. *Japan: An Account, Geographical and Historical.* London: George Routledge, 1852.
McCauley, Edward Yorke. *With Perry in Japan: The Diary of Edward Yorke McCauley.* Ed. Allan B. Cole. Princeton: Princeton University Press, 1942.
Maeda Ai. *Bakumatsu ishin-ki no bungaku.* Tokyo: Hōsei Daigaku Shuppankyoku, 1972.
[Maruyama Kunio.] *Ishin-shi.* 6 vols. Tokyo: Meiji Shoin, 1939–1941.
——. *Bakumatsu ishin gaikō shiryō shūsei.* 6 vols. Tokyo: Zaisei Keizai Gakkai, 1942–1944. (Referred to throughout as *BIGS.*)

Maruyama Masao. "Fukuzawa ni okeru jitsugaku no tenka." *Tōyō bunka kenkyū* 3 (1947).

———. "Nihon Fascism no shisō to undō." In *Sonjō shisō to zettai shugi. Tōyō bunka kōza,* 2. Comp. Tokyo Daigaku Tōyō Bunka Kenkyūjo. Tokyo: Hakujitsu Shoin, 1948.

———. "Kaidai." In *Fukuzawa Yukichi senshū,* 4. Tokyo: Iwanami Shoten, 1952.

———. *Nihon seiji shisō-shi kenkyū.* Tokyo: Tokyo Daigaku Shuppankai, 1952.

———. *Gendai seiji no shisō to kōdō,* 1. Tokyo: Miraisha, 1957.

———. *Nihon no shisō.* Tokyo: Iwanami Shoten, 1961.

———. *Thought and Behavior in Modern Japanese Politics.* Ed. Ivan Morris. London: Oxford University Press, 1963.

———. "Fukuzawa Yukichi no tetsugaku — toku ni sono jiji hihan tono kanren" (1951). Reprinted in *Kindai shugi. Nihon shisō taikei,* 34. Tokyo: Chikuma Shobō, 1964.

———. *Studies in the Intellectual History of Tokugawa Japan.* Trans. Mikiso Hane. Princeton: Princeton University Press, 1974.

Matsudaira Ietada. *Nikki* (1577–1594). 2 vols. *Zoku shiryō taisei,* 19–20. Comp. Zoku Shiryō Taisei Kankōkai. Kyoto: Rinsen Shoten, 1967.

Matsudaira Tarō. *Edo jidai seido no kenkyū* (1919). Ed. Shinji Yoshimoto. Tokyo: Kashiwa Shobō, 1964.

Matsumoto Sannosuke. "Kindai shisō no bōga." In *Kindai shisō no bōga. Gendai Nihon shisō taikei,* 1. Tokyo: Chikuma Shobō, 1966.

———. "Dentō to kindai no mondai: Amerika ni okeru Nihon-shi kenkyū o chūshin ni." *Iwanami kōza: Nihon rekishi* [2nd ser.], 24 (Bekkan 1). Tokyo: Iwanami Shoten, 1977.

Matsuura Rei. *Katsu Kaishū.* Tokyo: Chūōkōronsha, 1968.

———. *Yokoi Shōnan.* Tokyo: Asahi Shinbunsha, 1976.

Matsuzaki Kōdō. *Kōdō nichireki* (1823–1844). 6 vols. Ed. Yamada Taku. Tokyo: Heibonsha, 1970.

Matsuzawa Hiroaki. "Eikoku tansaku shimatsu." In *Seiyō kenbun shū. Nihon shisō taikei,* 66. Ed. Numata Jirō and Matsuzawa Hiroaki. Tokyo: Iwanami Shoten, 1974.

———. "Samazama na seiyō kenbun — 'ijō tansaku' kara 'yōkō' e." In *Seiyō kenbun shū. Nihon shisō taikei,* 66. Ed. Numata Jirō and Matsuzawa Hiroaki. Tokyo: Iwanami Shoten, 1974.

Mayo, Marlene. "The Iwakura Mission to the United States and Europe, 1871–1873." In *Researches in the Social Sciences on Japan,* 2. New York: Columbia University Press, 1959.

———. "Rationality in the Meiji Restoration: The Iwakura Embassy." In *Modern Japanese Leadership: Tradition and Change,* Ed. Bernard S. Silberman and H. D. Harootunian. Tucson: University of Arizona Press, 1966.

Meiji ishin-shi kenkyū kōza. Ed. Rekishigaku Kenkyūkai. 7 vols. Tokyo: Heibonsha, 1956–1969.

Miner, Earl. *Introduction to Japanese Court Poetry.* Stanford: Stanford University Press, 1968.

———. *Japanese Poetic Diaries.* Berkeley and Los Angeles: University of California Press, 1969.

Mitamura Engyo. *Goten jochū.* Tokyo: Shunyōdō, 1930.

Mitford, Algernon (Lord Redesdale). *Memories.* 2 vols. New York: E. P. Dutton, n.d.

Miura Baien. *Miura Baien shū. Dai Nihon shisō zenshū,* 8. Tokyo: Dai Nihon Shisō Zenshū Kankōkai, 1933.

———. *Miura Baien shū.* Ed. Saegusa Hiroto. Tokyo: Iwanami Shoten, 1955.

Miyazaki Michio. *Arai Hakuseki no yōgaku to kaigai chishiki.* Tokyo: Yoshikawa Kōbunkan, 1973.

Miyoshi, Masao. *Accomplices of Silence: The Modern Japanese Novel.* Berkeley and Los Angeles: University of California Press, 1974.

Mizukuri Gempo. *Gyokuseki shirin.* Reprinted in *Gaikoku bunka hen. Meiji bunka zenshū,* 16, ed. Yoshino Sakuzō. Tokyo: Nihon Hyōronsha, 1928.

Mizukuri Seigo. *Konyo zushiki.* Edo, 1845.

———. *Konyo zushiki ho.* Edo, 1846.

Mori Katsumi. *Ken-Tō-shi.* Tokyo: Shibundō, 1972.

Morison, Samuel Eliot. *"Old Bruin": Commodore Matthew C. Perry, 1794–1858.* Boston and Toronto: Little, Brown, 1967.

Morley, James William, ed. *Japan's Foreign Policy, 1868–1941: A Research Guide.* New York: Columbia University Press, 1974.

Morosawa Yōko. *Onna no rekishi.* 2 vols. Tokyo: Miraisha, 1970.

Morrow, Dr. James. *A Scientist with Perry in Japan: The Journal of Dr. James Morrow.* Ed. Allan B. Cole. Chapel Hill: University of North Carolina Press, 1947.

Morse, Edward Sylvester. *Japan Day by Day.* 2 vols. Boston: Houghton Mifflin, 1917.

Moss, Michael. *Seizure by the Japanese of Mr. Moss and His Treatment by the Consul-General.* London, 1863.

Motoori Norinaga. *Motoori Norinaga zenshū,* 16, 18. Ed. Ōno Susumu and Ōkubo Tadashi. Tokyo: Chikuma Shobō, 1974, 1973.

Murai Masuo. *Edojō: Shōgun-ke no seikatsu.* Tokyo: Chūōkōronsha, 1964.

Muramatsu Shikō (Roshū). *Kōshū sōwa.* Tokyo: Kenkōkaku, 1936.

Murayama Tamotsu. *Shūkō koto hajime. Nichi-Bei ryōkoku kankei-shi,* 1. Tokyo: Jiji Tsūshinsha, 1970.

Murray, Hugh. *The Encyclopaedia of Geography.* 3 vols. Philadelphia: Carey, Lea & Blanchard, 1837.

Mushakōji Minoru. "Boshin-eki no ichi-shiryō." *Shigaku zasshi* 61 (1952).

Nagai Hideo. "Tōitsu kokka no seiritsu." *Kindai,* 1. *Iwanami kōza: Nihon rekishi* [2nd ser.], 14. Tokyo: Iwanami Shoten, 1975.

———. *Jiyū minken. Nihon no rekishi,* 25. Tokyo: Shōgakkan, 1976.

Nagashima Konshirō and Ōta Takeo, eds. *Teihon: Edojō ō-oku* (1892). Reprint. Tokyo: Jimbutsu Ōraisha, 1968.

Najita, Tetsuo. "Ōshio Heihachirō." In *Personality in Japanese History,* ed. Albert M. Craig and Donald H. Shively. Berkeley and Los Angeles: University of California Press, 1970.

———. *Japan.* Englewood Cliffs, N.J.: Prentice-Hall, 1974.

———. "Intellectual Change in Early Eighteenth-Century Tokugawa Confucianism." *Journal of Asian Studies* 34 (1975).

Nakae Tōju. [*Selected Works.*] Ed. Yamai Yū et al. *Nihon shisō taikei,* 29. Tokyo: Iwanami Shoten, 1974.

[Nakae Tōju and] Kumazawa Banzan. [*Selected Works.*] Ed. Itō Tasaburō. *Nihon no meicho,* 11. Tokyo: Chūōkōronsha, 1976.

Nakagawa Kazuo. *Nihon josei-shi ron.* Tokyo: Dai Nihon Tosho Kabushiki Kaisha, 1926.

Nakahama Manjirō. *Manjirō hyōryū-ki.* Reprinted in *Kinsei hyōryūki shū,* ed. Arakawa Hidetoshi. Tokyo: Hōsei Daigaku Shuppankyoku, 1969.

Nakahama Tōichirō. *Nakahama Manjirō den.* Tokyo: Fuzanbō, 1936.

Nakane Yukie, ed. *Sakumu kiji.* 4 vols. Tokyo: Nihon Shiseki Kyōkai, 1920–1921.

Natsume Sōseki. "Danpen." *Natsume Sōseki zenshū*, 13:23–28. Tokyo: Iwanami Shoten, 1941.

Neumann, William L. *America Encounters Japan: From Perry to MacArthur.* New York: Harper & Row, 1965.

New York Herald.

New York Illustrated News.

New York Times.

Nezu Masashi. "Bakumatsu no France gaikō bunsho kara mita France no tai-Nichi hōshin." *Shigaku zasshi* 69 (1960).

Ninagawa Shin. *Ishin zengo no seisō to Oguri Kōzuke no shi.* Tokyo: Nihon Shoin, 1928.

———. *Zoku ishin zengo no seisō to Oguri Kōzuke.* Tokyo: Nihon Shoin, 1931.

Nitobe, Inazō. *The Intercourse between the United States and Japan: An Historical Sketch.* Baltimore: Johns Hopkins University Press, 1891.

Norman, E. H. *Andō Shōeki and the Anatomy of Japanese Feudalism. Transactions of the Asiatic Society of Japan*, 3rd ser., 2 (December 1949).

———. *Origins of the Modern Japanese State.* Ed. John W. Dower. New York: Pantheon, 1975.

Notes from the Japanese Legation in the United States to the Department of State, 1858–1906. File microcopies of records in the National Archives, no. 163. 3 rolls.

Numata Jirō. *Bakumatsu yōgaku-shi.* Tokyo: Tōkō Shoin, 1952.

———. *Nihon to seiyō. Tōzai bunmei no kōryū*, 6. Tokyo: Heibonsha, 1971.

———. "Bakumatsu no kengai shisetsu ni tsuite." In *Seiyō kenbun shū. Nihon shisō taikei*, 66, ed. Numata Jirō and Matsuzawa Hiroaki. Tokyo: Iwanami Shoten, 1974.

———. "Tamamushi Sadayū to *Kō-Bei nichiroku.*" In *Seiyō kenbun shū. Nihon shisō taikei*, 66, ed. Numata Jirō and Matsuzawa Hiroaki. Tokyo: Iwanami Shoten, 1974.

Numata Jirō et al., eds. *Yōgaku*, 1. *Nihon shisō taikei*, 64. Tokyo: Iwanami Shoten, 1976.

O'Conroy, Taid. *The Menace of Japan.* New York: H. C. Kinsey, 1934.

Ogata Hiroyasu. *Seiyō kyōiku inyū no hōto. Noma Kyōiku Kenkyūsho kiyō*, 19. Tokyo: Kōdansha, 1961.

Ogata Tomio, ed. *Rangaku to Nihon bunka.* Tokyo: Tokyo Daigaku Shuppankai, 1971.

Ōhira Kimata. *Sakuma Shōzan.* Tokyo: Yoshikawa Kōbunkan, 1959.

Oka Yoshitake. *Kindai Nihon no keisei.* Tokyo: Kōbundō Shobō, 1947.

———. *Sōmeiki no Meiji Nihon.* Tokyo: Miraisha, 1964.

Okada Akio, ed. *Bakumatsu, ishin. Gaikokujin no mita Nihon*, 2. Tokyo: Chikuma Shobō, 1961.

Ōkubo Toshikane, ed. *Iwakura shisetsu no kenkyū.* Tokyo: Munetaka Shobō, 1976.

Oliphant, Laurence. *Narrative of the Earl of Elgin's Mission to China and Japan in the Years 1857, '58, '59.* 2 vols. Edinburgh and London: William Blackwood & Sons, 1859.

———. *Episodes in a Life of Adventure: Or, Moss from a Rolling Stone.* New York: Harper & Brothers, 1887.

Oliphant, Margaret Oliphant W. *Memoir of the Life of Laurence Oliphant and of Alice Oliphant, His Wife.* 2 vols. New York: Harper & Brothers, 1891.

Ōno Susumu. *Taidan: Nihon-go o kangaeru.* Tokyo: Chūōkōronsha, 1975.

Osatake Takeshi. *Kokusai hō yori mitaru bakumatsu gaikō monogatari.* Tokyo: Bunka Seikatsu Kenkyūkai, 1926.

——. *Bakumatsu tōzai fūzoku kan. Nihon fūzoku-shi kōza*, 7. Tokyo: Yūzankaku, 1929.

——. *Iteki no kuni e: Bakumatsu kengai shisetsu monogatari*. Tokyo: Manrikaku Shobō, 1929.

——. *Kinsei Nihon no kokusai kannen no hattatsu*. Tokyo: Kyōritsusha, 1932.

——. *Meiji ishin*. 2 vols. Tokyo: Hakuyōsha, 1943.

——. *Bakumatsu gaikō hishi kō*. Tokyo: Hōkōdō, 1944.

——. *Ishin zengo ni okeru rikken shisō*. Tokyo: Hakuyōsha, 1948.

Osborn, Captain Sherard. *A Cruise in Japanese Waters*. Edinburgh and London: William Blackwood & Sons, 1859.

Ōshima Nobujirō. *Nihon kōtsū-shi ronsō*. Tokyo: Kokusai Kōtsū Bunka Kyōkai, 1939.

——. *Nihon kōtsū-shi gairon*. Tokyo: Yoshikawa Kōbunkan, 1964.

Ōshio Heihachirō. *Ōshio Heihachirō shū. Dai-Nihon shisō zenshū*, 16. Tokyo: Dai-Nihon Shisō Zenshū Kankōkai, 1933.

Ōtsuka Takematsu. *Bakumatsu gaikō-shi no kenkyū*. Tokyo: Hōbunkan, 1952.

Ōyake Sōichi. *Honoo wa nagareru: Meiji to Shōwa no tanima*. 4 vols. Tokyo: Bungei Shunjūsha, 1964.

Ozaki Hideki and Ozawa Kenshi. *Shashin hiroku: Katsu Kaishū*. Tokyo: Kōdansha, 1974.

Parke-Smith, M. *Western Barbarians in Japan and Formosa in Tokugawa Days, 1603–1868*. Kobe: J. L. Thompson, 1930.

Parks, E. Taylor. "The First Japanese Diplomatic Mission to the United States (1860)." U.S., *Department of State Bulletin* 42, no. 1089 (May 9, 1960).

Plutschow, Herbert. "Some Characteristics of Medieval Japanese Travel Diaries." Lecture given at the Regional Seminar, Center for Japanese and Korean Studies, University of California at Berkeley, December 5, 1975.

Preble, George Henry. *The Opening of Japan: A Diary of Discovery in the Far East, 1853–1856*. Ed. Boleslaw Szczesniak. Norman: University of Oklahoma Press, 1962.

Pryor, Mrs. Roger A. *Reminiscences of Peace and War*. New York: Macmillan, 1904.

Reischauer, Edwin O. *Ennin's Diary: The Record of a Pilgrimage to China in Search of the Law*. New York: Ronald Press, 1955.

——. *Ennin's Travels in T'ang China*. New York: Ronald Press, 1955.

Rekishigaku Kenkyūkai, comp. *Meiji ishin-shi kenkyū kōza*. 7 vols. Tokyo: Heibonsha, 1956–1969.

Saegusa Hiroto. *Miura Baien no tetsugaku*. Tokyo: Daiichi Shobō, 1941.

Sakamaki, Shunzō. *Japan and the United States: 1790–1853. Transactions of the Asiatic Society of Japan*, 2nd ser., 18. Tokyo: Kyōbunkan, 1939.

Sakata Seiichi. *Harris*. Tokyo: Yoshikawa Kōbunkan, 1961.

San Francisco *Daily Alta California*.

San Francisco *Daily Evening Bulletin*.

Sanjōnishi Sanetaka. *Sanetaka kōki* (1474–1535). 13 vols. Tokyo: Taiyōsha, 1931–1963.

Sansom, G. B. *Japan: A Short Cultural History*. London: Cresset, 1932.

——. *The Western World and Japan: A Study in the Interaction of European and Asiatic Cultures*. New York: Random House, 1949.

——. *A History of Japan*, 3 (1615–1867). Stanford: Stanford University Press, 1963.

Sasaki Takayuki. *Hogo hiroi: Nikki*, 5 (1870–1872). *Dai-Nihon kokiroku*. Comp. Tokyo Daigaku Shiryō Hensanjo. Tokyo: Tokyo Daigaku Shuppankai, 1974.

Sashi Tsutae. *"Kanrin Maru* tōjōsha Nagao Kōsaku no shōgai." *Shigaku zasshi* 36 (1963).

Satō Naosuke. *Seiyō bunka juyō no shiteki kenkyū.* Tokyo: Tokyodō, 1968.

Satō Seizaburō. "Seiō no shōgeki e no taiō: Kawaji Toshiakira o chūshin to shite." *Kindai Nihon no seiji shidō.* Ed. Shinohara Hajime and Mitani Taichirō. Tokyo: Tokyo Daigaku Shuppankai, 1965.

———. "Bakumatsu Meiji shoki ni okeru taigai ishiki no shoruikei." *Kindai Nihon no taigai taido.* Ed. Satō Seizaburō and R[oger] Dingman. Tokyo: Tokyo Daigaku Shuppankai, 1974.

Satō Shōsuke. *Yōgaku-shi kenkyū josetsu: Yōgaku to hōken kenryoku.* Tokyo: Iwanami Shoten, 1964.

Satow, Ernest. *A Diplomat in Japan.* London: Seeley, Service, 1921.

Scheiner, Irwin. *Christian Converts and Social Protest in Meiji Japan.* Berkeley and Los Angeles: University of California Press, 1970.

Schwantes, Robert S. *Japanese and Americans: A Century of Cultural Relations.* New York: Harper & Brothers, 1955.

Semmel, Bernard. *Jamaican Blood and Victorian Conscience: The Governor Eyre Controversy.* Boston: Houghton Mifflin, 1963.

Shiba Kōkan. *Saiyū nikki.* Ed. Kuroda Genji and Yamaga Seinosuke. Tokyo: Sakamoto Shoten, 1927.

Shibahara Takuji. *Kaikoku. Nihon no rekishi,* 23. Tokyo: Shōgakkan, 1975.

Shibama Chikakichi, ed. *Man'en gannen dai ichi ken-Bei shisetsu nikki.* Tokyo: Nichi-Bei Kyōkai, 1920.

Shibusawa Eiichi. *Tokugawa Yoshinobu-kō den.* 8 vols. Tokyo: Fuzanbō, 1918–1919.

Shigehisa Tokutarō. *Kyōiku, shūkyō. Oyatoi gaikokujin,* 5. Tokyo: Kashima Kenkyūjo Shuppankai, 1968.

Shikano Masanao. *Nihon kindai shisō no keisei.* Tokyo: Shin-Hyōronsha, 1956.

Shimada Saburō. *Kaikoku shimatsu: Ii Naosuke den.* Tokyo: Yoronsha, 1946.

Shimane Kiyoshi. "Bakumatsu gaikō no suishinsha Iwase Tadanari o chūshin to shite." *Kaikoku no kurushimi. Meiji no gunzō,* 1. Ed. Ichii Saburō. Tokyo: San'ichi Shobō, 1969.

Shimizu Masashi. "Amerika-yuki kōkai nikki." In *SS,* 4.

Shinji Yoshimoto. *Edo jidai buke no seikatsu.* Tokyo: Shibundō, 1961.

Shinji Yoshimoto, ed. *Edo jidai bushi no seikatsu.* Tokyo: Yūzankaku, 1969.

Shively, Donald H., ed. *Tradition and Modernization in Japanese Culture.* Princeton: Princeton University Press, 1971.

Shōji Kichinosuke et al., eds. *Minshū undō no shisō. Nihon shisō taikei,* 58. Tokyo: Iwanami Shoten, 1970.

Siebold, Philipp Franz von. *Geographical and Ethnological Elucidations to the Discoveries of Maerten Gerrits Vries.* Trans. F. M. Cowan. London: Trubner, 1859.

Skeel, Emily Ellsworth, and Edwin H. Carpenter, Jr., eds. *A Bibliography of the Writings of Noah Webster.* New York: New York Public Library, 1958.

Smith, George (Bishop of Victoria). *Ten Weeks in Japan.* London: Longmans, Green, Longmans, and Roberts, 1861.

Smith, Thomas C. "Ōkura Nagatsune and the Technologists." In *Personality in Japanese History,* ed. Albert M. Craig and Donald H. Shively. Berkeley and Los Angeles: University of California Press, 1970.

Soviak, Eugene. "On the Nature of Western Progress: The Journal of the Iwakura Embassy." In *Tradition and Modernization in Japanese Culture,* ed. Donald H. Shively. Princeton: Princeton University Press, 1971.

Spalding, J. W. *Japan and Around the World: An Account of Three Visits to the Japanese Empire.* New York: Redfield, 1855.

SS. See Nichi-Bei Shūkō, *Man'en gannen* . . .

Statler, Oliver. *The Black Ship Scroll.* San Francisco and New York: Japan Society, 1963.

——. *Shimoda Story.* New York: Random House, 1969.

Steiner, Jesse Frederick. *The Japanese Invasion: A Study in the Psychology of Inter-Racial Contacts.* Chicago: A. C. McClung, 1917.

Strong, George Templeton. *The Diary of George Templeton Strong.* 4 vols. Ed. Allan Nevins and Milton Halsey Thomas. New York: Macmillan, 1952.

Sugimoto Tsutomu. *Edo jidai Rangaku-go no seiritsu to sono tenkai.* 4 vols. Tokyo: Waseda Daigaku Shuppanbu, 1976–.

Sugita Genpaku, Hiraga Gennai, and Shiba Kōkan. [*Selected Works.*] *Nihon no meicho,* 22. Ed. Haga Tōru. Tokyo: Chūōkōronsha, 1971.

Suzuki Tōzō. *Kinsei kikō bungei nōto.* Tokyo: Tokyodō Shuppan, 1974.

Taguchi Masaharu. *Miura Baien.* Tokyo: Yoshikawa Kōbunkan, 1967.

Takahashi Ryūzō Sensei Kiju Kinenronshū Kankōkai. *Takahashi Ryūzō Sensei kiju kinenron shū.* Tokyo: Zoku Gunsho Ruijū Kanseikai, 1970.

Takahashi Shin'ichi. *Yōgaku ron.* Tokyo: Mikasa Shobō, 1939.

Takamure Itsue. *Josei no rekishi.* 2 vols. *Takamure Itsue zenshū,* 4, 5. Tokyo: Rironsha, 1966.

Takasaka, Masaaki, ed. *Shisō, genron hen. Meiji bunka-shi,* 4. Tokyo: Yōyōsha, 1955.

Takayanagi Kaneyoshi. *Bakumatsu no ōoku.* Tokyo: Yūzankaku, 1974.

Tamai Kōsuke. *Nikki bungaku no kenkyū.* Tokyo: Hanao Shobō, 1965.

Tamamuro Taijō. *Yokoi Shōnan.* Tokyo: Yoshikawa Kōbunkan, 1967.

Tamura Eitarō and Tanaka Eitarō. *Shiryō kara mita Katsu Kaishū.* Tokyo: Yūzankaku, 1974.

Tanabe Taichi. *Bakumatsu gaikō dan* (1898). 2 vols. Ed. Sakata Seiichi. Tokyo: Heibonsha, 1966.

Tanaka Akira. *Meiji ishin. Nihon no rekishi,* 24. Tokyo: Shōgakkan, 1976.

Tanaka Sōgorō. *Katsu Kaishū.* Tokyo: Chigura Shobō, 1940.

Tatsuno Sakito. *Sakuma Shōzan.* Tokyo: Shinjinbutsu Ōraisha, 1975.

Taylor, Bayard. *A Visit to India, China, and Japan in the Year 1853.* London: Sampson Low, 1855.

Tokutomi Iichirō. *Kinsei Nihon kokumin-shi,* esp. 30–44. Tokyo: Min'yūsha, 1929–1933.

Tokyo-to Tosei Shiryōkan, comp. *Tokyo no Eigaku. Tokyo-to-shi kiyō,* 16. Tokyo: Tosei Shiryōkan, 1959.

Tominaga Makita. "Amerika Hikozō 'narrativu' shohon o megutte." *Biburia* 1 (1969).

Tōyama Shigeki. *Meiji ishin.* Tokyo: Iwanami Shoten, 1951.

——. "Kaikoku, taisei hōkan." In *Meiji ishin kenkyū kōza,* 3, comp. Rekishigaku Kenkyūkai. Tokyo: Heibonsha, 1958.

——. *Fukuzawa Yukichi: Shisō to seiji to no kanren.* Tokyo: Tokyo Daikaku Shuppankai, 1970.

Toyoda Minoru. *Nihon Eigaku-shi no kenkyū.* Tokyo: Iwanami Shoten, 1941.

Toyoda Takeshi and Kodama Kōta, eds. *Kōtsū-shi. Taikei Nihon-shi sōsho,* 24. Tokyo: Yamakawa Shuppansha, 1970.

Treat, Payson J. *Diplomatic Relations between the United States and Japan, 1853–1895.* 2 vols. Stanford: Stanford University Press, 1932.

Tsuda Sōkichi. *Jukyō no jissen dōtoku.* Tokyo: Iwanami Shoten, 1938.

Tsurumi Shunsuke. *Takano Chōei.* Tokyo: Asahi Shinbunsha, 1975.

Tsurumi Shunsuke, ed. *Goisshin no arashi. Nihon no hyakunen,* 10. Tokyo: Chikuma Shobō, 1964.

Tsurumine Boshin. *Meriken shinshi.* 5 vols. Edo, 1855.

Tu, Wei-Ming. "*Li* as Process of Humanization." *Philosophy East and West* 22 (April 1972).

———. "The Confucian Perception of Adulthood." *Daedalus,* Spring 1976.

Uete Michiari. "Sakuma Shōzan ni okeru jugaku, bushi seishin, yōgaku." In *Nihon shisō taikei,* 55, ed. Satō Shōsuke et al. Tokyo: Iwanami Shoten, 1971.

Umezu Masakage. *Nikki* (1612–1633). 9 vols. *Dai-Nihon kokiroku.* Comp. Tokyo Daigaku Shiryō Hensanjo. Tokyo: Iwanami Shoten, 1953–1966.

U.S. Congress, Senate. *Bills and Joint Resolutions of the Senate of the United States for the Thirty-Sixth Congress, 1859–60 and 1860–61.* Washington: George W. Bowman, 1861.

W., E. S. "The First Voyage to Japan." *Historical Collections of the Essex Institute* 2 (1860):287–292.

Wajima Yoshio. *Shōheikō to hangaku.* Tokyo: Shibundō, 1972.

Walworth, Arthur. *Black Ships Off Japan: The Story of Commodore Perry's Expedition.* New York: Alfred A. Knopf, 1946.

Ward, Robert E., ed. *Political Development in Modern Japan.* Princeton: Princeton University Press, 1968.

Watanabe Ikujirō. *Meiji tennō.* 2 vols. Tokyo: Meiji Tennō Shōtokukai, 1958.

Watanabe Kazan, Takano Chōei, Sakuma Shōzan, Yokoi Shōnan, and Hashimoto Sanai. [*Selected Works.*] Ed. Satō Shōsuke et al. *Nihon shisō taikei,* 55. Tokyo: Iwanami Shoten, 1971.

Watts, Talbot. *Japan and the Japanese.* New York: J. P. Neagle, 1852.

Webb, Herschel. *The Japanese Imperial Institution in the Tokugawa Period.* New York: Columbia University Press, 1968.

Wei Yüan. See Gi Gen.

Williams, Frederick Wells. *The Life and Letters of Samuel Wells Williams, L.L.D.: Missionary, Diplomatist, Sinologue.* New York and London: G. P. Putnam's Sons, 1889.

Williams, Samuel Wells. *A Journal of the Perry Expedition to Japan (1853–1854). Transactions of the Asiatic Society of Japan,* 37, p. 2. Tokyo: Z. P. Maruya, 1910.

Wood, William Maxwell. *Fankwei: Or, the San Jacinto in the Seas of India, China and Japan.* New York: Harper & Brothers, 1859.

Yajima Suketoshi and Nomura Kentarō, eds. *Gakujutsu hen. Meiji bunka-shi,* 5. Tokyo: Yōyōsha, 1954.

Yamaguchi, Muneyuki. *Hashimoto Sanai.* Tokyo: Yoshikawa Kōbunkan, 1962.

Yamaji Aizan. *Katsu Kaishū.* Tokyo: Kaizōsha, 1929.

Yamashina Kototsune. *Nikki* (1576–1601). 9 vols. Comp. Tokyo Daigaku Shiryō Hensanjo. Tokyo: Iwanami Shoten, 1975.

Yamazaki Masashige. *Yokoi Shōnan.* 2 vols. Tokyo: Meiji Shoin, 1938.

Yanaga Chitoshi. *Japan Since Perry.* New York: McGraw-Hill, 1949.

Yasunaga Toshinobu. *Andō Shōeki.* Tokyo: Heibonsha, 1976.

Yoshida Tsunekichi. "Nonomura Tadazane no *Kōkai nichiroku* ni tsuite." In *SS,* 3.

———. "Masuzu Shunjirō no *A-kō kōkai nikki* ni tsuite." In *SS,* 2.

———. "Murayama Hakugen no *Hōshi nichiroku* ni tsuite." In *SS,* 2.

———. "Shimmi Masaoki no *A-kō-ei* ni tsuite." In *SS,* 2.

———. *Tōjin Okichi.* Tokyo: Chūōkōronsha, 1971.

INDEX

227